MUSIC POWER

MUSIC POWER

Creative Living Through the Joys of Music

Barbara Anne Scarantino

Foreword by
Paul Anka

Dodd, Mead & Company • New York

First Edition

1   2   3   4   5   6   7   8   9   10

Library of Congress Cataloging-in-Publication Data

Scarantino, Barbara Anne, 1942–
    Music power.

    Bibliography: p.
    Includes index.
    1.   Music   therapy.   2.   Music—Psychology.   3.   Music—
Physiological aspects.   I. Title.
ML3920.S297   1987   615.8'5154   87-15729
ISBN 0-396-08969-0

*Dedicated with love
to my son, Jonathan,
who is my music*

Contents

Part II—Emotional and Psychological Effects: *how music affects moods and behavior; the* yin *(feminine) and* yang *(masculine) aspects of music; effects of various instruments; manipulation of behavior and buying habits by music and advertising industries; music aids learning and concentration.*

4. The Musical "Score"   47

Lust versus romance; erotic responses to disco and African rhythms; relaxation aids sexual dysfunction.

5. The Song Is You   55

How to release tension, get rid of hostilities, enhance physical and mental energy, and achieve total well-being through the power of your own voice.

6. Music Makes It Better   69

Healing and regeneration of the mind and body through the use of music and guided imagery; rock/art therapy for troubled teens; energy balancing; the seven chakras and music.

7. Balancing the Scales   83

Music completes the ``Circle of Health'' to help you lose weight, enhance exercise and athletic training programs, manage stress, elevate your consciousness, achieve spiritual fulfillment; music and your Zodiac sign; personality types and music choices.

Close-Up: Gilda Marx

> **The "Grande Dame" of Aerobics Speaks Out
> on Music   103**

8. The Key to the Perfect Exercise Class   107

*Exercise P.M. and A.M.; music motivates the body to move; good and bad
choices of exercise music; choreography; matching music and exercise
energy; sequentializing your exercises and your music.*

Close-Up: Vassili Sulich

> **Children Come to Life Through Dance
> and Music   123**

9. All God's Children Have Music   127

*Music through prenatal life, infancy and adolescence; music and singing
aid child's speech; music education systems; music training enhances
physical health and emotional upbringing; the peer group phenomenon;
drugs, sex, and rock and roll; musical illiteracy.*

10. Life's Song   145

*A suggested full day of music to fit your life style and schedule at home,
at work, at mealtimes, with the children, at exercise class—wherever you
are, whatever you do.*

Acknowledgments

I wish to express my heartfelt gratitude to the following people for their invaluable contributions to this project:

Mr. Paul Anka, for graciously consenting to lend his name and personal views to my book; Margaret and Andy Anka for their love and friendship (and for bringing my book to Paul); Gilda Marx and Vassili Sulich for giving me their valuable time, their enthusiasm, and their personal and professional insights; Buddy Hill and Sharon Deitz, for being special friends, caring teachers, and willing interviewees; Carelia Bower, for bringing my "dream" from spirit energy into physical reality; Dr. Jacqueline Joy Borkin, for keeping my body together to endure the agonies and ecstasies of writing a book; Mom and Dad, for giving me the right chromosomes and genes to choose music and writing as my life's work; and to Michael, for his song.

Foreword
by
Paul Anka

Music has been my lifelong companion. Some of my earliest memories are of the profound stirrings I felt when listening to certain songs. Growing up in Ottawa, Canada, which isn't exactly the music capital of the world, and being the son of restaurateurs, it's not as though music was an expected career choice for me. But even as a young boy, I knew that music was to be my life's work. I taught myself to play the guitar and pick up tunes on the piano, and at the age of thirteen I left home and headed to Los Angeles to cut my first record. The fact that it was a complete failure didn't stifle my enthusiasm. I started playing nightclubs, and at the age of fifteen I wrote my first song, "Diana." And the rest, as they say, is history.

But music is infinitely more to me than a career. It is my love, my passion, the gift I have been blessed with that makes me who I am. Without music there would be no Paul Anka. Always eager to learn more about this great love of mine, you can imagine how intrigued I was to be handed a copy of Barbara Scarantino's *Music Power.* I took it home and read it in one sitting. The next day I read it again. While there are numerous fine books that have been written about the wonders of music, this book adds a new dimension to our knowledge of it. It's like holding a prism and watching the colors change as you look at it from different angles. *Music Power* takes some of this musical knowledge and holds it up to the light, looking at it from a different point of view. What results is further enlightenment on a subject whose ingredients and uses are fathomless.

Don't let the fact that I am some hot-shot composer deceive you. I have no classical training or degree in musicology. (Many of you probably know as much about music as I did when I first started out.) Music experts may learn a few new things from Barbara's book, but it is primarily written with the layperson in mind. The information and insights are all put forth in a manner everyone can easily understand, and it is done with warmth and a surprising amount of humor.

Music Power tells you how to use music to improve the quality of your life. It tells you how to listen to music and what to listen for; how to use music to stimulate creative thought, inspire you, give you energy, strength and courage, and enhance many other aspects of your everyday life. And I hope parents who are reading this book will take special note of the chapter on music and children. I have five daughters who have been raised in an atmosphere of music and I know that it enriches a child's life.

I am especially impressed with the balanced viewpoints expressed in this book. While there are guidelines on how to tell ''good'' music from ''bad,'' never is there the recommendation that we limit ourselves to only certain types of music, for this would limit our experiences in life. However, I think many listeners may agree with her that heavy metal and punk music contain more negatives than positives. Heavy metal, with its sinister trappings, and punk, with its rebellious tirade against society, are really pretty empty musically (although I must admit that I was flattered when the late Sid Vicious of the Sex Pistols recorded his version of ''My Way'' a while back!) The most unfortunate aspect of these types of music is that often some young people become so devoted to it they won't dare consider listening to anything else. If only they knew the exciting ''high'' they could get with other kinds of music, they would switch instantly.

I myself started out as a rock and roller, coming of age to the tunes of Chuck Berry and Fats Domino. As I grew older and matured, it was only natural that my music did, also. I still keep abreast of contemporary music and its innovations, and I like much of what I hear. And I have had the privilege and pleasure of working with such talented pop figures as Michael Jackson, Kenny Loggins, and Michael McDonald. But rather than being concerned only with what is ''in'' at the moment, I try instead to express sentiments that are universal to all people and all ages. Music is a means of communication, and if I expect people to listen to my songs I know that what I have to say better be worth listening to. And the one emotion you will find in nearly all my songs is love. What could be more universal than that?

There is this feeling of love in *Music Power*—in Barbara's love for music and love for you, her readers. Mostly, she projects love and respect for the composers and artists who give their lives over to creating music of *all* kinds, from classical to new age to jazz and rock.

Most importantly, *Music Power* reinforces the belief that all of us who create music hold: that music is more than a commodity to be bought and sold, used and discarded. It is a precious gift, whatever its form. It holds the answers to the mysteries of the universe and puts us in touch with higher powers of inspiration and love.

Whatever your taste in music may be, Barbara will show you how to get the most out of it. And if you take her up on her suggestions and use music as more than mere background filler or physical stimulation, your life will surely be enriched.

Music Power has something for everyone who listens to music. And I think that is just about everybody.

Overture

Music.

The very word is music to my ears. It has come to mean infinitely more to me in these past few years than just another sound in the cacophony of sounds in my environment. It has come to be a life-giving force, a mentor to my creative abilities, a stimulator to my physical and mental energies, an inspiration to my higher mind, a friend, a comfort, the expression and manifestation of my very essence—my soul—a source of joy, humor, and anticipation to each new day, and a great humbler of my healthy ego!

Music is a "high" like no other. Indeed, it can raise you to such heights it is an awesome experience. And when you give yourself over to it, elevate your consciousness through it, and hone your senses with it, you begin to realize your own spiritual potential. On the more earthly level, music is the quintessential stimulus, calming fears and other painful emotions, bringing dormant sensualities to the surface, inspiring passion of thought and deed, bringing forth physical strength and healing power, instilling laughter, prompting tears that cleanse and renew the soul.

There is music in every living thing, in all things organic and inorganic. It exists in all the vibrations and rhythms of the universe—in the juxtaposition of the planets, and in the gentle "silent" growing of a blade of grass. We can *hear* it if we learn to listen for it. We can *make* it if we let it work through us.

Music is all things, and yet it can be a "no thing" if we fail to recognize its purpose and its message, and its impact upon us. If we fail to pay attention to it and, instead, consider it merely one-dimensional (such as only for our passive amusement), then music is no more than any other superficial commodity available for sale, use and discard. But if we learn to express, renew, and rejoice through it, music can be an invaluable means through which we can improve the quality of our health and our lives.

In our own personal program of health, music can serve as a preventive measure by keeping the body in balance physically, emotionally, and spiritually. Through various clinical and scientific studies, researchers have learned that music penetrates the electromagnetic field that surrounds the body (the aura), that the body can differentiate between beneficial and detrimental sound vibrations, that our health can be affected both positively and negatively by the music it hears, and that music is a valuable tool to use in the healing process of the body and the mind.

For decades, Hollywood, Madison Avenue, the recording industry, employers, and retail businesses have manipulated our moods, behavior, and buying habits, often without our conscious consent, or at least without our full awareness of the mind control game that was being played. It's time we reassumed control over our lives by tapping into music's power for our *own* benefit. If we choose to be active listeners instead of passive receptors, music can work its wonders through us as *we* choose. Otherwise, music is "done unto us" by people who know very well how to use its powers to benefit their own interests.

Music is pervasive. It has infiltrated every aspect of our lives. But our awareness of it, our knowledge of its intricacies, history, beauty, and connection to all living things is at an all time low. Are we truly a society of "musical illiterates"? And are we perpetuating generations of children whose only knowledge of music is a beat that emanates from an electronic box to stimulate or pacify them? Has the value we place on music diminished to the point where it is of no more importance to us than a new pair of Reeboks, or a jolt of adrenaline to arouse our senses? Perhaps we can answer those questions best by looking to our own individual values and those we instill in our children, and by the appreciation we have of music as a means of education as well as an art form.

When I sang for a living some years ago, I was privileged to express the words and melodies of composers whose "inner pulse" was in harmony with mine. But somehow, I felt incomplete and inadequate. Later, when I began to write music, it was not out of a cultivation of my own musical abilities, for I had little knowledge of where the notes were on the piano. Rather, the music somehow found me, spoke its message through me in a mystical experience that happens only when you tune in to the powerful voice that urges you on, and inspires you to do things you never dreamed you could do. It was then that I realized that music was not a "thing" outside of me that I listened to and enjoyed, it was an integral, definitive part of me, just as my genes and chromosomes are part of what makes me the person I am.

It was this revelation that gradually led me to writing *Music Power.* I hungered to learn more about this "thing" that stirred me, moved me, and inspired me so. And as I researched and learned, I realized I had so much *more* to learn (and still do). But the knowledge I gained I soon began sharing with my friends, who in turn began to use music to enhance their professional lives as well as their personal lives. Teachers, writers, holistic health practitioners, facialists, executives, exercise instructors—they all desired to know more and more.

Thus, *Music Power* is written for the layperson, the person who loves music but knows little about it and perhaps does not know where to begin to develop a basic understanding of its powers and uses. I do not purport to be an expert on music and how it works its wonders, nor can I examine in painstaking detail all the pertinent aspects of music in just one book. But most of us do not need to read volumes on music history or theory to know how to apply music to improve the quality of our lives. So, think of *Music Power* as a primer, a basic handbook of practical knowledge, and from there you may "graduate" to more indepth studies, if you desire.

I also hope *Music Power* will give the average music fan a deeper appreciation of the people who create music, so that these artists may continue to express themselves freely and independently of corporate restraints, the same restraints that have resulted in a lot of "formula" or "cookie cutter" music to create that "hit song" sound. The more we know about music, the more we will demand quality and innovation instead of mediocrity.

Music Power is somewhat different from other music therapy books in that it recognizes and recommends popular forms of music as being therapeutic, as well as classical and "serious" music usually recommended by professional music therapists. To ignore popular music and its positive qualities would be like erasing the past fifty years of music history, and negating the efforts of some of the greatest artists and composers of all time. Music, like life, is dynamic and ever changing, and our knowledge and awareness of music's powers must grow and evolve with the times.

However, please note the following: there is a heavy push in our society to have us worship all things high tech—including music—that separate us from the true essence of life-giving forces, and the creative genius and sensitivities that are inherently human. But we can never forget the human element in both the creation and appreciation of music, for what has been given to us by supernal forces can never be replaced by a micro chip (especially if there is a massive power blackout!). So, be wary of computerized, synthesized music that is devoid of color, imagination, and heart, and don't ever substitute sterile electronic imitations for genuine instruments or live, flesh and blood composers and artists. But do become familiar with such artists as Vangelis, Jean Michel-Jarre, Kitaro, Mannheim Steamroller, and others who sensitively and skillfully use synthesized sounds that are stimulating, motivating, and in tune with music's creative life forces. Remember, a computer can duplicate the <u>sound</u> of music, but it takes a human hand and human mind to give that sound heart and soul.

From the womb to the death experience, music can enhance and enrich our lives. There is music for every activity—from cleaning the house to learning a foreign language, from exercise to sleeping, and for every environment: home, office, car, bedroom, and operating room. Once you understand music's functions and its influences, you will hear music in ways you never heard it before, use it in ways you never imagined you could use it, and be in touch with yourself and with life in a way that always seemed beyond your grasp.

That's *Music Power.* And it's yours for a song.

1

Let's Take It From the Top

L ALA was a lonely cave girl. All her sisters were married, happy little cavemakers with babies, and husbands who brought home teradactyl steaks every night. but LaLa felt no attraction to most of the men she met. They were all the same: big, hulking, hairy brutes with only one thing on their primitive minds. LaLa wanted more than just to be dragged into a dark crevice in the mountain to be mated like a wild sow. But since candlelight and seduction had not yet been invented, LaLa didn't know what she was missing. All she knew was, so far no one made an offer she couldn't refuse.

Then, along came DeDah, a stranger from a distant tribe who had lost his family to a herd of mastodons. He was to reside with LaLa's tribe, but he was not readily accepted into the fold. LaLa felt sorry for him, identifying with his loneliness. One day they saw each other across a crowded plain. Perhaps it was the way the sun shimmered on LaLa's waist-length hair; perhaps it was the way DeDah stood—tall and erect and defiant. But sparks flew between them. Slowly they ventured toward each other, their bodies naked and sinewy, until they were face to face, breath to breath, untouching, yet afire with desire.

DeDah shook his club and grunted excitedly at LaLa (DeDah may have been different in LaLa's eyes, but he was still like every other caveman: hormonal). Aroused by the lascivious leer in DeDah's eyes, LaLa emitted a lilting untrained soprano's "oooohhh" from her voluptuous mouth. This set DeDah crazy. He could hardly wait to get his hands on her. LaLa had no time to wait either. In seconds their bodies were encircling each other, embracing each other, moving and bobbing in a rhythmic mating dance as they dazzled each other with sweeping passion.

Each time they touched, LaLa sang out, "Oooohhh," in that silken voice of hers.

Finally, in a crescendo of ecstasy, LaLa hit an admirable "High C" in harmony with DeDah's exuberant tenor:

"Oh, LaLa..." "Oh, DeDah..." "Oh La..." "DeDah..."

All together now: "Oh, LaDeDah!"

And thus, music, out of love, was born.

If it didn't happen precisely that way, who's to say? Although Charles Darwin would have been pleased with this prehistoric vignette (he believed that music evolved from sexual instincts and was originally a mating call), all the theories as to music's origins remain just that: theories, some based on anthropological discoveries, others on spiritual beliefs, but all of them fascinating and with more than a small grain of truth.

Aside from Darwin's mating-call theory, there is the hypothesis that music originated as a result of man's imitation of bird calls and songs. Another suggests music started as a means of communication in the form of calling signals or shouting sounds. Or it could have begun as a work song to ease the burdens of heavy tasks. Still another premise is that music existed in the universe since the dawn of Creation, and that it is a reflection of man's thought processes and memory through the eons of time. In essence, man did not *invent* music, rather he *rediscovered* it through his evolving awareness of life, love and God.

While all of these theories have their proponents and opponents, it is obvious that music as we know it today did not spring fully formed from the head of Zeus. It had to evolve, just as all things on earth evolved, from the lowest simplest form.

At the first awakening of life on Earth, there were sea creatures who experienced sensitivities to light, touch and the presence of food. There were sounds to be heard in the various vibrations emitted by light and its spectral colors, and in the rhythm of the sea tides, but no creatures with ears with which to *hear* these sounds. Rather, they were *felt* as part of the rhythm of all life.

Through the eons of man's evolution, he became possessed of a primitive brain capable of simple awareness and emotions, able to feel states of pain, and pleasure. Hearing was the last of man's senses to develop fully, and this hearing opened up new vistas of awareness, giving him a desire to understand, utilize and recreate all the sounds in his environment.

Music, not art or language, is the oldest form of expression, borne out of man's need to communicate to others his emotions, desires and state of being. For the mythical LaLa and DeDah, music was borne of their need to express love (or lust) and to satisfy physical and emotional desires.

The first instrument was man's voice, chanting imitations of the sounds of nature, perhaps grunting out expressions of anger, sorrow, hate, fear, or passion. Perhaps man hummed to imitate a swarm of bees, or bellowed loudly in concert with the cry of an animal of prey. These vocal sounds came to represent things and feelings that became recognizable to man's peers, and a "language" began to develop.

But although he was primitive, man was insatiably curious and fascinated by the sounds that "things" made. As far back as 35,000 years ago, man fashioned instruments from animal horns and bones, logs, reeds, natural fibers, and other resonating materials. And here, too, music became a natural extension of all the sounds of nature. There is no doubt that the babbling brook came before flute, or the bellowing of a bull before the brass.

"The Hills," wrote Oscar Hammerstein, "are alive with the sound of music." Listen and you will hear the siren's song in the wind, the hum of the ocean waves as they ebb and flow on the shore. This is nature's music. And man, in his unending quest to "connect" with all things natural and supernatural, began to imitate these sounds of the earth with his voice and his primitive instruments to become one with his Creator.

There is nothing new on earth. There are no new ideas, no new words, no new music. It's all been thought, written, and said. But with each new culture and civilization, with each new age and level of consciousness, we rediscover that which has always existed and find new ways of expressing it. Looking back to the earliest times, we can see how music has been influenced *by* and has had an influence *on* society, and that these influences are no different today than they were throughout the ages.

In the pre-Christian era, people were acutely aware of the powers locked within music and in *all* sound. In looking at ancient Egypt, China, India and Greece, there is evidence that these cultures believed music had the power to magnificently develop or completely degrade the psyche, and thereby strengthen or bring down entire civilizations. Ancient Chinese philosophy expounded that music was the basis for *everything,* that it could mold the individual and thus society itself into whatever mood the music projected, be it wistful and romantic, strong and militant, or stable and unchanging.

But no civilization held music in higher esteem than classical Greece, where an "educated man" was synonomous with a "musical man." The word music is derived from the Greek word *musiki,* meaning all the arts of the nine Muses. The Muses were the goddesses of all the arts in Greek mythology, and their leader was Apollo, the master athlete, warrior and musician. Apollo and the Muses lived on Mount Parnassus, which came to be thought of as the home of music. The Temple of Apollo at Delphi on Mount Parnassus established the link between music and mystery, and the *Hymn to Apollo* is one of the few pieces of early Greek music that has survived, having been carved onto a stone at Delphi.

In the fifth century B.C., the Greek philosopher/mathematician Pythagoras was busy researching the precept that music was all powerful, but from a different viewpoint—that of numbers and geometric ratios— and ultimately created the mathematical formulas for Western European music as we know it today. Pythagoras believed that the phenomenon known as "numbers" held the key to the secrets of the universe.

In looking at all the universal manifestations (the circling of the planets, the lunar cycle, the rhythm of the tides, the growth cycles of plant and animal life), he found them to be harmoniously interconnected. In applying his concept to the distances between the sun, moon, and stars, Pythagoras and his fellow scientists developed a set of geometric ratios and proportions that they believed, if used in the composition of music, would resonate in harmony with the universal forces and enhance life physically, emotionally and spiritually. (If you have ever suffered through learning chord combinations, intervals, time signatures, the seven- and twelve-note scales and tonic systems, and the rest of the "numbers game" called Music, you can thank Pythagoras and his fellow Greeks!)

But the ancient scientists and philosophers' understanding and appreciation of music went beyond the purely academic. Pythagoras, Aristotle, Plato, and others of their ilk, also helped music come full circle in its meaning by endowing it with ethical values, and determining its place in society as an aesthetic art form and means of expression. Their tremendous wisdom and inner spiritual development with respect to music's powers has been carried down through the ages, and is exhibited in the works of composers called the Great Masters.

Unfortunately, little of the original music of ancient Greece remains, as it was often improvised and passed on to others by *ear* rather than notation. When Greece was defeated by Rome, the importance of music diminished. While they enjoyed good music, the Romans were not on a creative par with the Greeks, nor were they as aesthetically sensitive. The Romans loved loud music and spectacular shows, but many of these spectacles became increasingly cruel and soon people came to associate music with vulgarity. Due to the Roman persecution of the Jews and Christians (who sang psalms of the Bible accompanied by instruments) religious music became "purified." That is, it became separated from music as a form of enjoyment. We still see this division today between classical music and popular music—one being music for the mind and the other music for entertainment.

The Roman Empire finally fell, but centuries would pass before music as we know it would evolve and take shape, and before Pythagoras' work would be rediscovered and celebrated in the Middle Ages.

Our knowledge of pre-Western European music is sketchy at best, due to a lack of adequate methods of notation. But experts believe that music among primitive as well as civilized peoples long ago was improvisational and without structure. So, composers and performers were free to do their own thing. To a point. Whether music was utilized, merely tolerated or banned outright depended upon the whims of whatever religious organizations were dominant in a particular culture. The more primitive the society, the more music was tied to religious rituals, ceremonies and festivities. Much use was made of monotonous vocal incantations and instrumental rhythms for the purpose of inducing a magic hypnosis. Music was also used in the spoken dramas of the Chinese and Greek theatres. And there were folk dances and songs of love and work in all cultures.

This was the age of the lyre (seven-string, hand-held harp), and the wind instruments such as the flute, as well as primitive percussion instruments. The only composer-performer of record was David in the Old Testament, who serenaded and soothed King Saul with his poetic psalms and harp playing. As early as 3,000 B.C., sophisticated musical theories had been developed in China, and by the time of the Great Crusades, the music of India had reached its peak. But music's evolvement in the West was very slow. In fact, it took more than 1,000 years to possess the logic, structure and harmony that we today exalt in its most perfect form (such as in the music of Johann Sebastian Bach).

Through the periods of time known as Romanesque, Gothic, and Renaissance (twelfth to sixteenth centuries), music developed magnificently with the rise and spread of Christianity, especially liturgical music. It progressed from single-note melodies to combinations of sounds and dual melodies, although rhythms were still free of strict metrical phrasing (no beats to the bar, no time signatures, etc.). Secular music provided a highly cultivated group of amateur performers both in the aristocracy and upper middle class who were very adept at singing and/or playing.

The most important musicians were priests, and an important occupation in thousands of monasteries was liturgical singing. After the twelfth century, the organ became a very important instrument. Primitive at first (played with heavy blows of the fist), it soon evolved into a more flexible instrument that could play intricate polyphonic sounds. The violin also evolved at this time into the instrument we know today, crafted with skill by men whose ideals of beauty reflected those of the ancient Greeks.

With the advent of the Renaissance period, the Catholic Church was far less powerful (due to Protestant Reformation led by Martin Luther). This period was truly the era of Humanism, and focused on the accomplishments of life instead of the foreboding Christian afterlife of heaven or hell. This humanistic attitude spilled over into the music of the times. While medieval composers had cared little about the emotional aspect of music, Renaissance composers wrote music to enhance the meaning and emotions of the text. If words expressed sadness, pain, or heartbreak, the harmony and melody of the music coincided with these human feelings.

Secular music became increasingly popular during the Renaissance period, with poems of various languages (Italian, French, Spanish, German, English, etc.) being set to music. Music was an important leisure activity, and all educated persons were expected to study, play, and read music adeptly.

Musical "love poems" (madrigals) were published in Italy by the thousands and found their way to Elizabethan England. This created a wave of English madrigals—lighter and more humorous than their Italian counterparts, making them a joy to sing and play.

The Baroque period (1575-1750) was a landmark era in the history of music. The term "baroque" (alleged to be derived from the Portuguese, meaning an irregularly shaped pearl) was originally one of scorn for the works of art from this period, considered excessively decorative, dramatic, flamboyant, and emotional. This was a period of violent and revolutionary upheavals, with Catholicism and Protestantism at bloody odds (sound familiar?). These characteristics spilled over into the music, which contained complex harmonies, rapid scale passages, decorations, and chord configurations composed in a solid structure, but with joyful exuberance and free-fantasylike fashion. Even if you know nothing of music from this period, you are probably familiar with the powerful, intricate Bach fugues played on gigantic cathedral pipe organs (seen in many Bela Lugosi films).

Most of the acoustic instruments that we know today were in use during the Baroque era. Even though vocal music was still important, composers began to express feelings and emotions in their works that gave instrumental music its own prestigious place in the arts.

Aside from its flamboyant style, the Baroque period is a landmark one for another important reason: composers of this era were schooled in the Pythagorean principles of harmony and in the philosophy that contended music was the bridge linking all things in the universe.

Johann Sebastian Bach was one of the greatest composers of the Baroque era, even though he was barely recognized in his own time. His music had not only passion, but achieved a level of perfection in its construction that some believe has never been surpassed. Bach was especially adept at composing music for relaxation and healing. One of his most famous works, "The Goldberg Variations," was composed for Russian Envoy Count Kayserling, who suffered chronic bouts of insomnia. Bach composed something "calm, yet bright," as requested by the Count, and upon hearing it played by his favorite musician, Johann Goldberg, Keyserling was soon restful, relaxed, and sleeping peacefully.

While religion still had a strong influence on music of the Baroque period, a good deal of music was written for other purposes such as marriage ceremonies, the dedication of a new building, and as entertainment to be performed in the homes of the wealthy and aristocratic. Now we saw small bands of musicians (combos?) performing for dining, dancing, and pure listening pleasure. And with the origination of the dramatic opera, we saw the development of the orchestra and chorus, as well as the featured solo singer.

Aside from Bach, some of the most important composers of this era were Corelli, Purcell, Vivaldi, Telemann, and Handel, with whose death the Baroque period ended. But it ended in magnificence with Handel's most enduring creation, *The Messiah*. Ever since its most popular "Hallelujah Chorus" brought King George II to his feet in uninhibited enthusiasm, *The Messiah* has represented the spirit of Christmas more than any other piece of music (more than "Silent Night," or "O Little Town of Bethlehem"). Revered by Beethoven as "the greatest composer that ever lived," Handel created this masterpiece in 24 days, while (as legend tells it) alternately weeping and praying, and finally declaring that "...I did see all of heaven before me and the Great God himself." When hearing this majestic composition, it is not difficult to believe Handel's declaration.

To most of us, any music that isn't popular or commercial is "classical." But classical music denotes that period of time (Classicism, 1750-1820) when we were blessed with the talents of Haydn, Mozart, Cherubini and Beethoven, among others. It was also known as the Age of Elegance, of grace and style in all aspects of life and art. Now we were hearing the symphony, the sonata, chamber music, the overture. The church bowed out of its heavy involvement with music at this time, and patronage of the arts and artists by the upper classes is what now nourished music, with Austria and Germany becoming the center of a vital musical activity.

However, even though this society was sophisticated and elegant, it was also emotionally cold. The Age of Reason, as it was called, coveted intellectual pursuits and looked condescendingly and suspiciously upon any reliance upon or display of feelings (could Mr. Spock have been a Classicist and not a Vulcan?).

Thanks to the establishment of the publishing houses (the precursor of the booking agent and recording company), musical performances became widespread, and publishers were in a position to champion certain composers—often at the expense of others. Concert halls and opera houses became established institutions and made it possible for all classes to enjoy the music of noted composers.

With classical music, rhythms became simpler, with structured measures and cadences; and the tempos were constant from beginning to end. Now we could tap our feet to the music. Instruments were divided into four major groups: strings, woodwinds, brass, and percussion. With the exception of the latter group, each became a complete choir in itself, with its own part to "sing." Now, the piano superceded the harpsichord as the household instrument. Dynamics and phrasing were explicit, giving little opportunity for improvisations or imagination on the part of the performer.

Mozart, however, was so versatile in his abilities, being both musically disciplined and innovative, that his compositions possess a passion, elegance, and humanity that is unparalleled. His work was exalted by his contemporaries, such as Haydn, and even Beethoven longed to be

Mozart's pupil, but this desire was thwarted by Mozart's death at age thirty-six.

Just as music is the bridge linking all things in the Universe, Mozart's music was the link between the structured musical style of Bach and the volatile power of Beethoven, who himself bridged the Classical period over to the Romantic era.

Romantic was, indeed, the word for the period of 1800 to 1910, as was the music, with sentimental melodies, intimacy of style, and emotion as a primary function of composition. It was at this time that Beethoven created some of his most important works. It was Beethoven who extended the variety and range of the symphony orchestra by writing parts for trombones, piccolo, and contra-bassoon, thus adding more depth and power to his compositions.

Constantly striving for purity, intensity and perfection in his works, Beethoven was responsible for leading the way to individualism and subjective feeling in music. This change mirrored the mood of the people and their attitude in all things political, religious, scientific, and artistic. Dramatic thought and action was the keynote of the day; the French Revolution had instilled artists with the ideals of liberty and individualism; the rules and regulations of Classicism were found intolerable; and "to be different" was the goal of everyone, especially the musical composer (sound like something out of the 1960's?). This meant creating music that was as much a representation of the composer's identity as his national origin or physical characteristics. Thus, the symphony and concerto were the favorite musical forms of the Romantic composer, allowing him to stretch his abilities beyond expectations, to create diversities of mood and color in the various movements, to take the listener on a journey to previously untraveled corners of time and space, then bring him back home again to familiar surroundings.

The economic and social life of the common man was drastically changed by the Industrial Revolution, and this era saw the rise of a wealthy, capitalistic middle class, and the decline of the aristocracy's power and influence. With the equalizing of social classes, the Romantic composer addressed his music to the masses more than at any other time in previous history, offering an escape from the pressing problems of reality. Serious music was "popularized" by small bands who played by ear or who learned simplified versions of the latest opera tunes, marches, and waltzes for the enjoyment of patrons of dance halls and other social establishments.

The music "biz" took hold during this time, and the composer's publisher and manager had a great influence on what the composer wrote, based on their own opinions as to what the public would accept and enjoy. The music critic became more overt as a liaison between the public and the composer and in setting the standards of musical taste. Usually, the composer and critic were at odds with each other. (As I said, there is nothing new in the world.)

The audience was now searching for new excitement and new experiences. Composers strove to stir up or calm down the listener's feelings with symphonic music and the extravagant spectacles of opera and ballet. Performers and composers alike loved to dazzle audiences with technical displays of virtuoso pieces, and with the Romantic era the "star system"—the worship of solo performers—was born.

Although the lovely, sentimental melodies of Brahms, Strauss, Mendelsohn, and Chopin are representative of the Romantic era, these were also the years of man's struggle for total control of his life and total freedom of expression, in every corner of the globe. Thus, music experienced a synthesis of styles and cultures, from the Russian folk-influenced music of Moussorgsky's opera, *Boris Gudenov,* to the Gypsy spirit of Spanish Flamenco in Bizet's *Carmen,* and the *Sturm und Drang* intensity of Richard Wagner's *Tristan.* Clearly, new forces were at work within society, being reflected more than ever in the music of the times and in the works of Paganini, Franz Schubert, Donizetti, Berlioz, Schumann, Tchaikovsky, Rimsky-Korsakov, Puccini, and Debussy.

Twentieth century music has seen so many upheavals and radical changes, and has served so many diverse functions and uses that it has experienced a culture shock of its own. Just as society has withstood two world wars, the age of technology, the space race, political and economic disaster, social revolution, and the nuclear age, so has music reflected these changes, progressions (in some cases, *re*gressions), and attitudes.

Perhaps nowhere on earth has music undergone so many transformations or spawned so many hybrids of style than in America, the melting pot of races, cultures, ideas and ideals. Even as early as 1620, when the Pilgrims arrived, there were music forms indigenous to the native peoples of the continent that were a homogenous blending of a variety of nations and tribes. Sadly, the newcomers totally ignored this rich heritage of music, supplanting it with the Western harmony of European music.

But by the nineteenth century, the population of American had increased dramatically, with millions of immigrants coming from Europe, Scandinavia and Canada to find new opportunities for a new life. Most of these people were peasants, and their music was the music of the people, filled with life, color, and diverse human emotions, as well as diverse rhythms and harmonies.

Through an experiencing and sharing of hard times, new forms of popular music took shape. Spirituals and the blues were created from the merging of earthy, African rhythms and melodies with European harmony. America's first great native composer was Stephen Foster born in Pittsburgh, Pennsylvania in 1826, on the fourth of July. Foster was on his way to a military career at West Point when he first began writing songs. And although he lived all of his life in the North, his songs are filled with the "plantation spirit" of the African slaves in the South: "Camptown Races," "Old Black Joe," "My Old Kentucky Home," and others.

The military-style march music of John Phillip Sousa has much of its roots in English operetta and church music. Still, one can feel the pride of America in such songs as "Semper Fidelis" and "Stars and Stripes Forever," given Sousa's own individual panache.

Who would think that one could mix the bold sounds of brass bands, the good humor of folk music, and the syncopated rhythms of Africa to create the "parlor music of white middle-class America." But, by the turn of the century, everyone wanted to play ragtime on the piano (or on the mechanical player piano roll). This music, brought to great fame by composer Scott Joplin (1868-1917), was bold, courageous, and optimistic, just like the times.

"Serious" music still continued to thrive, and some of the most noteworthy composers of this century are Charles Ives, Igor Stravinsky, Bela Bartok, Maurice Ravel, Serge Prokofiev, Dmitri Shostakovich, and more recently, Aaron Copland and Leonard Bernstein. But it was "popular" music—the music of the masses—that took the country by storm with a heartbeat and identity of its own.

Technological advancements early in the century, such as the phonograph and motion picture, made it possible for the average person to hear music and see entertainment forms that they previously might not have experienced. It all happened with such velocity that it soon became obvious Europe was losing its dominance over the arts. The American counterpart to the opera was the "musical," performed in vaudeville houses and on the stage of Broadway theatres. Here, the patriotic, foot-tapping music of George M. Cohan ("Yankee Doodle Dandy") held its own against the stylish European-influenced operettas of Victor Herbert (*Naughty Marietta*).

After World War II, jazz, the hard-driving energetic offspring of ragtime, made its way along the Mississippi River to dance halls around the world and usurped the turn-of-the-century ballads with amazing swiftness. This experimental new form of music was considered "dangerous" and denounced by moralists as a corrupter of youth (just as the waltz had been in the nineteenth century). But nothing could stop the music, and soon it began to influence even serious composers. George Gershwin brought jazz to the concert stage in a unique blending of white/black/popular/classical music (*Rhapsody in Blue, Porgy and Bess*).

As more and more artists strove to express the intensity of their feelings and their cultural roots, jazz experienced an outgrowth into five distinct styles: the happy energy of traditional Dixieland (Louis Armstrong); the elegance and sophistication of swing (Benny Goodman); modern jazz with its improvisational hybrids of be-bop, cool jazz and hard bop (Charlie Parker, Dizzy Gillespie, Dave Brubeck); the rawness of free jazz (Ornette Coleman); and the pulsating fusion known as jazz-rock (Miles Davis, Weather Report).

World War II, wars in Korea and Vietnam, the space race and nuclear arms race have all wrought stunning implications in our attitudes about music. Rapid communications systems, sophisticated recording techniques, and other "immediate gratification" inventions meant that music has had to meet the desires and demands of a highly informed, insatiable, confused, frustrated, and jaded society. We live in a world constantly on the brink of destruction, yet we are filled with eternal cockeyed optimism. We are glad to be alive, yet angry and disillusioned with the conditions of the world. We want to plan for the future, yet live only for today.

In the 1950's rock and roll picked up the driving beat of rhythm and blues (mixed with a little country-western) and intensified it with a sexual urgency that drove fans (and parents) into hysteria. Through rock's evolution over the years, no other form of music has so clearly shown a separation from the past, becoming music for the "now generation," and creating idols and legends of unprecedented worship (Elvis Presley, the Beatles, the Rolling Stones, Bruce Springsteen). Its subdivisions (pop, new wave, acid rock, electro-pop, etc.) and its fusions (jazz-rock, folk-rock, etc.) have given it a colorful musical history of its own, one that continues to explore new horizons of sound in synthesized and computerized "music."

While some pop music composers have come and gone like the wind, others have maintained their place in history along side the immortal greats who created earlier forms of music: Cole Porter, Jerome Kern, Irving Berlin, Fats Waller, Rodgers and Hart (and Hammerstein), Duke Ellington, Lerner and Lowe, Steven Sondheim, Alan and Marilyn Bergman, Marvin Hamlisch, Henry Mancini, Bob Dylan, Neil Diamond, Paul Anka, Burt Bacharach, Carole Bayer Sager, Harry Chapin, John Lennon, Paul McCartney, Paul Simon, Billy Joel, Maurice White, Stevie Wonder...the list goes on and on.

All of them have given us new expressions, new depths, new excitement and passions in their music that will never be outdated or forgotten. For they compose music not just for the "market," but from the heart. They have given us some of the happiest, liveliest, finger-snapping, foot-tapping music; the loveliest melodies; the most inspired and inspiring lyrics. And in a sea of musical garbage (such as heavy metal and punk), their works float gracefully like lilies on a pond.

Now there are the "new age" music composers, such as Vangelis, Kitaro, George Winston, Steve Halpern, Paul Winter, Jean-Michel Jarre, Andreas Vollenweider, and a number of others, who create music for the purposes of meditation, relaxation, healing, spiritual enlightenment, or pure listening pleasure. Just as in the Baroque era, new age composers are making music more than an entertainment phenomenon. They are combining their talents with the physical and spiritual laws of the universe, guiding us to the fathomless fountain of music's powers. The increasing popularity of new age music proves there is a huge and hungry audience for that which calls us to a "higher ground."

Perhaps (and it is my fondest hope) it is this hunger which will intervene and prevent music from succumbing totally to the high-tech advances of synthesizers, samplers, computers, and other musical machinery. In a nightmare I see acoustical instruments going the way of the dinosaur and live concerts being mere illusions, devoid of human form. There are no live musicians, just a collage of video and audio paraphernalia re-creating entire symphonies through software programs in some obscure laboratorylike booth, piping the sound into the theater. The dancers and singers are holograms—transparent images that appear and disappear from a projected light force. And worse, the audience is also a congregation of holograms, projected into their seats from their homes—the ultimate in passive, nonparticipatory "entertainment."

But then I awaken and recall a television commercial which featured Itzhak Perlman extolling the virtues of a Sara Lee croissant. As an embellishment, he displayed a dazzling few seconds of virtuosity on his violin. I thought, Let someone try *that* with a computer! And I realized there is still much musical promise for this twentieth century. And I can hardly wait until 2001.

2

What Is This Thing Called Music?

UNLESS you are a music scholar, you might have a hard time answering that question. And even the experts seem to disagree. Consequently, there is no one and only definition of music that is universally accepted. But every child and every adult knows in his own unique way what image to bring forth when we say the word "music." Very early in life we experience it in some form or another: nursery rhymes, lullabys, school and church songs, radio and TV jingles, and so forth.

As the years go by and we are exposed to a wide variety of musical compositions and forms, our definition of what music is *to us* will probably be the sum and substance of many subjective experiences feelings and opinions, depending upon what purpose music serves in our lives.

For most of us, music's appeal is primarily emotional and psychological, as well as physical. Music excites us, moves us, entertains us, soothes us, and it thrills us, perhaps more than any other stimulus. A survey published in the December 1985 issue of *Psychology Today* resulted in a startling discovery: ninety-six percent of the respondents stated that musical passages gave them more thrills than scenes from a movie or ballet, sex, special moments at sporting events, success in competition, parades, or a variety of other activities.

Yet, the average person can't really explain why this is so. Nonetheless, many people agree that music's impact is profound. Because music is so pervasive in our society (in fact, we have to make an effort to get *away* from it), the more we know about it, the better able we are to use music to benefit and enrich our lives. And in order to answer the question, "What is this thing called music?" we have to take a look at all its components from an objective, as well as subjective, point of view.

OBJECTIVE

Rarely does music happen spontaneously or by chance. Rather, it is ordered, controlled, and shaped according to specific rules of harmonics and the laws of physical science. Technically speaking, music can be described as a continued series of sounds with sustained constant frequencies (pitch), created by an instrument or a human voice, arranged in specific patterns of rhythm, melody, and harmony.

Sound complicated? I won't dare make it as complicated as it really is (then I wouldn't be able to understand it myself). Volumes have been written on just the scientific aspect of music as "sound." But in simple terms, let's take a look at "sounds."

A sound is made by disturbances in the air pressure that excite sensations in the ear. *Sound* is a general term, encompassing sensations of all qualities (slamming doors, yelling, falling trees, etc.). A *tone* is a sound of definite pitch caused by vibrations of predominantly one frequency (the musical tone "C" for example). *Noise* is a sound lacking pitch and is caused by vibrations of different and dissonant (harsh, inharmonious) frequencies. Hal Lingerman, author of *The Healing Energies of Music*, states, "Noise is the opposite of music: it is 'sound gone crazy,' [for it fails] to find any agreement or harmony with the universe in which it is moving." An artistically-played trumpet is *music* to our ears, while a blaring car horn is an annoying *noise*.

Pitch, according to the *Harvard Dictionary of Music*, is the location of musical sound in the tonal scale, preceding from low to high. Pitch is determined by the frequency of the tone; that is, the number of vibrations per second.

You'll read a lot about "vibrations" in this book, so I'll explain: *Vibrations* are the moving back and forth (oscillating motions) of an elastic or rigid body suddenly released from tension (the plucking of a violin string, for example). These "bodies" vibrate in the air at so many cycles per second. The slower the cycles per second, the lower the sound (or pitch). The faster the cycles per second, the higher the sound (or pitch). For example, on the piano the highest frequency tone (at the far right of the keyboard) is 4,186 cycles per second, while the lowest (at the far left of the keyboard) is about 27 cycles per second. We humans can hear sounds which vibrate from a low of 20 times per second to a high of 20,000 times per second. Other "animals" can hear frequencies much higher.

To produce notes of music, a string (on a violin, guitar, etc.), a column of air (in a flute, horn, etc.), a surface (cymbal, drumhead, etc.), or loudspeaker (amplifier) vibrates at its own distinctive pitch. The length, tension, and weight of the instrument will determine the pitch: the longer and thicker a string, for example, the deeper the pitch. Short, taut, thin strings produce a much higher and "thinner" sound. The same principle holds true for all instruments, as well as for natural objects (a thin stick has a thinner, higher sound when struck than a large, hollow log).

"But what has all this to do with what I think or how I feel when I switch on my favorite song?" you may be asking.

A great deal. What we *hear* has a direct bearing on how we *feel*. The sensitivity of the human ear is such that we can separate one sound above all others, such as hearing only one person's voice in a crowd of voices, or one instrument in an orchestra of many instruments. We can choose what we wish to hear consciously, and dismiss what we do not wish to hear. However, all the "dismissed" sounds are still felt, recorded and stored in our subconscious mind, waiting to be retrieved by our memory system. In order to understand the infinite power that music has, and how to tap into that power, it is important to know what is happening in our "sound environment" when we hear musical sounds. Only then can we learn how to choose music that is beneficial over music that is potentially harmful.

A vibration is not merely an intangible element, of importance only to a physics professor. Everything in the universe is in a state of vibration: atoms, chemicals, colors, and musical sounds. They affect everything in us and around us and lead to (or destroy) our physical, intellectual, emotional, or spiritual harmony with our environment, and with other people in our environment.

This brings us back to my "technical" definition of music: A continued series of sounds with sustained constant frequencies (pitch or vibrations) created by an instrument or a human voice, arranged in specific patterns of rhythm, melody, and harmony.

Without these *sustained* frequencies, melodic and harmonic music could not exist. This is what makes the difference between Nature's Music and Man's Music. In nature, sounds and frequencies are constantly changing and are controlled only by the whims of nature. Man's music is controlled by the structure of a composition, which must follow the laws of harmonics, and by the skills and talents of the musician or singer.

The combinations of sounds that we hear and call "music" are also created by applying certain rules of mathematics set forth by Pythagoras who, as you will recall, studied all the rhythms and cycles of the universe and created the formula for music as we know it.

These mathematical principles are evident in every aspect of music (scales, chords, time signatures, tempos, and rhythms) and have a corresponding "cosmic connection." For example, Pythagoras developed the seven tones of the scale (do-re-me-fa-so-la-ti) by calculating the distance from the moon to the earth (one tone), the distance from the moon to Mercury (semitone), from Mercury to Venus (one and a half tones), the sun to Mars (one tone), Mars to Jupiter (semitone), Jupiter to Saturn (semitone), and Saturn to the fixed stars or zodiac (one and a half tones). The eighth tone of the scale (also known as "do") completes a full octave. This final tone actually vibrates at twice the frequency of the first "do," but it is so perfect in consonance that it appears to be merely a duplication of the original "do" tone. The whole range of musical sounds is divided into almost identical segments, each called an octave. For example, the note "C" to the next higher "C" is one octave. And the note "D" to the next higher "D" is also an octave.

There are five major elements of music that have profound effects on us: rhythm, melody, harmony, tone color, and form. Of these, rhythm and melody are closely related. While it is possible to have rhythm without melody, there is no way to have melody without rhythm. Rhythm is the framework on which the melody is hung. Without rhythm, melody would have no shape, no form, and no meaning. Sort of like an umbrella without the metal ribs. It would only be a series of notes and tones free-floating and going nowhere. (I would like to note that meditation music often consists of melody—or rather strategically chosen "tones"—without any discernible rhythm, but this is another form which we will discuss later).

Rhythm is what makes us want to dance; melody is what makes us want to sing while we dance. Rhythm moves "in time" and becomes largely a physical stimulus, while melody moves "in space" and appeals more to our emotions and sense of aesthetics. Rhythm—which is the flow and movement of the music, also known as "the beat"—was part of the earliest stages of man's development. Back at least as far as the Stone Age, man discovered that his emotions and his body could be stimulated by the beat of a drum. He could be excited to war, aroused sexually, and put into hypnotic trances by an insistent, incessant rhythm. Obviously, little has changed through the centuries. Today, similar effects are achieved through the monotony of pop music beats using computerized drum machines to "hypnotize" (or is that "lobotomize") us.

But rhythm is more than just the ticking off of beats (one, two, three, four). It also means the organization of *notes,* and how long they are played (quarter note, half note, etc.), as well as the *rests* (length of silences when no notes are played). Different instruments in a band may have their own individual set of notes and rests, strategically connected to form a very colorful and unique rhythm (boogie woogie, samba, reggae, etc.). Popular music beats and rhythms are usually constant so that people can move and dance in ordered cadence. In classical music, however, the rhythms may slow down and speed up under the direction and interpretation of an individual conductor. Musicians being human, they may not always play time values as accurately as written. Only computerized music is metrically precise, which is why it sounds so artificial and monotonous.

Another element of music is harmony. When several notes are played simultaneously on the piano, they form a chord. If the chord is structured properly and sounds pleasant, the notes are said to be "in harmony," or *consonant* with each other. A simple triad chord consists of the first (do), third (mi) and fifth (so) notes of the scale, and they sound harmonious when played together. There are many more sophisticated chords (sevenths, elevenths, diminished, minors, etc.) that consist of four, five, and six or more notes played together, that produce lovely harmonies as well. A song's melody notes are found within the chordal tones as well as in the passing tones of the chord's own scale (major scale, minor scale, etc.) In other words, the melody must relate to the harmonic structure of the chords.

The music forms of the Far East have their own distinctive harmonic structures, some of which are pleasant to our ears (music of India, for example) and some that may be unpleasant.

Harmony must also occur when several instruments play together, or when voices are singing together. If chords are *dissonant,* or instruments are "out of harmony" with each other, they sound annoying to us. When one person sings out of tune or hits a "sour note," he or she is also out of harmony with the other voices. (I must add that dissonant chords are often used in some forms of music, such as in progressive jazz, to create a special effect or denote a certain style or technique. In these instances, the chords are correct, even though they may be out of harmony with the natural laws of music.)

Prior to 1900, most music was essentially consonant, and when a composer deviated from that form there were outraged cries from the critics and masses. Such was the case with the music of Wagner in the 1850's and later with the music of Richard Strauss. Igor Stravinsky's *The Rite of Spring,* considered his most celebrated composition, caused one of the most famous riots ever to take place on musical grounds when it debuted in Paris on May 29, 1913. Recognized as revolutionary in form, it consists of complex, assymmetrical rhythms and harsh dissonances that caused fistfights between his opponents and supporters in the audience.

Today, listeners have become adjusted to music that previous generations would consider ugly and incomprehensible, especially the various forms of rock and jazz music.

Tone color in music is also important in how we respond. All the various instruments have their own unique sound identity, or tone color. For example, the twang of a guitar has a different tone color than that of a classical violin, even though they may be playing the same note (a-b-c-d, etc.). A flute has a different tone color than a saxophone, and so forth. This is due to the difference in materials of which the various instruments are made, their size, and whether they are struck, plucked, banged on, or blown into.

Tone colors can be rich, warm, bright, dark, mellow (such as oboes, flutes, bassoons, cellos). Or they can be brilliant, like a trumpet. The piano is one of the most highly versatile of all acoustic instruments, with a broad range of pitches, tone colors and dynamics. It can whisper a melody or bellow it loudly. It can resonate one pure and fine tone, or a rich, vibrant combination of colors.

When several different instruments are combined, it results in an entirely new and beautiful palate of tone colors. Think of the magnificent landscape an entire orchestra paints with twenty or a hundred different instruments!

Individual instruments can be used to denote different moods, emotions and even represent characters, human or animal. Remember *Peter and the Wolf,* or *The Three Little Pigs,* or the poignant dying swan in *Swan Lake?* Tchaikovsky had perhaps his greatest challenge as a composer when he was commissioned to score the ballet, *The Nutcracker.* It is said that he cried out in frustration, "How the devil do you expect me to compose music to represent a kingdom of lollipops!" But he did. And although Tchaikovsky decried it as his worst work, *The Nutcracker* is considered his best. In it, he used a rather new instrument in his day called a celesta to represent the delicate and sweet Sugar Plum Fairies.

Today, electronic instruments, synthesizers, and computers give us an entirely new spectrum of tonal colors resulting in both agonizing and thrilling musical experiences. Electric guitars and keyboards do not produce musical sounds themselves. Rather, they produce a weak electrical signal that is amplified through a loudspeaker, resulting in the music you hear. Volume and tone controls on these instruments allow the musician to soften, intensify, or modify the sounds at will. What results (pleasant and mellow or shrieking and nerve-shattering) depends upon the style and genre of the music to be played.

Synthesizers make music by "building up" sounds, by creating their own various harmonics through the use of oscillators or computer components, and amplifying the signal through a loudspeaker. Some synthesizers can "sample," or recreate, any live or recorded sound fed into it, and store the sound into their memory banks. A skilled musician/programmer can "synthesize" the sound of an entire orchestra so precisely that even a trained ear would have difficulty in telling the manufactured music from the real thing. This technological advancement has caused countless musicians to lose their jobs, as many showrooms and recording companies make personnel cutbacks to save money.

Computers have taken over our lives and have made a profound impact on the art and profession of music. Computers can produce simple musical tones and notes or entire musical scores. Because they can handle electrical signals at enormous speeds, they can process them in a variety of ways. They can take these signals and change them, add new tones, alter the quality, and even create a modern piece of music in the style of a composer who lived centuries ago. Computers can produce meticulously constant rhythms of all kinds and at speeds a drummer or percussionist could never execute. But the tone color of computerized music is, in my opinion, infinitely inferior to that of acoustic instruments. Much of what we hear in modern music today should be labeled "special sound effects," rather than music, for it is heartless and cold, something true music should never be.

Music's *form* takes on many forms (not to be confused with genres: classical, jazz, ragtime, pop, rock, etc.). Musical form means the organization and careful plotting of all the elements we have discussed (rhythm, melody, harmony, and tonality) into a certain structure as designed by the composer. Consider it the same as the foundation of a building. Without form, the musical structure would collapse into a blob of indistinguishable sounds known as "noise."

In Western European and American music, compositions have a definite form—there is a beginning, middle, and end. You can count phrases and movements, feel when one is ending and the other beginning. There are a vast number of musical structures—or forms— from sonatas, rondos, cantatas, and symphonies in classical music; to simple ballads and ditties with two verses and a "hook chorus" in popular music.

When a piece of music is sung by a vocalist who is, in essence, telling a story, the form is more easily recognizable. The more familiar the story, the more impact the music has on us, the more we remember it, and the more satisfying the musical experience for us.

Understanding what music is from an objective point of view is merely the first step in answering that question, "What is this thing called music?" We must also explore the remarkable subjective aspects of music and what it means to us as individuals and to society as a whole.

SUBJECTIVE

While musicians usually must be more concerned with mastering the physical and technical elements of music than with understanding the *meta*physical aspects of it, how "connected" they are to cosmic influences is revealed in the way their music affects us. A technically flawless composition or performance may evoke our admiration, but it is music with heart and soul that moves and inspires us.

Music truly gets to the essence of what and who we are, because we create it, and we create our relationship to it. It serves many functions, has many uses and elicits many responses in us—physically, emotionally, and spiritually—that are both conscious and subliminal, tangible and intangible.

Here are some of the most common ways in which we utilize music:

1. As *emotional expression,* music gives us the vehicle to express feelings and ideas we might not reveal through normal conversation. We can tell someone we love them in a song, express our loneliness or despair as well as our joy and optimism. Frustration and anger felt by entire groups of people can be demonstrated with music, such as the protest songs of the sixties. With music we can let off steam and touch upon subjects that are taboo without suffering personal rejection and chastisement. Remember Johnny Paycheck musically inviting his boss to "Take This Job and Shove It" or Madonna's lament to unwed motherhood, "Papa Don't Preach"?

2. As *aesthetic enjoyment,* music satisfies man's basic need for creating and contemplating beauty. This is not only true for the artist, or creator of music, but for those who dream and *wish* that they were artists. It verifies the existence of the dedicated composer, and it enhances the otherwise banal existence of the average person.

3. As *entertainment,* music amuses us and diverts our attention away from the stresses of everyday life. It can make us laugh, cry, stand up and cheer, dance, stamp our feet in rhythm, and let us feel just plain good all over.

4. As a means of *communication,* music is universal, but it is not a universal language. The emotions and meanings music conveys and the responses to it depend largely upon the culture and background of the composer and the listener. For example, one may actually feel the joy or sadness of a piece of music, but that feeling and its meaning are based largely upon the mental images and past experiences of the individual.

5. As a *symbol,* music can represent things, ideas, and behaviors. "The Star-Spangled Banner" represents our forefathers' fight for freedom. Neil Diamond's "America" represents the immigrant's desire for and willingness to make sacrifices for freedom. Graduation ceremonies are given even more dignity with the traditional "Pomp and Circumstance."

6. As a means to *integrate society,* music is a phenomenon. It invites and encourages people to participate in group activities and to rally around a cause or support an event that needs group cooperation. Prime recent examples are the "Live Aid" concerts to raise money for starving Africans, the "Farm Aid" concerts to aid the American farmers, and "Hands Across America" to aid the homeless.

7. Music offers *gratification* for both children and adults by allowing them to achieve in a noncompetitive environment. The joy of playing a musical instrument results in high self-esteem and contributes greatly to a state of physical and emotional well-being.

So, now we basically know what music is, how we use it, and, in a general sense, what it does for us. Do we like it? Obviously. But how much do we like music? And why?

We can reduce everything in the universe to cold, empirical scientific data, analyze it, measure it, and label it. But the intangible mystical experiences, the visions, the feelings, the sensations and inspirations of even one person cannot be measured.

We can take a human heart and examine its physical components and functions, but we can never see or measure or know what is *in* that heart, what it feels, why it laughs or cries, strengthens or crumbles. We can take a brain and analyze its cells, its function, know that it thinks and rules the body; but we cannot see the images—physical and metaphysical—that it sees, or travel to the vast depths of despair and ascend to the boundless heights of ecstasy that the mind can travel, merely by examining tissue slices under a microscope. All of these intangibles belong only to the soul of the individual person who possesses the heart and the brain.

It is the same with music. We can reduce it to its numerical values, to its physical laws of vibrations, but we cannot measure completely the profound emotional and spiritual effects of music in the same way you measure the fluctuation of the heartbeat, brain waves, or breathing rhythms. The only way you can know the true power of music is to *know* it, to *feel* it, *see* it, *become* it. And this truly is an individual experience.

Everyone reacts to music. To what degree of passion is as unique as the human being who is reacting. People vary in their preferences for everything under the sun that appeals to their sensory nature: food, clothing, movies, home decor, art, and music. These preferences have their roots in a person's individual biological design and emotional needs, cultural experiences, age, education, and even geographic location. There is also a wide variance in what people consider "good" music and even why they think it's good. It might be safe to say that one person's music is another person's madness.

Some people won't recognize any music with a pop-rock beat as music to be taken seriously. Still others wouldn't be caught dead listening to Mozart. For some, country is the *only* music (if you're any kind of American!), and for others, well, it takes a little swing to put them "In The Mood."

Then, there are those who aren't sure: "I don't know what I like, but I'll know it when I hear it."

We may love a song one day and hate it the next. As our personalities, moods, lifestyles and needs change, so do our tastes and our evaluations of what is "good" or "bad," pleasant or unpleasant, inspiring or dull. We all listen to music in different ways and for different reasons. Some of us, however, *listen* but do not *hear*. But our body hears and our subconscious mind hears.

It's been said that man is not corrupted by what goes into the mind, but by what comes out of it. While this theory is debatable, it does hold a large grain of truth. Certainly it is desirable to expose ourselves only to the best and most positive thoughts, ideas, words, and music. But we can't always control our environment. We can, however, be more aware of its influences and learn to turn negative experiences into positive ones.

I stated in my Overture that the "good" or "bad" in music lies in its *purpose* and not in its *form*. And I truly believe that. A music scholar or critic may analyze a piece of music by asking objectively, "Does it follow the rules of harmony, or does it break these rules? If the latter, is it with the purpose of expanding on the basic foundation to find a larger truth, or does it rebel for the composer's sake alone? Is it serious music or is it frivolous?"

But you and I, concerned with more subjective purposes of music may ask: "What is the motive behind this song? Is it to provide a physical or emotional experience that helps me explore my own inner feelings, that makes me break out of my skin, so to speak, and discover latent depths of my personality? Does it make me feel good about life or inspire me to find more creative solutions to life's problems? Does it stand the test of time and strike a responsive chord in me of love, joy, or reverence as it has for countless others through the years? Does it make me feel just plain good all over so that I treat everyone around me with the same love and respect that I would like to receive?"

Whatever questions you may ask of it, music is far too important to life not to have a purpose, and it should always be a purpose for good.

Saturating our body and mind with the best music we can find isn't a one-way street:

"Music is a moral law," said Plato. "It gives a soul to the universe, wings to the mind, flight to the imagination, a charm to sadness, gaiety and life to everything. It is the essence of order and leads to all that is good, just and beautiful, of which it is the invisible, but nevertheless dazzling, passionate and eternal glow."

Fortunately, Plato could never have heard the music of Twisted Sister. But I am certain you get his drift. When we use music to tune up inside, the positive feelings we enjoy will flow forth from us and positively affect everything around us. By understanding what music is and how we can use its power to our benefit, what "comes out" of us will be a "dazzling, passionate and eternal glow."

3

The Musical Bridge

OUR life here on earth has a vital connection to all of universal life. You and I cannot reach out and physically touch a star or capture a rainbow, but we know they exist and have an effect on our earthly existence. Our connection to the universe can be bridged by our spiritual beliefs—the thoughts and precepts we carry around in our head and heart but cannot touch or see—or by one of life's "tangibles" known as music.

With music, we have the best of both worlds: We can experience it physically, in the stimulation and energy it provides, and we can bathe in its ethereal qualities, feeling it emotionally and spiritually. Music is a bridge of profound strength and substance and allows us to be in touch with the entire world of vibrations.

PART I: PHYSICAL EFFECTS

Think of the loud pounding of a hammer smashing against a nail as it is driven into a board. Would you want to listen to that pounding for hours on end. I doubt it. It makes your head throb, which is probably why we coined the expression, "My head is pounding like a hammer" to describe a headache.

On the other hand, try to imagine the light tapping of a sculptor's chisel on a delicate piece of stone. This sound can be a very pleasant one, partly because of the subtlety of the sculptor's touch, and partly because we know he is creating something of beauty, something that will always be there enriching our lives.

Now recall the riveting noise of a pneumatic drill ripping up the street outside your window. How many metal fillings have you cracked hearing that abominable noise? Wouldn't you rather hear the rhythm of the falling rain, gently showering the earth with love, refreshing and invigorating the air? Of course you would.

That's the way it is with music. Some musical sounds and tones are more pleasing than others, and consequently more beneficial to our health and well-being. The ancient philosphers and scientists believed it; long ago, musicians and physicians incorporated this belief into their respective arts.

Of course, previous civilizations didn't have to deal with the music(?) of Motley Crue, wrecking balls, or those horrific little dirt bikes that buzz around and around and around. Everything was relatively quiet. Perhaps a bird chirped a bit zealously now and then, or the wind whistled fiercely through the logs in the cabin, but all in all it was pretty darned quiet.

Today, we are overassaulted with noise from morning till night, whether we choose the assault or not. Living in high-density-noise environments (near the airport or industrial center), plays havoc with our health. There are more noise-related headaches, respiratory disorders, nervous breakdowns, cardiac problems, and digestive upsets than ever before. Too much exposure to this irritating cacophony of environmental sounds gives people a feeling of agitation, anger, and frustration—even when they are not consciously aware of the noises, and when they think they have tuned them out.

Just think about all the "normal" noise you are subjected to every day: planes, trains, dual exhaust mufflers, honking horns, machinery, humming generators, computer terminals, ringing phones, crying babies, screaming adults, the dishwasher, washing machine, air conditioner, ad nauseum. (And if you work in a Las Vegas casino, add slot machine bells, buzzers, and sirens.)

To add insult to injury, we compound the problem by blasting our senses with overamplified TV's, radios, and stereos in an attempt to "get away from it all" and "relax." In reality, your body never gets a chance to fully calm down from one frenzied sound experience before it is jolted into another.

The music we listen to—by chance or by choice—has immediate and long-lasting impact on us for both good and ill. These effects are no longer just theories, as some skeptics might suppose. There is much empirical evidence to substantiate what the ancients knew instinctively: that music is the bridge linking all things physical, spiritual, and emotional in the universe.

For many years, scientific studies on music's physical effects focused primarily on relaxation or stimulation of the body via the beat of the music: slow music retarded the pulse and respiration and slightly reduced blood pressure; faster music quickened these vital signs. Music was used for psychological therapy based mostly on the relaxation/ stimulation response.

But in 1970, when Dorothy Retallack released her historic findings on the effects of music on plants, research in this area took a tremendous turn, and the beat was no longer the essential focus of experimentation. Now, it was the *sounds* of the music that became important.

Retallack was a music major in college in 1968 and required to take a biology class in order to receive her degree. While contemplating what to do for the required experiment, she remembered reading about the effects of prayer and the human voice on plants. It was reported that plants that were prayed over and loved thrived beautifully. The plants that received "hate vibrations" deteriorated.

Based on these findings, Retallack decided to embark on an experiment to see if certain tones affected plants more than other tones. First she began by playing certain single notes to the plants in an environment where light, temperature, soil, and water were controlled. After several weeks of being exposed almost constantly to music tones every day, most of the plants died. Later, when certain other tones were played for about three hours at a time intermittently, the plants responded better, even better than those plants kept in complete silence.

From there, Retallack progressed to playing recordings of actual musical compositions using pop, rock, acid rock, classical, jazz, country, and East Indian music. The plants grew lush and abundant on almost all the music (especially classical, jazz, and Ravi Shankar), but they withered and died in the rock music chamber. Of the classical music played, Bach was by far the plants' favorite composer (remember his training in Pythagorean principles?). The acid rock music, which had detrimental effects, included selections by Led Zeppelin and Jimi Hendrix.

While Retallack's music selections in all genres were limited, and by no means representative of a total bias for or against any one kind of music, still her findings were provocative. Experiments with music became almost a national pastime in the academic world as researchers sought to discover the effects of music on plants, animals, and people.

In his book, *The Secret Power of Music,* David Tame recounts experiments conducted by psychologists who wantd to test the effects of rock and Bach on rats. The rats were given free rein of two connecting boxes; in one box, Bach's music was piped in, while the other box was racked with rock music. By and large, the rats chose the Bach box—even when the music was switched from one box to the other.

Other experiments have found that certain pieces of music (such as "The Blue Danube") cause hens to lay more eggs, and music also helps cows give more milk. In the Soviet Union and Canada, researchers discovered that wheat grows faster at the sound of certain musical and ultrasonic tones. At Century Seafood in Philadelphia, lobsters are serenaded with such selections as "Old Cape Cod" to tenderize the critters for consumption.

Through experiments with sound vibrations and matter, science is learning how the sound vibrations of music affect our bodies, vital organs, and cells. Cymatics, a science developed in recent years by Dr. Hans Jenny of Switzerland, allows us to actually *see* the results of different sounds on such things as metal filings, liquids, and powders. By exposing them to certain vibrations, these *inorganic* elements rearranged themselves to form intriguing geometric *organic* shapes such as spirals, hexagonal cells of honeycombs, and pentagonal stars.

Although Jenny spent ten years on the study of wave forms and their relationship to matter, his work was based on the discoveries around 1800 of German physicist Ernst Chladni, who developed violin-shaped metal plates that made visible the kinds of vibrations that are natural to violins.

So, it seems that the ancient teachings and philosophies on music are being borne out by scientific experiments. Today, modern biochemists and astrophysicists, as well as yogis, agree that our bodies are systems of vibrating atomic particles, and that the cells in our bodies resonate automatically to incoming sound vibrations. If sound vibrations can affect and rearrange the patterns of sand particles and metal filings, it is safe to presume that music vibrations produced by instruments and our own voices can have an effect on how the cells of our body are arranged and rearranged. It's certainly not unknown that music of a high, shrill frequency can shatter glass (remember the Memorex tape commercials?), so why could it not have the same effect on the human body? Apparently there is little doubt that it does.

Our bodies themselves are instruments, the cells and organs are vibrating masses, the bones in our heads are resonators. Dr. Steven Halpern, noted researcher and composer of the "Anti-Frantic Alternative" series of recordings, offers a very simple experiment by which we can verify the resonance of sound vibrations on our own body. Using the vowel sound "O," sing a low note, as low as you can, in a hearty but not forced voice. Close your eyes and feel where in your body you experience the tone. Most likely you will feel it somewhere around your stomach area or below. Sing a higher note and see if it doesn't settle around your chest cavity. Your highest note following that one (come on, sing out!) should resonate somewhere in your head.

In his fascinating book, *Tuning the Human Instrument,* Halpern describes his research, which focused mostly on the relaxational response to music. Halpern designed the first experiments back in 1973 that involved both GSR (galvanized skin response), biofeedback, and Kirlian photography (which photographs the colorful aura—electromagnetic field—around the body). He and a team of associates played music for test subjects that had been classified by the National Music Therapy Association as being highly relaxing and meditative (such as "Leibestraum No. 3" by Liszt). They also used some music that Halpern himself had been working on aimed specifically at achieving relaxation ("Spectrum Suite"), and compared the test subjects' responses to these compositions.

The results demonstrated that Halpern's music was far more conducive to actual physiological relaxation than the classical pieces, and the Kirlian images obtained with "Spectrum Suite" paralleled the results of studies that involved meditation and healing.

Of course, Halpern composes his music specifically to be beneficial to your health and primarily to relax you. Most music, however, is created for aesthetic (or monetary) reasons. This doesn't mean it is good or bad. It simply means that music that is truly beneficial to one's health and well-being does not come about by chance. It must contain the right elements so that the body involuntarily responds in a healthful, positive way, without mental suggestions or anticipation of a desired result.

Music to relax to or mediate to is pretty easy to come by. Just walk into any metaphysical book and record store and take your choice from a wide selection of tapes and records. And it is fairly easy to see (or *feel)* why this music is so soothing. On the other hand, it takes some intriguing testing methods to determine what happens to the body when exposed to popular—especially rock—music.

One of these testing methods is Behavioral Kinesiology, used by physical therapists, physicians, and chiropractors to test the strength or weakness of a patient's muscles and organs. You might have undergone this testing procedure at one time or another and not have known what it is called. The doctor has you stand up or lie down, extend your arm while he touches a specific pressure point on your body, pushes down on your extended arm, and tells you to resist his efforts. Since every muscle in the body relates to an organ, if muscles test weak it can be an indication that there is some internal malfunction or imbalance.

Dr. John Diamond, an Australian psychiatrist and physician practicing in New York, tested thousands of recordings on subjects using various types of music and found a direct correlation between music and muscle strength or weakness. As explained in his book, *Your Body Doesn't Lie,* Diamond demonstrated that our bodies can discriminate between various performances of the same musical compositions, can distinguish between beneficial and deterimental sounds, and can be helped enormously by certain sounds.

He found this to be so even if we cover our ears and block the sound, because we hear with our entire body, not just our ears. He also affirms that music enhances our general well-being and that surrounded by the right sounds we can be "invigorated, energized and balanced...Music can be an important part of our program of primary prevention of illness at a prephysical, energy-imbalance level."

He cited the long and healthy lifespan of music conductors (such as Stokowski, Toscanini, Fiedler, and Ormandy) who were active, productive, and creative even into their eighties and nineties while the average age of death of the American male is 68.9 years, and attributed much of this longevity to the conductors' exposure to the healing qualities of the music of the Great Masters.

Through the course of testing thousands of recordings of hard rock artists (such as The Doors, The Band, Janis Joplin, Queen, Alice

Cooper, Bachman-Turner Overdrive and Led Zeppelin), Diamond found that the "stopped anapestic beat" of this music caused all the muscles in the entire body to go weak. The anapestic beat (which sounds like da-da-DAH) is contrary to the human heartbeat (which goes DAH-da).

The body operates optimally at its own natural rhythms, but being a highly sensitive instrument, the body feels and adapts itself to the rhythms of its surroundings. If those rhythms are unnatural (such as the da-da-DAH beat), and the exposure is prolonged, there is a potential for physical damage, such as weakening of the muscles.

Another phenomenon occurs when the anapestic beat is played. It's called "switching" of the brain. This means that the symmetry between the two cerebral hemispheres is lost and the entire body is thrown into a state of alarm, causing a host of disorders to manifest in the form of behavioral and learning disabilities in children, as well as poor work performance, fatigue, and general malaise in adults.

Diamond found that not all rock music had this effect, nor did a particular group's music have a detrimental effect consistently. Certain selections by the Beatles, fifties and sixties rock and roll, country, jazz, and some other music styles did not weaken muscles. It appears that when music is swift and constant with no hesitation of the beat between measures...in other words when it's really rockin' and rollin'...it creates a forward motion that your mind and body respond to with extra energy and physical strength.

In today's music, especially computerized funk, soul, and disco (also called "dance" music), this anapestic beat is very noticable, mainly because it is played at a moderate tempo for a specific style of dancing. Michael Jackson's "Billy Jean" is a prime example of the anapestic beat, as well as some of the music of the Culture Club, Madonna, Eurythmics, The Cars, etc. Music of the Doobie Brothers, Huey Lewis, or Chuck Berry's classic "Roll Over Beethoven" are good examples of music with a forward motion that really rocks and rolls.

Erratic beats are not the only elements in music that have a detrimental effect on the body. Ultrahigh (shrill) frequencies found in heavy metal music can be especially hazardous. Christian minister and former rock guitarist Bob Larson recounts experiments conducted by Drs. Earl W. Flosdorf and Leslie A. Chambers demonstrating that shrill sounds projected into a liquid medium coagulated proteins. Larson also recalls that a teenage fad (in the seventies) was to take raw eggs to rock concerts and place them at the foot of the stage. Before the concert was over, the eggs could be eaten hard-boiled as a result of the raucous rock music.

Rock music may be the most pervasive, but it is not the only culprit. When music is chaotic and dissonant, muscles test weak. Diamond cited Stravinsky's *"Rite of Spring"* and Ravel's *"La Valse"* (specifically the endings of the compositions) as especially debilitating because they disintegrate into a crescendo of dissonance and confusion. Another example was a short segment of Haitian voodoo drumming.

According to anthropologist Ralph G. Locke and experimental psychiatrist Edward F. Kelly at Spring Creek Institute in North Carolina, rhythmic drumming at certain frequencies can make the brain's rhythms become synchronized to them. This is similar to "photic driving," in which flashing strobe lights (a popular effect in many discos) can impose their rhythm on the brain.

But while most other music forms are not addictive, rock music is, and many people insist that they can't "get up" to anything but rock music. This is probably so. Rock is addictive because the drumbeat has gotten increasingly louder over the years and overshadows the melody and lyrics and other instruments. (This beat has even found its way into country music). We become hypnotized and caught up in this urgent rhythm, and it becomes "natural" to us even though it is out of sync with our natural body rhythms. While we are undergoing this music-induced stress, the flow of adrenaline is heavy and, as with any "drug," we can get hooked on this excitation and become adrenaline junkies. But eventually this stress takes its toll.

But just as effectual as the overpowering rhythms and drumbeats of rock, et al., is the volume at which they are played. When instruments were purely acoustical and unamplified, we heard music with our ears and brain, and could decide for ourselves whether or not is was good or bad, pleasing or annoying, stimulating or dull. But with the advent of the electronic instrument, stereophonic sound and its accoutrements, the whole body became the ear. At high decibels—more than 90— sound begins to be dangerous to your health. And at 120 to 130 decibels—the level at which most modern music is played—it not only literally hurts your ears, but the vibrations rack your body from the inside out.

The Better Hearing Institute in Washington, D.C., estimates that it takes as little as fifteen minutes of exposure to loud rock music for damage to occur. When you consider that the body has no defense against loud and repetitive sound (except to get as far away from it as possible), it's a scary proposition. This is true whether it is a rock concert, a Las Vegas showroom, or a booming, acoustically dynamic symphony hall. Loud is loud. And the hazards imposed on the performer as well as the audience are well known.

When you hear a ghetto blaster moving down the street attached to the body of a young music fan, or hear a car radio broadcasting for the entire Western hemisphere to hear, have you ever wondered why in the world these people need to play the music so incredibly loud? While some music lovers blast their music because of how it "feels," they are alos wrapping themselves in an emotional security blanket of sounds, protecting themselves from physical or psychological intrusions, according to music therapists. Perhaps this is why some insecure *adults* prefer a deafening disco to a quiet restaurant for their romantic encounters. It keeps them from getting too close to another person and therefore "protects" them.

Unless you are an insecure, rebellious teen, or an adult suffering from the Peter Pan syndrome, you'll have little trouble avoiding heavy metal and its hair-splicing electronics and histrionics (a la Judas Priest, Black Sabbath, Motley Crue, etc.). or the seamy violence of punk made infamous by the late Sid Vicious and the Sex Pistols.

But perhaps just as harmful as the anapestic beats, painful volumes, and metal guitars is the monotonous droning of computerized music and rapping songs. Even at low volumes, this tedious uninteresting type of music seems to be a form of physical and mental Chinese water torture (a continuous dripping of water on the brow—drip, drip, DRIP!)

One music assignment I had was to visit a popular Las Vegas Disco and monitor the music to perhaps suggest some changes in the programming. After two hours, I no longer heard any music. All I felt was the beat (da-da-DAH) as one song after another was mixed in non-stop for the dancing pleasure of the crowd. Every song had the same tempo and almost every one was in the same key—or so it seemed. I observed the people on the dance floor. They were mesmerized, out in some Never Never Land of physical excitation that transcended the here and now. Needless to say, attempts to add some diversity to the music were met with less than enthusiastic reactions.

Lest we annihilate rock music altogether and cause an uproar of indignation from rock musicians and fans, let me add that there is no reason to dismiss rock entirely from your life. There is much about today's music that is good. To say that all of it is harmful is a gross generalization and as erroneous (and pompous) as saying that all classical music is therapeutic.

What is rock music, anyway? It almost defies categorization. Is it the country-rooted music of Elvis Presley? The sophisticated art-rock of Moody Blues and the Beatles? The musical poetry of Paul Simon and Neil Diamond? Is it the frollicking rhythms of Elton John and Billy Joel? Or the blues-inspired rock of Bob Seger? The ear-splicing squeals of Ozzy Osbourne? The "machine" music of Janet Jackson or Klymaxx? The fusion of Chicago? The R&B/rock of Stevie Wonder?

It is all these and more. The trick is to separate the wheat from the chaff, discard the worthless and retain the nourishing. Through his experiments, Dr. John Diamond noted that the weakening effects of rock music ceased when the music itself ceased. The key, therefore, is to avoid prolonged exposure to the negative elements of rock (or any music) to the exclusion of all other forms. Be selective and vary your music. To do otherwise is to cheat yourself of many new and memorable experiences.

PART II: EMOTIONAL AND PSYCHOLOGICAL EFFECTS

The physical effects of music are decidedly powerful, and there seems to be little—if any—disagreement among scientists and researchers that this is so. There is also a widespread consensus among psychologists, philosophers, and musicologists that music influences the mind and emotions in very profound ways, even though there is no universal agreement on just how it manages to do so. The creation of music and our responses to it depend largely on cultural learning, our exposure to, and training in music.

Most people respond to the familiar and are reluctant (or have little opportunity) to avail themselves of new and alien forms of music. Their responses, then, may be limited, much the same as when one limit's his perceptions of color's impact by choosing only primary (red, blue, yellow) or neutral (black, white) hues. The more varied the colors of your clothing, makeup, home, and other environments, the more kaleidoscopic your life experiences will be. The more you allow yourself to bask in the multifaceted sensual experiences of music, the more depth and creativity your responses will engender.

Music can make us feel happy, passionate, angry, reverent, sentimental, or sad. When we feel melancholy, nostalgic, and even teary-eyed, we are usually responding to minor chords in the music.

These "sad-sounding" chords and melodies trigger certain chemical reactions in our system that in turn bring forth more of these emotions.

Author and metaphysician Corinne Heline relates these feelings to the life cycles of the universe and the annual seasons that alternate between a "major" and a "minor." At the Autumn Equinox, the earth changes from the major tones of spring and summer to the minors that prevail during autumn and winter.

In music, major cords are said to be masculine (*yang*): strong, extroverted and outgoing. Minor chords are said to be feminine (*yin*): sentimental, expressing inner emotions, gentle. Generally speaking, the white keys on the piano are natural notes while the black keys are flats or sharps. Looking at the note "D" on the keyboard, you see that it is surrounded by two black keys; the one to the left creates D flat, the one to the right creates D sharp. Flatted notes (lowered a half-tone from the natural note) are described as minor and feminine; sharped notes (raised a half-tone from the natural) are major and masculine.

The ancient Chinese believed strongly in the concept of two opposite, balancing polarities of *yin* and *yang*, or the *T'ai chi*. The entire system of their philosophy posits that everything in the universe—including music—consists of varying combinations of these two (masculine, feminine; positive, negative) forces.

Beethoven's Fifth symphony is surely *yang*, while Franz Schubert's *Ave Maria* is undoubtedly *yin*. In the popular music vein, Jacque Brel's poignant, "If You Go Away," feels decidedly *yin* to me, as does George Gershwin's "Summertime" from *Porgy and Bess*. On the other hand, the songs, "My Way" and the theme from "New York, New York" feel very *yang*.

These two fundamental opposites have a very strong effect on men and women alike, perhaps in varying degrees, for we are all possessed of both masculine and feminine hormones, chromosomes and emotions.

Our emotional responses to music have been labeled "Essentic Forms" by Dr. Manfred Clines, an Australian neuropsychologist and concert pianist, who has recorded them on a graph via a computerized push-button device.

Clynes, author of *Sentics (The Touch of Emotion)* and *Music, Mind and Brain: The Neuropsychology of Music*, claims that codes in the nervous system may explain why certain musical compositions evoke specific feelings in us. This neurobiological influence may not only condition one's *responses* to the emotional and rhythmic quality of the music, but it could affect the initial *creation* of the qualities themselves.

To illustrate, Clynes asks why a single piece of music when performed by a great artist can "move and transform the state of listeners, penetrate their defenses and make them glad to be alive"— while the same piece performed by a lesser artist, does not have this power?

Clynes asserts that the answer is not to be found in the musical *score*, but in the performer's *feel* for the composition. The greater the musician's empathy, the more clarity in his expression, and the deeper the listener's response.

Research by Clynes further suggests that "essentic forms" have innate meanings that transcend cultural learning and conditioning and are therefore neurologically coded. He demonstrated this by instructing people in four different countries (the United States, Mexico, Japan, and Indonesia) to press the push-button transducer with each of seven emotions: anger, hate, greed, love, sex, joy, and reverence. The transducer then converted the *form* of the push—the pressure pattern of the finger on the button—to a tone or a line on the graph. The graphic representation for each emotion was approximately the same for all individuals regardless of their culture.

Clynes also suggests that musical compositions embody the unique "inner pulse" of their composers, that they are a reflection of the composer's own personality. And a performer whose own inner pulse is sensitive to the composer's can communicate the same emotions to the audience and reflect the visions of joy, love, and so forth that were created perhaps hundreds of years before.

The same can be said of orchestra conductors. Some are filled with a highly transmittable life energy that motivates and inspires the musicians to peak performance and can absolutely electrify the audience. Others are merely technically proficient and make no emotional connection to the composer's work. Thus the entire performance is cold.

In the recording studio, it is the engineer who ultimately is responsible for capturing the essence and "inner pulse" of the composer, musician, conductor, and performer. If he is attuned to their inner feelings, he will enshrine the moment forever on tape. If he doesn't get the "message," the meaning will be lost, the mix will be bad, and, if it gets to the market place, the buyer of the record will be ultimately cheated.

(It might be an interesting experiment for you to conduct at home or at a concert, or anywhere you might be able to listen to music of your

choice. Check your emotional reactions to a particular artist's performance, then compare the performances of the same works with another
artist. See if you feel the same as you did the first time. See if your inner
pulse matches theirs. This can be a very important tool in self-discovery
which we will discuss in a later chapter.)

Each group of instruments, indeed the individual instruments
themselves, evoke a variety of physical and emotional responses in us
and are deliberately used for such a purpose. When artfully played,
woodwinds and stringed instruments such as the flute, oboe, harp,
piano, cello, and so forth, have a very soothing, mind-clearing effect.
These instruments voice the cry of the soul for love, God-awareness, and
total well-being. Wind chimes and bells, such as the sistrum used in
some religious ceremonies to cast away evil spirits, lift us to higher
levels of consciousness with their pure, clean tones.

The thrilling sound of the trumpet and other brass instruments
still represent "The Word," or power, stimulate our feelings of potency
and nobility, and sometimes arouse a sense of terror and foreboding.
The Bible recounts how Joshua destroyed the walls of Jericho through
the use of sound produced in sequences of seven. Joshua and his
legions headed by seven priests blowing seven trumpets of rams' horns,
circled the city for seven days. On the seventh day, they circled seven
times, and when Joshua's people shouted along with the blare of the
trumpets, the walls of Jericho came tumbling down. To this day, the
assault on the enemy in every movie is accompanied by the rousing
sound of trumpets, bugles, and brass.

The organ, known as the "king of the instruments," is powerfully
connected to that Cosmic Life Force that lifts the soul to greater
heights and inspires us to fulfill our destinies. It is still the dominant
instrument in churches and cathedrals, but in the twentieth century it
became affiliated with "soul" music of another kind: the blues. Used
only rarely prior to 1951 by Fats Waller and Count Basie, the Hammond
organ was spotlighted by Wild Bill Davis who performed blues-oriented
works on it. But the real potential of the instrument was proven by jazz
great Jimmy Smith, who helped the instrument obtain wholehearted
acceptance in the Funky Era.

The heavy percussion instruments, such as the bass drum,
influence our emotions by arousing our base passions. And the sound
vibration of the electric bass guitar, with its very low frequency levels
powerfully amplified, acts as a sexual stimulus because it resonates
right at the "crucial point" between the thighs. The drum and the bass

guitar combined offer a musical aphrodisiac that has popularized popular music more than any other element.

Certain sounds created by instruments or synthesizers are used in television and movie films to elicit a wide range of emotional responses from us. Remember the foreboding, stomach-churning music to denote the approach of the unseen shark in *Jaws?* Or the shrill, nerve-shattering "musical screams" in a *Psycho*-genre murder scene?

Using music to achieve altered states of consciousness is not a new phenomenon, although it is becoming a significant trend in popular music today. Lab research shows that certain drumbeats act as a kind of pacemaker, regulating brain-wave rhythms and breathing, and leading to biochemical changes that alter one's conscious awareness. Certain primitive cultures in the Third World, and in Asia and the Orient, all knew how to use music to induce trances, control pain, and perform extraordinary physical deeds, such as sprinting across a bed of coals without burning the soles of their feet.

The war dances of the early American Indians, accompanied by incessant drumbeats, stamping of the feet and ardent chanting, awakened their deep animal instincts, worked them into a mental frenzy, and preceded the killing of their enemies. Some of today's rock bands use a similar hypnotic rhythm in order to hook you on the stimulus of their sound so you will be urged to buy their records. Which leads us to the twentieth-century version of Altered States of Consciousness—or rather Manipulation of the Mind through music. And it is not only the rock groups who are the guilty ones here.

Music is no longer mainly an intellectual stimulus—something the ears hear and the mind imagines. Now, it is a total sensory experience. It is imagination brought to life through films, videotape, and live performances. Music is lasers, sensitizers, prismatics, and other special effects. Not only can we hear it, but we can see it and feel it. We can even taste it and smell it as it summons forth the craving for a Godfather's pizza and a Sugar Free Dr Pepper.

Using a precise number of beats per minute, the most penetrating vibrational frequencies, mind-boggling visual effects, and irresistibly suggestive lyrics, music Svengalis from Hollywood and Vine to Madison Avenue wield us into euphoric states, rebellious exhibitionism, and wild spending sprees. This is the era of the great seduction, and the seductive sounds of music begin—and end—with "dough."

Whether it's our favorite record or video, background music in a store or restaurant, Muzak at work or in the elevator, or those ubiquitous radio and television jingles, music today is composed primarily to cause certain chemical reactions in the body (such as a boost in adrenaline flow), to alter brain waves, manipulate blood pressure and respiration, stimulate sexual desires, and render us malleable to the dictates of the music and its message.

The scientific programming of music to affect subliminal control of large numbers of people became prevalent—and lucrative—in the 1930's with the invention of that aural ozone known as Muzak. The Muzak people resist the notion that their service borders on mind control, and call it a "subliminal motivator." But, to coin a phrase, "One man's subliminal motivator is another man's manipulator." And manipulate Muzak does.

Every tone and rhythm pattern is carefully synchronized to complement patterns of human productivity and behavior. In the workplace, Muzak begins with a slow tempo in the morning, increases its pace just before lunch, slows down again, then quickens in the late afternoon. Thus, our energy flow is massaged and regulated to make us work more efficiently and productively, primarily to benefit our employer.

In stores, restaurants, and other commercial establishments, Muzak and similar music services regulate the pace at which we eat and run, linger and buy, or relax and wait. Up-tempo music is used to make us move more quickly through our meal in a restaurant where they want a high turnover of customers (usually to the dismay of our digestive tracts). But in a department store, fast music makes us move through the aisles and pass over merchandise more quickly. This results in lower sales volume. Soft, slow music is used, therefore, to make us relax, linger and empty our wallets.

Because the emotional dynamics in music causes spontaneous and "human" reactions in the listener, Muzak is careful to squeeze all the emotion, color, and meaning out of their selections, leaving us with musical white bread. The best thing that can be said for this dead form of music is that it gives live musicians a job. (I think!)

Noted author and television personality, Edwin Newman, proposes that background music (Muzak, et al.) sounds as though it has been composed by someone who had been *told* about music, but had never *heard* any. "Over the centuries," Newman writes, "many have managed to do this, but only in our time have composers set about it deliberately." He doubts that anyone really listens to it, including the producers of it themselves. But he also laments that, because of the computer process of composing, there are so many possible arrangements of notes and instruments, "the material for background music will never run out."

It may seem to be an innocuous presence in our lives, yet when we have no say as to when it will be inflicted upon us and how it will be used, the control of our sound environment is taken away from us and placed in the hands of those with self-serving interests.

Taking a cue from Muzak's laboratory application of tempo to manipulate our behavior, Madison Avenue, et al., created those literally unforgettable 72-beats-a-minute radio and television jingles. While jingles are more of an art form than background music, and contain a dash of emotional appeal here and there, the sole purpose of a jingle is to get us to buy a product.

If we hear the jingle often enough (and God knows we do!), we'll be singing it to ourselves all day long. And when we get to the store and see the product on the shelf, our computer brain clicks that peppy little tune into place and we reach for that box of doughnuts, detergent, or doggy bones, convinced we made a wise buying decision on our own.

If some of us are impervious to the strains of "Ring Around The Collar," most of us are apparently vulnerable to the pulsating sounds of the Top 40 tunes of the day. Ever wise to the music tastes and desires of the buying public, ad agency whiz kids have now decided that all commercials should sound like hits on the radio and look like rock videos.

Transcending its own boundaries (often those of good taste), rock is used not only to sell itself, but to peddle everything we eat, wear, drive, drink, and play with. By taking what is popular on the charts, composers of jingles (which they prefer to call "songs" these days) mold, knead, and squeeze the music into 29.5 seconds of what is known as "Agency Rock." Add to this Top 40 sound the vision of our favorite entertainers (Michael Jackson/Lionel Ritchie for Pepsi, Kool and the Gang for Wendy's Chicken Nuggets, Whitney Houston for Diet Coke), and not only do they have us ready to buy the commercial's product, but the clothes, hairstyles, and life-styles of the performers.

Legendary composer-singer Bob Dylan stated (*Los Angeles Times,* August 1984), "Just as food can be bad for your system, music can be bad for your spiritual and emotional feelings...we're constantly being bombarded by insulting and humiliating music, which people are making for you the way they make those Wonder Bread products."

Too much of today's music comes off the factory production line computerized and lobotomized. We hear only an infinitesimal fraction of the wonderful music available—whether it is classical, rock, jazz, country, etc.—and, unless we have the desire and knowledge to dig through record-store inventories for new and exciting sounds, we will continue to hear only what the producers and distributors want us to hear. We are force-fed cookie-cutter music that fits a hit record "formula," and are thus deprived of the opportunity to experience the works of truly creative and inspired composers of all genres.

Of course, there is no crime in enjoying the music that is being foisted upon us, or in submitting to its enticements, if we do so with conscious consent. If we have full knowledge of the purpose of the music and the motives of its progenitors, we can then refuse to be manipulated to the benefit of others. Instead, we will learn to monitor and direct our own responses and know how to balance any negative influences with positive alternative choices. Which brings us to the plus side of musical mind control.

New age music composers, are exploring rhythms and modes of music that induce relaxation, contemplation, euphoria, and other high-level conscious states. Most of their work is based on yoga theories that support the proposition that various types of music, sounds, and tones have vastly different effects, some beneficial and harmonious with natural body forces, and others harmful.

Since there is a basic relationship between our own level of awareness and the vibrations in the universe, we can achieve a particular state of consciousness by tuning these vibrations to the state of mind we want. This is the principle behind mantra meditation—meditating with sounds such as "Ohm"—or *toning* (vocalizing certain words or sounds so that they resonate in certain parts of the body and balance our energy centers).

To the Hindus, om, also called the Cosmic Sound or Primal Vibration, is the origin and basis of all the matter and energy in the universe. When uttered, this syllable or sound is believed to attune the individual to the Celestial Tones themselves or, to the Music of the Spheres, as they were called by the Pythagoreans of Greece.

If research studies have indicated that the "wrong kind" of music can harm the body and hinder the learning process, it has also demonstrated that the "right kind" of music can have positive effects on the body and further the learning process significantly. In experiments detailed in the book, *Superlearning,* the right kind of music is considered to be selections by Baroque-era composers such as Bach, Telemann, Handel, Vivaldi, and Corelli.

In the 1970's, Bulgarian researchers, under the direction of Dr. Georgi Lozanov, discovered a holistic approach to learning that allows the body and mind to work in harmony through the linking of music and verbal suggestions. It is well known that tension can create a barrier to optimal concentration and retention of information. Relaxation is vital to learning, but while profoundly relaxed people can't concentrate intently, and learning and memory skills are inadequate. To create the most effective atmosphere for learning, Lozanov and his associates developed a program of breathing techniques, rhythmic and carefully timed narration of information to be learned—from foreign languages to mathematical principles, etc.—with music playing in the background to enhance learning and memory retention.

While listening to largo movements from works of Baroque-era composers, with tempos slower than the average heartbeat (sixty beats per minute or slower), the vital signs of test subjects slowed down in rhythm with the music, relaxing them physically but leaving their minds alert for the assimilation of information. When the various educational data was presented to the students while the music played in the background, the students experienced significant increases in awareness and retention of information, and a whole repertoire of health benefits, including relief from pain and headaches (often associated with the stress of learning).

The key is the right brain/left brain/body connection: occupy the creative right brain with music to keep it alert, feed the analytical left brain with data to be learned, and do it at a pace that keeps the body relaxed and receptive to this input.

Vocal music or chants were ruled out lest the lyrics compete with the material to be learned. The best results were obtained using music with a slow, constant rhythm, a nondistracting melodic structure, and harmonic patterns based on specific ratios. That the scientists chose baroque music, therefore, is not surprising. Although they do suggest that much more research needed to be done to find other types of suitable music, such as music from Asia, the Orient, India, and the Middle East.

Subsequent to their experiments, special music was composed in Bulgaria to meet the requirements of the program. In the United States, Steven Halpern states that his composition, "Comfort Zone," can be used in conjunction with the "Superlearning" concepts.

Combining music with verbal suggestions is not new, nor is it limited to "Superlearning" techniques. There are hundreds of audio cassette tapes on the market to help you modify undesirable behavior, improve health and well-being, or achieve specific personal and professional goals. There are tapes for headache relief, conquering bedwetting, improving sports performance, or achieving harmony in marriage. On the side of the ridiculous, there are tapes to increase breast measurements, while on the side of the sublime there are tapes that take you on the spiritual journey to God (self) realization.

The music provided on these tapes is usually classical, easy listening, or meditative. Obviously rock music would not be appropriate here, yet there are some people today who believe subliminal messages are embedded very skillfully in some rock records—messages with demonic undertones. These are probably the same people who believe there are Satanic messages contained in the "Mr. Ed" theme—but only when played backward!

While subliminal *visual* images have been outlawed (such as flashing "Pepsi Cola" or "You want some popcorn" on the movie screen so quickly that it is not seen with the eye but is absorbed by the subconscious mind), subliminal audio tapes (containing subaural messages that only the mind can hear) have burgeoned forth on the market in recent years offering the same opportunities for behavior modification and life enhancement as the regular cassette programs. I personally prefer not to buy those, even though the person who created the taped program may well be legit. If I'm going to have my mind controlled, I want to be consciously aware of it.

Unless we have access to EEG and EKG machines, GSR biofeedback and Kirlian photography equipment, or can have someone test our muscles to music, we must rely upon ourselves to gauge the effects of music on our body and mind. There are few things more exciting than being enveloped by the total sensory experience of music; to be swept away by its dynamics, and to transcend the mundane realities of everyday life. But with this seduction of the self comes a responsibility: to bear the consequences of our actions and reactions.

We must take control of our own sound environment, be aware of the music we hear and how we respond to it. Instead of salivating like Pavlov's dog every time a musical bell goes off, exercise your right of free choice and free will based upon the knowledge you have acquired as to music's physical, emotional, and psychological effects. *Choose* to be stimulated or not to be; *choose* to buy or not to buy; *choose* to be impassioned or not to be moved.

See if you can answer these questions knowledgeably and objectively:

Do your ears throb, does your head pound, or your stomach churn when listening to your favorite music?

Are you jittery and agitated during mealtimes when music is playing in the background?

Do you lie awake at night while listening to the radio or that special classical record to relax you?

Are you buying products that you don't particularly care about and spending money you don't have?

Do you lose your cool and drive erratically when the Top 40 station is on the radio?

And how's your concentration lately?

Check the music you are exposed to. Listen to the elements contained in it: the instruments, the beat, the *volume.* Be aware of *when* you are listening to certain music. It could be the right music played at the wrong time that's causing the problems. Or it could be that *nothing* you are hearing is doing you any good at all. If so, you need to broaden your musical horizons, experiment with different genres of music, expand and refine your music tastes, perhaps with some of the music suggested at the back of this book. I guarantee you'll be listening to music you may have never heard before, or be listening to it and actually *hearing* it in ways you have never heard it before: with your ears, your body, your mind, and your heart.

4

The Musical "Score"

In the "olden days," the scenario went something like this:

> The couple are taking a romantic canoe ride on a moonlit lake. They toy with words. She is demure. He has restraint. Lazily, she runs her fingers through the gold-flecked water. A harp arpeggios. Now the strings tiptoe in. He sings his plaintive words of love. She swoons. He moves closer (without tipping the canoe over). Hollywood kiss. Fade to black.

Cut to this scene:

> The couple stand apart waiting for their cue. First comes the sound of the

drum—primitive, urgent. A chorus of voices fills the air with a mesmerizing chant. The couple move their feet to the rhythm, coyly, marking their territory. Their shoulders sway; then hips, smoothly, coquettishly, then bolder, undulating. Their minds in a trance-like state, the couple slip into another world, one of musical erotica, a frenzied passion, without ever touching each other.

Is this the pagan fertility rite of a primeval tribe of people? No doubt it has its roots there. But this scenario is taking place in discos and night spots around the world, with men and women getting more aroused dancing *apart* from each other than *with* each other.

But who has the potential for a more satisfying romantic experience: the couple on the lake or the couple on the dance floor? While the convertible has since replaced the canoe, and the Jacuzzi has become a substitute for a moonlit lake, romantic music and a quietly seductive atmosphere can do more for fulfilling sexual relationships than all the disco dance floor gyrations can ever do. If the sexual revolution has taught us anything at all, it is that there is much more to love and to sex than just the biological act itself. But try to tell that to some record producers and their sensation-hungry customers.

Using music to arouse our sensual passions is not a 1980's phenomenon. For centuries, composers of "love songs" have inspired romantic notions with poignant melodies and heart-rending lyrics. The tug of music on our heartstrings is as strong today as it ever was, with one overriding difference: the major thrust of today's music is raw sexuality. Instead of having our erotic appetites gently massaged, we are being assaulted with a heavy hand.

Ever since Elvis Presley emerged on the music scene, rock and roll has been given a bad rap. Presley's popularity spawned a new generation of gyrating singer/musicians whose performances were considered lewd, inspired by the devil, and contributing to the corruption of morals in our society. But compared to the performers of today, the fifties and sixties rockers were but mere innocents in both motive and expression. Today, exploitation of our baser animal instincts purely for the love of money is the *raison d'être* behind most of today's popular music.

It's called the "bedroom lure" in the music industry, where most songs are deliberately composed with seduction in mind.

Before structured music ever came into existence, musical tones and rhythms were used by primitive cultures, primarily to attract a mate. Such was the theory of Charles Darwin. But he was not alone in his assumptions. Other theorists believe that all music is an imitation of animal cries. (And what do animals cry for besides food?)

Recall the love legend of Lala and DeDah (from Chapter 1). Were their moans and cries of ecstasy not music to *their* ears, even if they didn't know what "music" was at that point? Now, move forward in time a few million years to about 1975 when soon-to-be-Disco Queen Donna Summer wrote and recorded her steamy version of "Love to Love You, Baby." For nearly seventeen minutes she panted and moaned orgasmically, repeating "Love to love you, Baby" over and over. Obviously, the basic erotic instincts and expressions of homo sapiens had not evolved very much since Lala let out her "high C" of ecstasy. And if she and DeDah had had the accompaniment of pulsing drumbeats and orchestral music, they would have hit Number One on the charts as well.

Suggestive lyrics, pulsating rhythms, and sensual singing are what turn people on today. And when they say, "I like the way this music makes me feel," they don't know how right they are. Popular music (especially soul and rock) *feels* sexually arousing because its low bass guitar frequencies and dominant drumbeats are actually vibrating the very organs we seek to please. With the advent of electronic music, high fidelity sound systems, and dangerously high decibel levels, our entire bodies became the listening instrument, not just our ears. We *feel* the music just as much as we *hear* it. And more and more, the primary focus of popular songs is the insistent beat, which overshadows the melody, lyrics, and other instruments.

Music is pure energy and, as such, it consists of vibratory frequencies that resonate in various energy centers of the body depending upon their *pitch.* High notes resonate in the upper areas of the body, while lower-pitched notes are felt in the lower areas of the body. The *bass* is the lowest part you can sing or play in music, and the body's lowest energy center is from the hips down. It's no wonder that discos and dance clubs are so popular. They are the perfect (and socially acceptable) arena for what has been called "musical masturbation." And squealing young rock groupies are probably as enamored of the bass player's "low frequencies" as they are of the bass player himself.

But overexposure to the very vibrations that arouse people can leave them limp from the constant sound pounding on highly sensitive nerve endings and body organs, especially sexual organs. Composer and music researcher Steven Halpern reports in his book, *Tuning the Human Instrument:*

> "...an increasing number of Rock stars, former paragons of virility, are reporting problems in that area, which testifies to the destructive consequences of daily doses of high volume music."

Aside from the steady, monotonous assault of rock/disco/soul beats, the pulsations and syncopations of jazz music are also sexually arousing. With its primitive African roots, syncopated jazz rhythms (with the accent *off* the beat in four-quarter time) induce high physical and emotional energy and, in an attempt to release these tensions, the body just has to move (with activity centered primarily around the loins). This lower chakra (energy center) stimulation results in an outpouring of sexual hormones and a desire to fulfill sexual impulses as soon as possible. In some instances, people may even lose control. Author David Tame writes:

> "It is not unknown for those who are the chief producers of these rhythms, the drummers of modern music, to actually have music-induced orgasms after several hours of nonstop drumming."

Vintage though it may be (circa 1955), the classic "Voodoo Suite" by Perez Prado's orchestra, featuring Shorty Rogers, is a prime example of erotic, primitive African sounds and rhythms fused with jazz. A more contemporary (1982) example is Michael Jackson's "Wanna Be Startin' Somethin'" on the Quincy Jones-produced album, *Thriller* (actually more of a potpouri of jazz/African/rock/disco rhythms and sounds).

While jazz had its roots in African and European cultures, it had its own influence on other forms of music and on composers who successfully married classical and jazz forms to revolutionize music, including Aaron Copland, George Gershwin, and Maurice Ravel. Known primarily as a French Impressionistic composer, Ravel was destined to write a piece of music that was to become famous years later (1979) as the theme song associated with a frustrated male libido in the top-grossing movie, *10.*

Who could forget the outrageously smitten and determined Dudley Moore in hot pursuit of an air-headed blonde fantasy who liked to "do it" to Ravel's "Bolero"? As the music score pulsed and undulated repetitively (some eighteen repetitions of the basic two-part musical theme, to be exact), with increasing dynamic tension, Moore became more and more aroused, more and more obsessed. Finally, in Bo Derek's bed, with "Bolero" throbbing away in stereo, Moore never did complete the final act. Just what plot twists and turns prevented Moore from fulfilling this fantasy escapes me. But perhaps the music did more to *prevent* sexual fulfillment than *promote* it. Although the composition was greeted with an uproar of acclamation when it first was presented in Paris in 1928, the Spanish-flavored piece draws harsh criticism from author and music therapist, Hal Lingerman (*The Healing Energies of Music*):

> "I feel Ravel's 'Bolero' is a very harmful piece of music, which should be avoided. The particular rhythms and discord, repeated as they are so often throughout the piece, have the effect on some people of depleting energies and can be very scattering and stressful."

Be that as it may, from a therapeutic standpoint, I have witnessed the enrapturing effect *Bolero* has had on people when the sheer physicality of this piece of music has been visually interpreted by performers. A particularly sensual rendition of the Ravel classic was presented by the Nevada Dance Theatre a few seasons ago and the powerful choreography combined with the music literally lifted the audience up out of its seats with cheers and applause. And who can ever forget the magnificent masterpiece on ice created by Jayne Torvil and Christopher Dean, who won an Olympic Gold Medal in 1984 with their spellbinding ice dance to Bolero?

On the other hand, it does point out that highly stimulating music such as this is great for the arousal of the passions within us, but, just as in music there is the necessary polarity called "tension and release," our physical body also must be released from tension so that it may perform well. It is logical to presume, therefore, the most desirable atmosphere for a memorable and satisfying romantic interlude is one in which both partners are dreamy and relaxed, where they transcend the perimeters of time and space, and drift along in a surreal experience that is complemented by lush violins and poignant piano solos. At least this is what I have learned from years and years of viewing four-hanky, silver screen romances. Or perhaps it is because, no matter what wild, driving rhythms have been the foundation for many forms of popular music, it is the romantic, tender love song that has survived and thrived through the years.

For centuries, the grand ballrooms of the elite social class, and the community dance halls of the working folk, were a common setting for boy-girl meetings, courtships, and eventual marriages—emphasis *marriage.* Dances were attended by young men and women, with adults in attendance to provide an air of respectability to the social occasions. Boy and girl met, waltzed, kept an acceptable distance (even while dancing), and eventually married before having, or even *saying* "sex."

By the 1920's, the horse and carriage attitude toward female sexuality began to change (due to relatively efficient forms of contraception) and, sex as a means of emotional expression for both male and female became an accepted norm—but still within the confines of marriage. For the men who frequented clubs and dance halls, dancing was a means of escape, a way to suspend time, to display their physical skills and enjoy their bodies. The girls who smoked, drank, and danced wildly in flapper garb were considered loose and immoral, but they were blazing a new path for young, *single* women who also desired romance, love, *and* sexual freedom.

Popular music became more and more physically oriented (jazz, bebop, swing, etc.) through the succeeding decades, but it was not until the 1950's that the music itself became a sexual form of expression. The gyrations and movements of the performers were instinctual, free-spirited responses to the earthy rhythm and blues beats, and their fans began losing their inhibitions as well at dances, hops, and parties. Still, the sexual aspect of the music and social interactions that ensued emphasized the traditional objectives of love and marriage.

The 1960's, however, were more rebellious musically and sexually. Marriage and love were usurped by fleeting hedonistic pursuits, and rock music allowed young women equal channels with men for expressing their sexual needs and wants without the customary desire for commitment. Even though the girls were still being encouraged to maintain an old-fashioned attitude toward love, romance, and marriage, they were hard-pressed to ignore the seductiveness of groups like the Rolling Stones who explored the dark side of human passions. But their music, and the entire rock music scene, were male-dominated and exuded a feeling of sex as power—over women.

The sexuality of music is inherent in its rhythm, with the beat commanding a direct physical response from the body. Add this beat to the seductive tone of the lyrics and the caressing "touch" of the instruments, and you have a package that is as irresistible as a siren's song. Dressing up to the "nines" to impress the opposite sex, to go partying, to enjoy the sensual delights of the body, to dance the night away on Friday and Saturday evenings, have been the most intense of pleasures from the ragtime era to the present day. But it wasn't until the disco music craze of the 1970's that dancing became a source of what has been termed "whole body eroticism," where dancers were literally entranced by a series of musical repetitions, an endless droning of four-quarter beats without the beginnings, middles, and ends of traditional song structures.

Unlike hard rock music's emphasis on male-female sexuality, disco music created and exemplified an erotic, yet asexual, self-centeredness. It is said that, while disco music is not in and of itself homosexual in nature, its aesthetic experiences—fleeting emotional contact, one-night stands, narcissistic concern for appearances—reflected a gay consciousness. Although the music itself is gone, the Disco phenomena lives on in the non-commital, meat-market atmosphere of singles bars and dance clubs.

No doubt about it. Listening and dancing to music is certainly sexually arousing. But music composers and their fans are also a voyeuristic bunch, somewhat like Chance the gardener in the film *Being There,* who claimed innocently, "I like to watch." Take, for example, the following scenarios from some of the most popular musical works of all time:

A young man making love to his sister, several young men strip young women naked and carry them off to do heaven knows what, a beautiful seductress strips down to her G-string and dances for a roomful of salivating men, frisky monks cavort with virgins, a young boy tries to get it on with every woman he sees, and a string of lighthearted activities (attempted rape, sadism, and murder) packaged into one musical act.

The video lineup on MTV, you are thinking? Wrong. These scenes are found in the following famous operas, respectively: Wagner's *Die Walkuere,* Schoenberg's *Moses and Aron,* Strauss' *Salome,* Carl Orff's choral work *Carmina Burana,* Mozart's *Le Nozze di Figaro,* and Puccini's *Tosca.* Where were the music censors when all this was going on? (In the audience, perhaps?)

The psychological, emotional and biological differences between the sexes can also be a hindrance to satisfying relations. One therapist, who emphasizes that women need more time than men to be aroused, likens the male to a match and the female to a heating pad: "...he lights up immediately and she warms up slowly." Such as the difference between "(Come on, baby) Light My Fire" (The Doors) and "When it comes to love, I want a slow hand" (Pointer Sisters).

Relaxation precedes and enhances many wonderful, important, worthwhile experiences: learning, creativity, athletic performance, healing, birthing—and sex. Relaxation means allowing the body to come back down from the states of tension and anxiety to its natural, healthful vibrations and rhythms. Once in that "balanced" state, you are more responsive to sensory stimulation, such as the touch of another person, and much more perceptive to the emotional needs of that person as well. While calm and focused, your brain is given free rein to fantasize and experience all the pleasures of the moment.

When you warm up your body gradually to exercise, the end result is peak performance and a deeply satisfying, complete workout. In this most intimate of all mind and body "workouts"—sex—why not give yourself every advantage by warming up to *it* gradually and naturally?

Set the stage for romance with candles, a lighted fireplace, or muted lighting and floor pillows. Put on some soft, gentle music and let the slow easy tempo calm you, caress you. Let the emotion and color of the music create romantic, sensual images in your mind, then bring them slowly, magically to life. Whether you choose something lush and dramatic (*Claire de Lune*) or something popular and touching ("She's Got A Way" by Billy Joel), let it be music with *yin* qualities: flowing, sentimental, nurturing. Let it wash over you, bringing all your nerve impulses tingling passionately to the surface. Reminisce about old times, or create a new moment in time to be remembered forever.

When you can't say it with flowers, say it with music. (Sorry this chapter is so short. One can write volumes about music but, with romance...well, some things are best left to the imagination.)

5

The Song is You

TRY to recall the last time you stubbed your bare toes. When you yelled out, it probably went something like this: "Ouch! Ow! Arrgghh! Gad!" or some colorful expletives that cannot be printed here. But whatever sounds came forth, no doubt they were loud, strong, and purposeful: they released the tension in your body and eased the pain. Your yelling was also involuntary and uninhibited, and came from your gut. But when you became conscious of the "noise" you were making, you muffled your screams, rubbed your toes, and suffered the throbbing pain in whimpering self–pity.

Who would imagine that such a common occurrence as stubbing a toe, and our bodily response to it, would be a prime example of the power of the voice? But it is.

All living things have a "voice." Cows moo, birds sing, cats purr, dogs growl, pigs grunt, and people speak. Animals, being instinctual creatures, do not just moo, oink, meow, and so forth, frivolously. They use their voice to denote a basic need or condition. They are imploring their fellow creatures to "look at me...hear me...I am in pain...

55

I'm hungry..." They don't stop to think if they should voice their sentiments. They just do it.

People, on the other hand, use their voice in two distinct ways: 1) to communicate thoughts, feelings, and ideas, which is a controlled and conscious use of the voice, governed by intellect and restrained by the dictates of the mind; and 2) through uninhibited, involuntary expressions of self that are brought forth by a creative force from within, such as in shrieks of laughter, cries of grief and sorrow, screams of pain, and sighs of relief.

People are born with the ability to use this creative force properly without even thinking about it. The gurgles and murmurs of babies are expressions of their bodily feelings. They cry and babble in a natural response to what they are *feeling*—not to what they are *thinking*. But later, as they learn to combine mental images and words, these natural expressions are altered and even hindered by the restraints of conscious thinking. Now, "conscious thinking" is not all that bad. In fact, where would we be without it? Probably in some perennial never-never land of gurgles, babbles, and sighs—like a newborn babe.

But what if we learned to combine the *natural* flow of that voice of ours—the uninhibited sounds that come from deep within, from the soul, from the very essence of what and who we are—with our ability to *consciously* use it for expression? And in combining the two, we were able to energize and heal our bodies, clear and invigorate our minds, and put our lives in order and balance? There are two distinct ways to do this: toning and singing.

In her book, *Toning: The Creative Power of the Voice,* Laurel Elizabeth Keyes defines toning as, "giving release and allowing the natural flow of energy to move through one's body." Toning is a means by which we can achieve total harmony and balance within ourselves. From a health standpoint, toning has great restorative values and enables us to correct disharmonies and discord by the use of tonal vibrations that we create with our own voice. The articulation of certain vowel sounds or syllables have a stimulating effect on the glands and organs, a cleansing effect on the mind and body, and helps to balance the flow of energy within us so we may return to complete physical, emotional, and spiritual harmony.

For example, feel the effects of each of the following vowel sounds as you vocalize them:

Ah (as in *hard*) will stimulate the upper lungs

O (as in *go*) lower lungs

Ohm (as in *home*) the heart

Oo (as in *broom*) sex glands

Ea (as in *head*) the thyroid, parathyroid, and throat

Ee (as in *keep*) stimulates the pituitary and pineal glands, and the head area in general

Perhaps you are toning without even realizing it. People involved in sports or martial arts use certain yells, grunts, and shouts to give them that extra spurt of energy at a crucial moment. The karate yell, "Kiai" or "Kihap," is believed to bring forth extra power and is preferred to the mere silent exhalation of air when performing certain karate moves. Karate students learn to force the air out of their bodies, rather than holding their breath, to give them this extra power. In weight lifting, a groan that sounds like one of pain is expelled by the weight lifter when he (or she) needs to pump that iron to the maximum level. In aerobics classes, instructors will encourage students to yell "Hey!" at intervals when large amounts of oxygen and energy are needed during jogging or hard dancing sequences. Since most people hold their breath when punching, throwing a ball, lifting weights, or doing exercises, they often have to be *taught* and constantly reminded to exhale to give them more energy and to help clear out toxins from the system.

As explained in Chapter 3, sound vibrations in our *external* environment have a profound impact on our bodies, whether we are consciously aware of these vibrations or not. Tonal vibrations emanating from *internal* sources within our own body—that we create with our own voice—also have a dramatic effect positively or negatively on our physical and mental well-being. And again, whether we are aware of these internal vibrations or not, the effects are the same.

And just as it is vital for us to listen to sounds and music that are healthful, it is equally important to understand the power of our own voice, so we can learn to use its power to our benefit.

The wise ancient cultures knew that chants, mantras, and prayers helped to achieve the union of soul, mind, and body. The words "aum," "amen" (derived from aum), and "om" were not created just so they could hear themselves hum. Using these intonations, they believed that man could reach a higher consciousness through a connection with the Creative Life Force, or the "God-self" within. They looked upon the voice as the primary instrument, with its own unique timbre releasing different forms and forces of sound. The ideas, emotions, and attitudes expressed through the voice indicated the level of one's consciousness and the connection to—or separation from—God.

The scriptures state, "In the beginning there was the Word..." But before the Word came Creative Thought, which gave the Word its meaning. On the highest plane of consciousness (such as in the most profound meditative state), thought is unlimited, all-knowing, all-loving, all-giving, without judgment and in complete harmony with the Universal Spirit. On the lower planes of consciousness, the thought becomes an expression of our physical and emotional feelings, and its effects are manifested in strictly physical and emotional ways.

The sound of your voice is pure energy, the same as a musical note, a sonic boom, or any other sound, tone, or noise. It is subject to the same laws of physics: it creates and emanates vibrations, affecting both the sender and the receiver. Silently read the following sentences:

"I love you."

"I hate you!"

"I am afraid of the dark!"

"It's a beautiful evening."

"I am a stupid worthless idiot!"

"I am a wonderful, worthwhile human being."

Now, say these words aloud, inflecting the true emotions associated with the phrases.

Obviously, the written word is not as powerful as the spoken word, and the same words spoken by two different people can have profoundly different effects. We can all remember sitting through dull and boring lecture classes because the speaker had a dull, flat, uninteresting voice, void of expression. Consequently, we didn't remember much of what was said. Other speakers have fired us with enthusiasm through the effective use of their voice to express their feelings and ideas.

Think of the actor (Richard Burton comes to mind) whose vibrant, rich tones have captivated us during a performance. Or the singer (perhaps Beverly Sills) who reaches deep from within to project a breathtaking full-bodied final note.

Just as one's voice is indicative of the ability or inability to control and bring forth inner emotions, the *tone* of the voice is also representative of the state of one's physical and emotional health. The whiny, weak, monotone voice is not only annoying to listen to, it designates that the person has a negative health condition or a negative outlook. He or she emanates and attracts only negative vibrations and conditions in life.

Then there is the strong, forceful voice that disguises destructive emotions, such as hostility and resentment. This person uses his voice to project authority and demand respect, but actually often arouses hate, fear, and rebellion instead. This person's tone often attracts troubles to himself in the way of accidents, catastrophic illness such as strokes and heart attacks, and perhaps even violence.

Ideally, on the other end of the spectrum, there is the voice resonating with self–assurance, warmth, and love; musical with laughter and nuances of unbridled sensitivities. A voice such as this can only emanate forth and draw in vitality, health, and well-being.

Perhaps you have a personal list of people whose voices irritate you, bore you, or anger you. On the other hand, you surely must know some people who uplift you with the clarity, warmth, sincerity, and sparkle in their voices. Think, also, of the *words* these people use constantly. Are they positive about life? Chronic complainers? Bullies? What about their health? What kind of circumstances do they draw to themselves? Is their life like a soap opera, or is it fulfilled and pleasant? Now, apply all of those questions to *yourself.*

We can literally hypnotize ourselves with frequent subconscious utterings, because the mind is utterly fascinated with its own voice. If we consistently think or voice *negative* thoughts, these thoughts will manifest in unhappy, unhealthful conditions, even illness. Conversely, if we program our brain with *positive* ideas, they will manifest into positive realities. "Affirmations" are a form of positive programming. Verbal suggestions to affect changes in behavior, moods, beliefs, and life-styles are a very potent means to "hypnotize" ourselves with wholesome, uplifting ideas. (As discussed in Chapter 3, these verbal suggestions can be acquired on tape with music background for enhanced impact.)

In realizing the power of the voice and in the words it expresses, we must not forget the effect our words have on children. With their fragile egos and sensitive, impressionable minds, the damage that can be done to their self-esteem through constant criticism is heartrending ("You are stupid," "You are lazy," "Why can't you be like your sister," "You'll never amount to anything," etc.). Conversely, words of love, praise, and encouragement are far more desirable in shaping a child's character and instilling a feeling of self-worth.

We all suffer the effects of stress and *distress* every single day. We become frustrated with our lot in life, with our jobs, the state of the economy, the threat of nuclear war, the inability to control our own destiny, feelings of loneliness or unfulfilled dreams. If we cannot overcome these things, usually we cope. But sometimes the coping mechanism fails and we begin to feel physically and emotionally wrung out. If these tensions are not released, we can suffer a physical or emotional breakdown and possibly illness. Now is the time to use the power of the voice.

One of the most graphic examples of this power that I have seen was in the movie *Network,* when TV newsman Howard Beale urged everyone in the nation to throw open their windows and yell, "I'm mad as hell and I'm not going to take it anymore!" What a mass catharsis that was. If we could allow everyone the opportunity to vocalize their aggressions instead of acting them out, the world would be a saner, safer place to live. Even a hearty primal scream now and then would suffice.

But just as you can vocally affirm every emotion, good and bad, in a strong, authoritative manner through toning, you can find a *song* to express your feelings, thoughts and desires. Whether it's "I've Got Plenty Of Nothin" or "You Light Up My Life" or "May The Bird Of Paradise Fly Up Your Nose," there's a song for you. Singing and toning are closely aligned. They both require and inspire proper breathing—something most of us never do unless we are rendered unconscious. They both require learning certain techniques in order to be effective. And they both allow us to echo forth whatever emotions we've been suppressing and are yearning to get out.

Just as mantras and chants were created to allow man to realize his spiritual awareness, songs were created to give voice to body language and emotions. Laborers in the field sang or whistled while working in the hot sun. Mother hummed pleasant little ditties as she churned butter, spun wool, or baked bread. When she cradled her babe in her arms at night, she lulled him to sleep with sweet murmurings and melodies. Folk songs and spiritual hymns were borne out of man's praise for his Creator, or to express the joys and sorrows of life.

There was a time when families and friends joined around the piano in the evening to sing songs of the holiday season or whatever songs were the favorite of the day. This practice has all but ceased with the advent of the radio, phonograph, television, and videos—all designed to make spectators out of us instead of participants. Aside from singing an occasional national anthem at a ball game or other event, most of us rarely know the joy of lifting our voices loud and proud in song.

Who can sing? Anyone who can carry a tune can learn to sing well. If you can speak you can sing, because the vocal mechanics are the same for both actions. Once inhibitions are released from the mind and body, it is surprising how well most people can actually put forth a song. Of course, some people will sing better than others because they were born with a more natural musical talent and a stronger, more resonant set of vocal chords. Not everyone can be a Pavarotti, or even an Ella Fitzgerald. But not everyone is destined to be or needs to be.

Whether you wish to remain an amateur or a professional, studying voice can reap marvelous physical, emotional, and psychological benefits. The American Academy of Teachers of Singing offers at least a dozen important reasons for studying voice:

Singing provides insight into the thoughts and feelings of others and, thus, broadens our cultural understanding and experiences; it enriches the imagination; increases intelligence; improves the power, quality, endurance, and correctness of the speaking voice; strengthens health through deep breathing; develops and strengthens the memory and powers of concentration. Singing releases pent-up emotions; it develops self-confidence and leadership qualities, as well as a more forceful, vital, and poised personality. Singing is a cultural asset; and it gives pleasure to one's self and one's friends.

There are many methods of voice training, depending upon whether you aspire to singing arias, Broadway melodies, or pop ballads. Most of these methods are based on traditional techniques of proper breathing, articulation, vocal exercises, voice placement, etc. But in keeping with these innovative times, one singing coach developed a rather unorthodox method of training boys and girls who desire to become rock music singers.

Known as the "Auntie Mame of heavy metal," Elizabeth Sabine has aided such Los Angeles metal groups as Lizzy Borden, Slayer, Stryper, and Queensrych to achieve a vocal style and strength comparable to some of their favorite artists (such as Steve Perry of Journey and Dennis DeYoung of Styx).

Sabine has described her method of teaching as a combination of Primal Scream therapy and child's play. After studying some of the rock singers admired by her students, she realized they sing just like children on a playground and that they emphasized emotion over technique. Sabine then proceeded to add the Primal Scream theory of radical psychologist Arthur Janov to other theories linking voice with emotion, and devised a teaching method that focused on the gut-level emotions of hard rock. Instead of making her students sing scales, she has them scream phrases like "get lost" or "shut up," phrases frequently vocalized by youngsters.

"Children are uninhibited. They don't listen to their own voices," she states. "They have a passion within. When they feel something, they just tighten their tummies, open their mouths and out it comes."

Sabine's vocal training method is not far afield from toning. Although the goals are different, each method focuses on the *emotional* as a means to achieve the end result. As humans, we are, above all else, emotional beings. This is how we are born, this is how we live, this is how we die. Every day of our lives, we act and react according to how we feel. Ideally, these feelings can be properly expressed—at the right time, in the right manner, honestly and openly. Often, however, our emotions are repressed and suppressed because society, circumstances, and other people in our life's circle demand or command we hold our feelings in check. Thus, what we swallow is regurgitated in unhealthful, destructive ways: illness, depression, hostility, agression, withdrawal from life, perhaps even violence upon ourselves or others.

Singing for enjoyment and emotional release should be encouraged in children as early as possible, both at home with their parents and friends, and in school classes and chorus programs. Singing aids a child's speech development and offers opportunities for social development and enhanced self-esteem, as well. But vocal training for children is a delicate undertaking, especially before the onset of adolescence, and voice teachers should have a credible background in speech therapy, otherwise vocal damage can occur from improper training techniques.

The vocal instrument goes through many stages of development from the time of birth. The vocal folds change in boys at puberty and almost double in length and thickness from their original size (a baby's throat is the size of a little finger). Girls' voices also change at puberty, but not as dramatically. Consequently, they don't suffer the mortifying "squeaks" and "cracks" that boys do. Training methods, therefore, must match the stage of physical development of the child, with full, rigorous training possible a couple of years after adolescence when the vocal chords are matured.

Vocal damage is not just a hazard of the act of singing. There are many activities engaged in by children and adults that are causing increasing cases of severe and even permanent damage due to misuse and overuse of the voice. Cheerleaders are susceptible, as are aerobics instructors, salesmen, public speakers, actors, and kids who indulge constantly in playing video games. "Video game throat" today is akin to barroom throat, where one must speak over the noise of the crowd. In video arcades, children's voices must compete with the drone of the computer-created games (music, crashes, explosions, and other bizarre simulated noises) as well as the voices of numerous hyperactive kids.

Vocal training for everyone, therefore, may be a form of preventive therapy to guard against the hazards of being part of a yelling, screaming society where voices must rise above the din of crowds, machines, and amplified music.

Professional singers must be in good physical health to endure the rigors of touring or the nightly stress of performing for several hours at a time. They must take care of their bodies through proper nutrition and exercise. In essence, they are like athletes—*vocal* athletes—and good health is a prerequisite to a consistently good performance, as is adequate vocal training.

The act of singing is considered by some professionals to be superior to the instrumental expression of music for, through the marriage of music and words, we achieve a more intimate synergy with the music itself. We not only operate on an intellectual level, by remembering the lyrics, keeping in time with the rhythm, and singing on pitch, but we actually become one with the music as it resonates through our body physically, as it becomes an extension and expression of our emotions, and as it elevates our spirit with a profound sense of wholeness and completion.

Why do some people sing better than others, lower, higher, fuller, stronger? Although we can all be trained to sing better than we do at this very moment, not all people can be trained to sing as gloriously as others. This is because we are all born with a specific vocal structural instrument: the shape, size, and relationship of the resonating chambers of the mouth, throat, and head cavities. We may not know how poor or superior this instrument is, however, until we undergo an examination by a vocal physiologist, or until we embark on a training regimen and achieve the maximum vocal potential we are able to achieve.

The average speaking voice uses a pitch range of about one octave (an octave equals eight tones of the scale, do-re-mi-fa-so-la-ti-do). Singing voices are categorized according to the vocal range they can execute proficiently.

In children, the highest voice is the *high soprano,* possessing great clarity and purity. It ranges about two-and-one-half octaves from middle C on the piano to F above the higher C. The lowest child's voice is *treble.* It is fuller than the high soprano, and spans two octaves from middle C to high C.

Women have three basic vocal ranges. The *soprano,* which is the highest range, spreads about two octaves from middle C on the piano to the higher C. Noted sopranos are Beverly Sills and Kathleen Battle, as well as the late Maria Callas. The *mezzo-soprano* has the clear qualities of soprano as well as the rich, low tones of the contralto, and ranges from G below middle C to the G two octaves higher. The sultry title role of *Carmen* (Bizet's opera) was written for a mezzo-soprano and has been sung by such noted performers as Marilyn Horne. The lowest woman's voice is the *contralto,* spanning two octaves from E below middle C to the higher E. Barbara Streisand is considered a contralto.

Men basically have four singing ranges. The *counter-tenor* is unusually high and clear, but not shrill, and also employs the high falsetto register, or range. It spans the two octaves from low G to the higher G. Recall an Irish tenor singing "Danny Boy." The highest man's voice that does not use falsetto is the *tenor.* Very powerful, this voice spans two full octaves from low to high A. Famous tenors include Placido Domingo and Luciano Pavarotti. The rich, full *baritone* spans a two-octave range from G to the higher G. Many popular crooners are considered baritones, such as Sinatra, Perry Como, Neil Diamond, etc. And the lowest male voice is the *bass,* spanning two octaves from very low D to the higher D. There are few solo parts written for the bass vocalist, but at least one famous song comes to mind, "Asleep in the Deep."

In rare instances, singers are possessed with ranges of astounding proportions, spanning three and even four octaves. In the 1940's, Hollywood promoted a remarkable exotic singer, Yma Sumac, whose voice deftly executed a four-octave range, reaching notes well beyond the capabilities of the most skilled soprano.

Singer Morganna King is noted for a rich, full-bodied three-plus octave range, as is popular singer of the sixties, Jackie Wilson.

Each individual's voice is suited either naturally or through professional training for singing a specific type of music. The musical theater performer or opera singer must train his or her voice precisely to the vocal ranges inherent in those respective types of music. Theater and opera singing is emphatic; all songs must be sung exactly as written. But it is the individual artist's flair for drama as well as the resonance and tone color of his or her voice that set some of these performers apart from the other so that they become stars. Think of the late Gordon MacRae in *Oklahoma* and *Carousel;* Howard Keel in *Showboat* and *Annie Get Your Gun;* or Mary Martin in *South Pacific* and

Sound of Music. And of course opera's Joan Sutherland, Leontyne Price, or the late Mario Lanza and Enrico Caruso.

Compare this style of structured singing with the stylized vocals of jazz and ballads, where a singer's own unique phrasing and interpretation of the words and music creates an intimacy of mood and emotion. Artists such as Ella Fitzgerald, Sarah Vaughan, Mel Torme, Joe Williams come to mind.

Blues singing allows the vocalist to improvise, bend notes, slide in and out of them at will, while following a basic twelve-bar chord progression. This type of singing can only be learned by listening to other great blues singers, such as Bessie Smith and B. B. King.

Rock music singing, which is also as individual as the singer himself, incorporates the easy approach of folk singing, with the shouting and "note-bending" of the rhythm and blues singer. Note the differences in style of Bruce Springsteen, David Bowie, and Billy Joel, among others.

Soul singers, such as Ray Charles, James Brown, Aretha Franklin, and Tina Turner, have their roots in gospel music, and the style incorporates black American folk music as well as the rhythmic drive of rhythm and blues. Most of these singers have tremendous vocal agility as well as the necessary heart and "soul" to pull it off.

The easy conversational tone of folk music allows the singer to use his vocal talents naturally, with little need of extensive training for power and increase of range. But this certainly does not diminish the talents of such artists as John Denver, Harry Chapin, or Joni Mitchell.

Country music singers also have an easy, accessible style like the folk singer, but there are many country artists whose vocal abilities allow them to "cross over" and sing music requiring strong technique and control. Anne Murray, Barbara Mandrell, Charley Pride, Glen Campbell and Kenny Rogers, etc.

What actually happens when we sing? And how is the ordinary speaking voice transformed into the gloriously powerful or delicately flowing instrument that captivates us when we hear it?

The larynx, or voice box, primarily serves as a valve that regulates the air flowing into and out of the lungs. Its secondary purpose, however, is that of sound production. When you sing or speak, air from your lungs pushes against the vocal chords (the twin bundles of muscle and ligament that form the opening, or *glottis*, through which the air actually flows), causing them to vibrate. The vocal chords vibrate at a certain frequency, or pitch, depending upon the amount of air pressure flowing in and out, and also depending upon the degree of tension exerted on the chords by the muscles of the larynx. Strong air pressure and taut vocal chords produce a high-pitched sound, while lower-pitched sounds are created by lesser air pressure and relaxed vocal chords.

To produce the wide variance of pitches and the power they possess, singers must strengthen the muscles of their vocal chords through vocal exercises, just as one would strengthen a body muscle through physical exercise. But there is more than strength involved here. A singer must learn proper breath control techniques as well as manipulation of the vocal muscles to produce the desired resonance and tone color. "Voice placement" is also important in the development of vocal range and quality. High notes are "placed" in the head cavity, lower notes are placed in the chest cavity, and still lower notes originate farther down in the solar plexus. As a singer articulates the various vowel sounds in a song, the notes will resonate in various energy centers of the body (recall our exercises earlier in this chapter). The ability to manipulate the vocal chords so that vocal tones are placed properly and are projected proficiently requires a great deal of control, technique, and professional dedication.

As I stated previously, the professional singer should be in top physical health to endure the rigors of training and performing.

However, the average person—or *non*professional—can either add an entirely new dimension to his fitness program through singing, or embark on the road to good health by the act of singing itself. The following techniques are not a substitute for formal voice training, and should be carefully and sensibly applied. The voice, and all its components within the throat, comprise a delicate instrument that should be handled with care. If you suffer sore throats, hoarseness, problems with swallowing or breathing, please see a physician or speech therapist before beginning, just as you would see a trained health professional before embarking on an exercise program.

If all is normal with your throat and voice, you can begin by taking a few deep breaths, inhaling through your nose and exhaling through your mouth. Be sure to expel all the air in your lungs, but don't force it out. Be certain your arms, hands, shoulders, and front neck muscles are relaxed. Hold your body erect and flexible, not rigid; keep your weight evenly balanced on your feet, and lift your chest and rib cage comfortably high, stomach in, to allow the breath to move freely and easily up and out from your lungs. (For a unique, luxurious feeling, try all of this lying on your back.)

Now, start to vocalize a few tones. You may hum first if you like, (humming is very therapeutic and helps to balance the brain hemispheres), then open your mouth and sing a vowel sound (oh, ah, etc.). Be conscious of what you are doing so you do it correctly: breathe properly and easily, keep your body (if you're standing) erect, controlled, but slightly relaxed; and let the tones come forth in your most comfortable range without straining—not too high and not too low. Usually your natural speaking voice is the most comfortable range to sing in. If you sound like Alfalfa Swietzer (the Little Rascal with the squeaky voice and needlelike cowlick), you are straining on the upper end of your range. If, however, your tones come out raspy and barely audible, you may be singing far too low.

Next, proceed to something more musical, such as "la-la-la," going up and down the scale (do-re-me-fa, etc.). Keep repeating until you feel less inhibited and awkward to be singing aloud. (It's amazing how we can feel embarrassed or even frightened to express ourselves vocally, even when we are *alone*.) As you warm up, let the music in you come forth with vitality and energy. Sing those notes and scales with enthusiasm. Don't worry how good or bad you are. You have a right to sing out loud, even if you are lousy at it. Try to feel where the tones resonate within your body (in the stomach area, chest, throat, head, etc.).

Next, pick a well-known song, one that is fairly easy to sing, that moves easily up and down the musical scale at comfortable intervals and has long, open tones. The "Do-Re-Mi" song from *The Sound of Music* is fun to do and an effective vocal exercise as well. Moving on to something with more emotion, try singing "Oh, What a Beautiful Morning" from *Oklahoma*. Sing it out, and *believe* the words. It *is* a beautiful morning—even if it's really eight o'clock at night: *Feel* that warm, glowing sunshine on your face. Smell the clean, sweet air. *See* the open meadow where "the corn is as high as an elephant's eye."

Or choose something rousing and patriotic, such as Irving Berlin's "God Bless America," or our unofficial anthem, "America the Beautiful." I defy you to sing either of these songs and not feel a stirring inside your soul, a tingling of emotion through your entire body, and even misty-eyed at the sentiments expressed in the lyrics. When you have this kind of physical and emotional response to singing, you know what it's like to "become the music." And when you are finished, note how invigorated you feel mentally, how clear your head is, how vital your energy is. These are but a few of the positive, healthful benefits you derive from singing.

Now you are ready to truly let the joy of singing overtake you and let it become a natural, inspired, uninhibited experience. Now, you can sing with your favorite record, the piano, a cappella, in the shower, cleaning the house, driving the car—wherever and whenever you feel the urge. If you're still shy, sing when you are alone, but do it with gusto! If you sing in a group, a chorus, or a church choir, lift your voice to the sky and connect with the spirit energy of all the other voices around you. Don't just mouth a few words meekly. Give it all you've got. When you do, you'll be cleaning out your body and mind of all the physical and mental garbage that has lain stagnating inside you far too long. You will feel energized, refreshed, and renewed; filled with life, love, and complete atonement with the universe.

The late Edgar Cayce, world-renowned psychic healer, was a great believer in the healing qualities of music, including singing. He believed that the voice nerve center is the highest vibration, and that by giving expression in song, you would realize "a new experience, a new awakening within [your]self."

6

Music Makes It Better

USING music to facilitate the healing process is a remedy as old as the universe itself. Whether it comes from a hand-carved, primitive wooden flute or an ultrasonic instrument created by twentieth-century scientists, the music—its sound vibrations and energy—work hand in hand with universal forces to help the body heal itself physically, emotionally, and spiritually.

But for a rather bleak period in history—from the nineteenth century to the mid-twentieth century—music as an aid to healing was all but ignored in favor of drugs, anesthesia, and other examples of medical "progress." Today, a resurgence in the use of music in the practice of medicine, psychotherapy, and other alternative medical practices is nothing less than a phenomenon. Its many applications and the boundlessness of its effects are just now beginning to be discovered—or, rather, *re*discovered.

While ancient cultures relied on theory, faith, intuitiveness, and rather elementary forms of scientific experimentation to measure the effects of music on the mind and body, the sophistication of modern

69

technology allows us to hear, feel, and *see* these effects on us both *ex*ternally and *in*ternally. Still, the ability of music to bring the mind up and out of the depths of despair, and to help repair and regenerate a diseased body, boggles the mind of even the most erudite practitioner.

For the layperson, discovering the power of music to enhance life and health is a wonderment and a revelation. To become aware of music's cosmic connection and, in turn, *our* connection to the Cosmic Tones of the universe, can give us greater understanding. Once we realize that we ourselves are musical instruments—that we resonate and harmonize in our own unique way with all the tones and colors of the earth, moon, and stars, and that we move to the dance of the universal rhythms, it is easier to believe in the power of music and in the power that *we* have to *become* the music.

For centuries, music has been an integral part of medical practice, with the physician and musician often being one and the same. The Greek, Apollo, was god of both music and medicine. The tales of Orpheus (1300 B.C.), a Thracian man of great genius, tell how he quieted troubled minds, gave life to flowers and trees, calmed angry waters, and stilled the wild winds with his musical gift. In the Old Testament, stories recount how David, the singer of psalms, soothed the madness of Saul by using the celestial powers of his harp. To cast off the "evil spirit," Saul was advised to "...seek out a man who is a wise player on a harp, and it shall come to pass that he shall play with his hand and thou shalt be well." Saul then summoned David to him, and when David played his lyre for the king, "...Saul was refreshed and was well, and the evil spirit departed from him."

Pythagoras of Samos, as we pointed out previously, taught his students that certain musical sequences, chords, and melodies produced definite responses in the human organism, and could change behavior patterns that accelerated the healing process. He also prescribed daily regimens of music to work by, relax to, fall asleep with, and wake up to. And in recent centuries, physicians used music to regulate the heartbeat, and used a combination of music and singing to cure such ailments as melancholy and the "vapors" (depression, hypochondria).

But in the nineteenth century, when anesthetics and painkillers were developed, music to facilitate the healing process was cast aside and forgotten. It wasn't until those "happy days" of the 1950's that dentists began to use music in the form of piped-in, bland, mindless tunes (Muzak, etc.) to disguise the bone-chilling whine of the dentist's drill. Subsequently, using music to ease pain, ease the stress of medical treatment, and a host of other remarkable applications became popular once again.

Where is it being used? In private practice by psychiatrists, psychologists, counselors, music therapists, speech therapists, and holistic practitioners; and in hospitals around the world, including: Kaiser-Permanente Medical Center in Los Angeles; the University of Massachusetts Medical Center in Worcester; Beth Israel Hospital in Boston; Hahnemann University Hospital in Philadelphia; Bretby Hall Orthopedic Hospital in Derby, England; and Charing Cross Hospital in London.

What kind of music is used? Depending upon the human condition and the "healing" required, the music choices are vast and varied: Harp and flute music to place patients in a meditative state, to ease the physical and emotional trauma of terminal illness, as a substitute for painkillers; largo movements of baroque and classical music for general relaxation and stress-reduction; songs like "Chariots of Fire" for the pushing stages of delivery, and from Stevie Wonder to Handel's *Messiah* to celebrate the moment of birth; anything from *Sesame Street* music to Neil Diamond to prepare children for heart catheterization; religious music and songs with special lifelong meanings to help hospice patients resolve feelings about death; the Beatles and the Carpenters during surgery; hard rock music to help youngsters rid themselves of anger, hostility and self-destructive tendencies; jazz, blues, march music, electronic-synthesizer music—whatever music is needed to balance the body's energy, to relax it or energize it.

How does music work its wonders? Scientists and practitioners aren't completely certain *how* it does, but they are certain *that* it does, and research continues to provide empirical data as well as firsthand observation and testimony.

Physical and psychological responses to music involve complex changes in brain chemistry, in the emotional brain (limbic system); the primitive brain (brain stem) which controls heartbeat, respiration, and muscle tension; and in the thinking part of the brain. Some kinds of music produce the same endorphins that occur during running and meditation. Endorphins are the natural opiates—or "feel-good" chemicals—secreted by the hypothalmus that can minimize the degree of pain that we feel.

Music increases blood volume, decreases and stabilizes heart rate, lowers blood pressure, puts you in tune with your bodily sensations, and even takes your mind to another place so you can forget your body and its ailments completely. Music creates an environment for healing—a positive attitude on the part of the patient and the physician—that is a vital adjunct to the treatment or therapy being applied.

An article in *Prevention* magazine (October 1983) cited numerous examples of "Music to Get Cured By." At Kaiser-Permanente, for example, Walkman-like cassette players with earphones were given to patients containing specially designed music tapes to be used before cardiac (and other types) surgery. David Walker, one of the medical center's psychiatrists, stated that the inability to relax was a common problem in many illnesses, and it was not unusual for patients to stay awake all night, obsessed with what was happening to them.

"Just knowing they have a way [music] to reduce the anxiety helps," Walker said, and patients were advised to use the tapes anytime they needed them—even as they were being wheeled into the operating room.

Children are particularly fearful of undergoing medical treatment, and if they are placed in the hospital, their anxiety magnifies. There, among strangers who probe and poke their little bodies, hearing familiar music can help them feel more at ease. Cynthia Briggs, director of music therapy at Hahnemann University Hospital, has helped young patients choose the music to be played for them during heart catheterization procedures. The selections range from music from their favorite television shows, to songs by their favorite recording artists.

"It's a way to personalize the experience," Briggs states, "and, hopefully, make things more pleasant."

The free-flowing, almost celestial music of harpist Georgia Kelly is not only popular with people who practice meditation and yoga, but it has been used extensively in hospitals (including the University of Massachusetts and Kaiser-Permanente). Kelly never realized the medical potential of her music until people wrote to her that they were using it in such situations as childbirth, during surgery, and for relaxation and sleep.

"My music takes your mind to another place," she says. "It helps you move away from identifying with your body and reduces your awareness of pain." For burn patients, people with chronic back pain, crippling spinal injuries or other debilitating ailments, Kelly's music has provided blessed temporary relief.

Guided imagery combined with music is also a highly effective means to promote healing and to ease physical and emotional suffering. For years, music therapists have used hypnosis and guided imagery to help patients with a variety of complaints (and there are a plethora of self-help tapes on the market that combine music and verbal suggestions to help relieve tension, recover from surgery, uplift the psyche, etc.).

At the Shealy Pain and Health Rehabilitation Institute in Springfield, Missouri, Dr. Norm Shealy has used music on his guided imagery tapes because he believes "music helps occupy another channel in the mind." He says his voice speaks to the left hemisphere of the brain, while the music engages the right hemisphere, keeping patients focused, alert, and receptive to the verbal suggestions (this, you may recall, is the theory behind "Superlearning," discussed in Chapter 3). While music plays, patients with a broken arm, for example, are encouraged to "see" the bone knitting, the arm getting stronger, and the end result of complete recovery. This guided imagery technique is also being used on patients with tumors, cancer, and other serious illnesses.

The creator of this technique called Guided Imagery and Music (GIM) is Helen Bonny, founder and former director of the Music Therapy Department at the Catholic University of America in Washington, D.C. Bonny is currently in private practice, but worked in the 1970's with LSD-therapy researchers at the Maryland Psychiatric Research Center, where music was used to enhance drug responses.

Intrigued with music's ability to alter moods and with its potentially therapeutic effects, Bonny developed the GIM technique which "involves listening in a relaxed state to selective music, a programmed tape or live music, in order to elicit mental imagery, symbols and deep feelings arising from the deeper conscious self."

Just as the power of music to aid the *physical* body in the regeneration process is becoming more widely recognized, the use of music to repair the *emotional* and *spiritual* bodies is also gaining ground rapidly. There are about 4,500 music therapists on record today. But the profession's beginnings can be traced to musicians who volunteered their time and talents soothing the wounded veterans of World War II in Veteran's Administration Hospitals.

Recognizing the positive effects music had, particularly on the mental patients, the V.A., in the 1950's, installed music therapy programs in some of its hospitals. It wasn't long before music therapy was introduced in civilian mental hospitals and in residential care centers for the mentally retarded. And music has been particularly successful in breaking through the psychological isolation of autistic children, deaf children, and drug and alcohol abusers.

Legend tells us that Orpheus could tame wild beasts (man's passions), move rocks (touch the bottom of the most unfeeling hearts), and even revive the dead (spiritually speaking), using the celestial music of his golden lyre. Today, some therapists are using music that literally *could* raise the dead to help psychotic teenagers "break on through to the other side."

At the Horsham (psychiatric) Clinic in Pennsylvania, art historian and therapist John Sappington, and Dr. L. Donald Tashjian, the clinic's medical director, developed a unique therapy session combining art with a rock 'n' roll beat, to bring troubled teens out of their psychological isolation. As their favorite music plays, the teens are encouraged to draw pictures illustrating what the songs mean to them. Not surprisingly, the teens favor music from the sixties and seventies by such drug casualties as Jim Morrison of The Doors, Janis Joplin, and Jimi Hendrix. The results the therapists have had in breaking through the defenses of these kids using rock/art therapy has been quite remarkable.

Most of the teenagers (several hundred at this writing), suffer severe psychiatric disturbances, including suicidal tendencies, problems with drugs, and sexual abuse. In choosing music that they could relate to best—rock and roll—Sappington and Tashjian have been able to get a "clear window into what is going on."

"You take an art from, [such as] music, that is basically nonverbal," Tashjian explains, "and it appeals to the emotions. You then have the intermediate step of making a visual rendering of that aural emotion."

Some of the drawings that have come out of the rock/art sessions include: a lone bird gliding over a barren landscape (music: "Freebird" by Lynyrd Skynard); an empty room, tables, and chairs ("You Can't Always Get What You Want," by the Rolling Stones); and plenty of "beastly, bloody creatures from the metalheads (kids who love heavy metal music)."

From the birth experience to the death experience, music is an invaluable adjunct to treatment and therapy—physical or psychological. Therapist Nancy Hunt knows the extreme joys and pain of both of these profound human adventures, with the onset of death being the most poignant.

Working in a hospice, Hunt uses music to help the terminally ill come to terms with death and talk to their loved ones about it. She uses a technique called "life review" and plays songs that were popular during the patient's most active times, such as courtship, early days of marriage, or perhaps wartime.

Hunt says that the songs are like mileposts in their lives, evoking vivid memories and expediting communication between the patient and family members. She has often been known to simply sit at someone's bedside and sing along with him or her a favorite church hymn learned as a child.

"Amazing Grace," "The Old Rugged Cross," and "In The Garden" are requested often and give patients great comfort.

Music works. It soothes. It comforts. It reaches deep down and touches us on a biological level, an emotional level and a spiritual level. It heals. And it works its miracles through its vibrations, by balancing the [electromagnetic] energy field of the body and creating a harmony of mind, body, and spirit.

We discussed in Chapter 3 how these vibrations work on a *physical* level, how sound can move matter, how it can affect us on a cellular level, strengthen or weaken muscles, and so forth. And the physical uses of music in the form of sound vibrations of specific frequencies to diagnose and treat illness are becoming more and more sophisticated. For example, research is being done using electrical fields to facilitate the healing of bone fractures and to regenerate limbs. Sound waves (ultrasound) are used to detect fetal disturbances in pregnant women, and also to "crush" kidney stones (a desirable alternative to major surgery), and a host of other medical applications.

But it is through the *metaphysical* study of vibration, known as the Third Law of Hermes (Hermes being the messenger of the gods, in Greek mythology, as well as the god of science), that we can truly understand music's power to heal.

Disease comes from a blockage of energy in the body: emotional stress, infection by viruses and bacteria, a blow to the body, and any one of hundreds of other things that can disrupt the body's normal function. To treat or cure the disease, we must remember the old law of Cause and Effect. The symptoms (Effect) of any disease or condition will not disappear completely until the blockage itself (Cause) is corrected.

Certain schools of thought in medicine and philosophy maintain that the body is a dynamic interaction of mind, body, and energy fields. The energy fields are known by several terms, including "etheric body" and "aura." The aura surrounds the body and suffuses every cell with color and light. Disease in the physical body is thought to begin with a disturbance at the "etheric" or "auric" level. In the Egyptian school of

Imhotep, it was maintained that disease could be cured by treating the body's *etheric* body and, once balance there was restored, healing of the *physical* body followed naturally.

It is believed that Jesus healed this way. He had the superior mind energy to function on the spiritual plane which deals with energy and motion. Jesus could move his own vibrational aura into the etheric body of an ill person and, by mentally bringing that person into a healthy, balanced energy field, the person's own imbalanced, diseased field would be corrected.

Vibration. Light. Color. Energy. Harmony. Music. Music of the Universe, of the Creator of the Universe, of Man, of You, and I.

In the beginning was the Word—the Creative Sound—from which God brought forth Light, which filled the universe. And they complemented each other: Sound being audible Light, and Light being visible Sound. Through these two whirling, vibrating masses of energy, the worlds, planets, and stars were formed, and as they moved and orbited through their universal space they emitted specific tones and radiated specific colors. These colors and tones were unique unto themselves, yet they correlated with each other and ultimately formed a relationship with each one of us.

As the Light radiated throughout the universe, it broke into seven major colors, or Spirits of Light, that became known as the colors of the spectrum. They entered the bodies of man (*our* bodies) through our electromagnetic field, known as the aura. The seven colors and their seven corresponding Cosmic Tones relate to our body's seven main chakras (energy centers), each resounding and resonating at specific frequencies (cycles per second).

People who are skilled in the reading of the aura—who can actually perceive its radiance around the body—note that there are many gradations of auric colors, ranging from murky dark shades to pure crystalline blues, and they indicate a person's state of emotional and physical health and well-being (or disease and distress). Kirlian photography also allows us to see the aura and its spectral colors.

When Pythagorus created his "numbers game" called Music (rhythm patterns of energy), it was based upon the magic number "seven," which appears time and time again in its relation to universal vibrations and the well-being of mankind (and, quite possibly, this is where the term "Lucky 7" originated).

In ancient astronomy the Sun, Moon, Mercury, Venus, Mars, Jupiter, and Saturn are known as the seven heavenly bodies, and each has its own keynote, which is identical to each one of the seven keynotes of the musical scale. The keynotes are said to resonate in the seven chakras.

In the ancient practice of yoga, it is believed that man has three bodies and three minds: the physical body and its consciousness, which operates in association with the physical body; the astral body and its consciousness which experiences emotions and feelings; and the causal body and its consciousness that is expressed mainly as intelligence and wisdom. The three body/mind sets exist and operate in different dimensions, each maintained by the specific type of prana (vital energy) appropriate to that dimension, but they are not separate entities. Rather they co-exist holistically, each one's survival depending upon the health and wellbeing of the other.

Each body/mind has its own energy center, known as a chakra, which controls the flow of prana and acts as a "switch" for the higher centers of the brain. As the chakras are activated and awakened, man becomes aware of the higher realms of existence and gains the power to enter those realms. Through this spiritual (or higher dimension) awareness, support and life are given to the lower (or physical) dimensions.

The awakening of the chakras is achieved through yoga meditation and positions of the body that enhance the flow of prana through the body. In hatha yoga, breathing exercises as well as body positions are employed to awaken the chakras. And the vibrational frequencies in music are also keys to awakening the chakras.

Each chakra vibrates at a certain frequency, emits a certain color vibration, and responds to a musical keynote, as follows: The keynote "C" (midpoint on the piano) vibrates pure red at 261.2 cycles per second and resonates around the base of the spine. The Red chakra is the physical life force, that stimulates and reenergizes the body.

The keynote "D" vibrates about several inches below the navel with a vital orange at 292.1 cycles per second. The orange chakra is the bridge between the physical red and mental yellow, affecting the adrenals and other circulatory glands.

"E" is yellow, centered around the solar plexus, and vibrates at 329.1 cycles per second. The yellow chakra is known as the "seat of the emotions."

"F" corresponds to green, is felt in the heart region, and its vibrational rate is 349.2 cycles per second. The green chakra is the great balancer and harmonizer, and signifies an affinity with the earth.

"G" is located in the throat's energy center (thyroid), its color is blue and it vibrates at 392 cycles per second. The blue chakra represents spiritual awareness and is the first of the three highest energy centers.

"A" gives off an indigo hue and resonates at 440 cycles per second in the area of the brow, or pituitary gland (commonly referred to as the "Third Eye.")

"B" vibrates at 493 cycles per second, its color is violet and it resonates in the crown chakra at the top of the head. When the body is in a full state of regeneration, this area is said to emit a pure white light.

The ancient lyre used by David and Orpheus was seven-stringed, and believed to sound the Music of the Spheres. When Joshua and his followers brought down the walls of Jericho, they did so by using seven trumpets blown by seven priests who, on the seventh day, circled the city seven times. With seven blasts of the trumpets and a hearty shout from the crowd, the walls came tumbling down.

The metaphysical principles of music, color, and light play a very important part in the healing theories of the Rosicrucian order (a nonreligious fraternity devoted to the practical application of an occult philosophy to human affairs). They maintain that there is a "nerve note" and a "music note" for each of the spinal nerves between the vertebrae. At the very base of the spine, the music notes begin with "E" in the fourth octave below middle "C" as found on the piano. As we go all the way up the vertebrae to the very first cervical, we arrive at "C" above middle "C." These notes arouse certain connections in the sympathetic nervous system causing the nerves to function easily and completely.

"Spectrum Suite" earned him the distinction (in 1977) of possibly being the "only composer who works with a unique understanding of the human mind and body, that enables him to create music that is 'in tune' with the biological composition of the body itself" Halpern's music, which is free-floating and gentle and usually produced by flute and/or electric piano, has been used in hospital settings as therapy, and by laypersons who wish to relax, meditate, and revitalize the mind and body.

"Spectrum Suite" earned him the distinction (in 1977) of possibly being the "only composer who works with a unique understanding of the human mind and body, that enables him to create music that is in tune with the biological composition of the body itself " Halpern's music, which is free-floating and gentle and usually produced by flute and/or electric piano, has been used in hospital settings as therapy, and by laypersons who wish to relax, meditate, and revitalize the mind and body.

The principle behind his music drew upon the relationship between the ascending frequencies of both sound and color octaves of the electromagnetic spectrum. Musically, "Spectrum Suite" is a series of lilting tones and gentle "nonmelodies" based on each note of the scale, and, when played, help each energy center of the body (the human instrument) to tune up to the universal harmonies. In experiments Halpern conducted, there were noticeable changes in the aura of the subjects comparable to the changes that occurred during profound states of meditation (without music).

There is also said to be a relationship between the twelve zodiacal signs and specific keynotes in the twelve-note chromatic scale. (This scale includes the seven major notes as well as the flats and sharps that lie between, seen as the black keys on the piano.) Rosicrucians, such as Corrine Heline, assert that each sign of the zodiac has a major keynote to which we respond and that affects a particular area of the body:

ARIES—D flat, rules the head

TAURUS—E flat, governs throat, neck, and ears

GEMINI—F sharp, rules lungs, shoulders, arms, and hands

CANCER—G sharp, rules the stomach and solar plexus

LEO—A sharp, governs heart and spinal chord

VIRGO—C natural, rules the intestines

LIBRA—D natural, governs kidneys and adrenal glands

SCORPIO—E natural, rules the reproductive glands

SAGITTARIUS—F natural, governs hips, thighs, and sacral plexus

CAPRICORN—G natural, governs the knees

AQUARIUS—A natural, rules lower limbs and ankles

PISCES—B natural, governs the feet

At the time of our birth, the positions of the planets formed a musical score of harmonies and dissonances that have tremendous impact on the mind, our body, and our entire life. We can be in tune with the harmonies and "make music," or we can perpetuate the dissonances and "make noise." When we choose the latter, we clash with our environment and cause dis-ease, disease and poor human relationships. We have all had the experience of meeting people to whom we take an immediate liking. Most likely our keynote is in harmony with theirs and we get "good vibes." Those we dislike have keynotes that clash with ours and create discord ("bad vibes") in us and around us.

If all of this talk of vibrations seems difficult to relate to, try a little experiment. Close your eyes and remember the last time you were out in nature—in the mountains, the woods, by the ocean, a lake, in the desert, etc. Remember how totally quiet it was, undisturbed by man-made noises. Remember the calm you felt, the peace and utter contentment you experienced. This is how it feels to be in tune with the universe.

In its natural state, the earth's vibrational frequency is about 7.5 cycles per second. When you are in *your* most natural (healthful, undisturbed) state, your frequency level is about 6.8 to 7.5 cycles per second. Placing yourself physically in Mother Nature's nurturing surroundings helps to bring your vibratory level down from its usual frenzied condition to one of serenity and inner peace. This is when your mind and body can repair and regenerate themselves.

Unless you are Shirley MacLaine, you probably can't escape to a mountaintop the moment you are feeling stressed. However, meditation is another way to achieve a restful and beneficial state of being. And meditation performed while listening to harmonious, uplifting music will connect your physical self with the life-giving "Music of the Spheres."

When practitioners use music to help "relax" their patients and thus note a better response to treatment and therapy, it appears obvious that what we call "relaxation" in *physical* terms is really "balance and harmony with the universe" in *metaphysical* terms. And thus the healing process begins, is augmented, and achieved.

The type of music that we choose will depend wholly upon the type of "healing"—or energy balancing—that is needed. And the seriousness of our ill condition is another factor to be considered. While there is a great deal of information available on music and healing, it is not an endeavor to be undertaken lightly. Don't expect to sit down at the piano, plunk a "D-flat" and cure a headache, or something far more medically complicated. For the purpose of treating specific illnesses and conditions more serious than general stress or malaise, you should consult experts who understand the cosmic laws of harmony, the human anatomy, and the serious application of music therapy. But we can use music as a preventive measure to nip mild symptoms in the bud before they become acute or chronic ailments.

Remember the law of Cause and Effect. Until we can remove the *Cause* of a disease or condition, we cannot remove its *Effect.* All we can do is mask the symptoms. (In the case of terminal illnesses, or conditions of unbearable pain, however, masking the symptoms with music seems to be as effective as taking drugs and painkillers, and far more desirable an alternative).

We cannot live in a vacuum, and being exposed to health-hazardous conditions is inevitable. But we can try to reverse these negative conditions by learning which music brings forth our own regenerative powers. We must *listen* to the music, *feel* its effects, *become* the music, so that we have the power to renew ourselves again and again.

Music can make life inexplicably joyful. It can allow us to achieve a higher quality of living and health for as many years as we choose to live on this earth's plane. And when the time comes for us to move on in search of experiences on a higher plane, tuning in to the Music of the Spheres can make the "ascension" (what we commonly call *death*) the most profound, welcome, and least feared of all human experiences.

7

Balancing the Scales

IN music, the twelve keys of the chromatic scale are arranged in what is called the Circle of Fifths, or their natural order of sharps and flats that move in ascending fashion in intervals of five semi-tones. After you complete the twelve steps of the circle (going counterclockwise C to F, F to B flat, etc.), the initial key is reached again, and a complete unbroken circle is created (see Diagram #1).

I make this reference to demonstrate that, musically as well as metaphysically, the circle is the most perfect symbol signifying life, for it is ongoing and never ending.

The discovery of the interval Circle of Fifths was a great one to the Chinese, for they honor the number five as sacred, dividing the basic elements in five (earth, fire, water, wood, and metal), and recognize five basic human relationships, and five basic kinds of grain as vital to life. Their musical scale, called the pentatonic scale, is comprised of five notes (G,A,B,D, and E).

I think of fitness and well being, also, as comprising a series of five individual vital components that unite together to form a "Circle of

Diagram #1

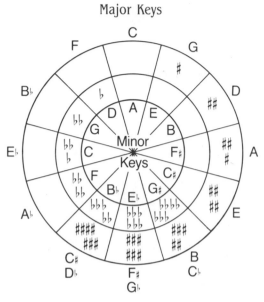

Major Keys

Circle of Fifths

Diagram #2

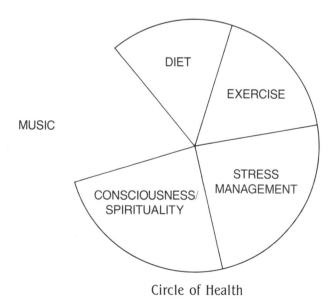

Circle of Health

Health." In Diagram #2, the components of diet, exercise, stress management, and consciousness/spirituality form part of the circle.

But without one final element—Music—the circle is incomplete and the other components are left without a connecting force that gives them strength and continuity.

Music is so powerful that it can harm you or heal you, drag you down physically and emotionally or lift you to heights of euphoria and total inner peace. Making music an integral part of your fitness and health program will keep the Circle complete, and allow you to succeed where in the past you might have failed.

One of the reasons there is such a high attrition rate on the part of health club members is that, after the novelty of sweat and strain wears off, there is no motivation to continue. The program loses its fire because it had no spark to begin with. Many health clubs are merely membership mills, or social clubs where people hang out for one reason or another. The word "health" is often a misnomer, with many of the clubs being merely beauty spas or exercise gyms where people free float in and out of workouts, classes, or treatments. The total "Circle of Health" is rarely addressed.

As health conscious as we Americans are, we still isolate our fitness programs from all of our other everyday activities, ignoring the holism that truly makes a fitness program work. We "go on" a diet, living for the day we can "go off" the diet, resisting the common truth that a diet is (or should be) our natural—and enjoyable—daily way of eating.

Exercise is that hour of torture we feel we must endure to be thin and fit, with many people exercising by rote, their minds wandering to the shopping list, the dinner date, or ruminating about how miserable the day was.

Stress Management is something we learn to practice only when the doctor says, "Do it, or else!" Thus, we add the anxiety of possible death or debilitation to all the other stress factors we must deal with.

Consciousness or our state of awareness of all the experiences we encounter in our life, is often thought of as something we *do* (such as in *elevate* it) only in group environments that are considered "weird," "faddish," or "occult."

Spirituality is usually equated with ritual and religious dogma, expressed only at appropriate times in appropriate "temples."

We all practice and utilize some of these components, or even all of them, at one time or another in the course of a day, a week, or a month. But unless they are all pulled together cohesively, our lives can be fragmented, our efforts futile, and our health and well-being jeopardized. Music relates to and connects all of these elements, bringing them together in one unified force that creates balance and harmony in our lives. Thus we enjoy health and well-being at its optimum.

MUSIC AND DIET

Obviously, when we think of diet, we fat-a-phobic Americans immediately think of weight control at the same time. But let's make one thing perfectly clear: there is no known music that can melt fat from the body. If there were, I couldn't be sitting down writing this book—not with a stereo speaker strapped to each hip! But, knowing how mood-altering music can be, specialists in weight control have discovered that music is a very effective tool to use in a diet program.

Dr. Stanley Title of the Stanley Title Clinic for Weight Control and Nutrition in New York City, stated (*Prevention* magazine, October 1983) that music can ease the stresses and irritability people suffer while on a diet program. Since anxiety can trigger a binge, he recommends playing music at specific times to "create a calm, stress-free environment" for the dieter. Most binges occur at home and, if a dieter feels one coming on, he or she can put on some soothing music, sit in a comfortable chair, take a few deep breaths, and concentrate solely on the music.

Music that is simple in melody and flows gently and freely works best. Environmental sounds—such as ocean waves, birds singing, raindrops, wind sounds—are also very peaceful and relaxing.

Music can also be an adjunct to proper nutrition and a physiological and psychological aid to reducing in these ways:

As an aid to digestion—light, pleasant music played before mealtimes regulates gastric juice production, calms the mind and body, and allows food to be digested, assimilated, and utilized in the system properly. Thus you avoid overacidity, indigestion, gas, and bloating, all of which hinder weight loss.

To help control appetite—slow, soothing music encourages you to eat slower. This stretches the mealtime and also gives the appestat (appetite control center) time to signal "I'm full" to the brain.

It was not coincidental that in ancient cultures court musicians played soft, soothing music while the nobility dined. This tradition carried over through the centuries to the higher class restaurants. Today, music is used as background in most eating establishments but, unfortunately, the *quality* of the music has deteriorated into "customer turnover overtures" of harsh, prerecorded songs. Noisy, unpleasant eating environments cause tension and anxiety and will interfere with digestion, and possibly make you eat and drink more than you really wanted to.

But there is more to successful weight control than good nutrition and proper digestion. There is the psychological aspect—probably the most vital aspect—that often spells the difference between success and failure in controlling your weight. Music properly chosen and applied can aid your diet program in these ways:

To boost self-esteem—inspiring, motivating music combined with positive affirmations helps to "reprogram" your thoughts and attitudes so that you perceive (and believe!) that you are a worthwhile human being. This music/mind exercise puts your outlook on weight control and life itself in the proper perspective so that you can set realistic and achievable goals.

To increase physical and mental energy—happy, up tempo music certainly stirs up the adrenaline, giving you an energy lift and psychological boost. You can be dragging your behind all day, but if you put on some peppy, uplifting music, your mind becomes alert and your body perks up immediately with increased heart rate and respiration, and a feeling of anticipation and excitement. This added vigor makes you more active and raises your metabolic rate so you burn up calories. The psychological lift you feel also encourages you to work more efficiently and productively, as well as contentedly.

To stimulate creative talents—music that is colorful and dramatic stimulates the imagination. It paints pictures in your mind of things you would like to do, places you would like to visit, and what you would like to become—even slim! You begin to think more inventively about everyday life, about how to solve your problems, and how to make the necessary changes in yourself to achieve personal and professional success.

To divert your attention away from food and diets—with all this increased vitality, heightened self-esteem, and resurgence of creativity, food becomes the least (and maybe *last*) thing on your mind. Think about a time that you were intensely involved in a sport, or a game of Trivial Pursuit, or working with your hands on some sort of craft or labor of love. How many hours went by before you realized you hadn't eaten? When you finally did eat, it was just a quick break for sustenance so you could hurry back to that exciting activity. Music, therefore, can be a marvelous behavior modification tool and diversionary tactic in your weight control strategy.

MUSIC AND EXERCISE

No matter what your present physical condition, there is a form of exercise that is right for you. And accompanying music not only gives you physical energy, but it can intensify your concentration, provide motivation, and enhance the results of your workout. Whether you are swimming, running, walking, playing tennis, doing aerobic dance, or lifting weights, it is important that your movements be rhythmical and deliberate so that you can learn body/mind coordination and not just throw yourself around in mindless, meaningless activity (and set yourself up for injury as well). This is why the choice of music is so important to your exercise or training program.

The ancient Greeks, who were a hearty athletic culture themselves, learned through their philosophers and scientists to associate high-pitched musical notes with swift motion and low-pitched notes with slow motion. It is logical to assume, therefore, that if you want your body to move quickly, decisively, and with great vigor, your choice of music will lean toward instruments and vibrational frequencies that resonate above the solar plexus, music that lifts you both physically and psychologically. Music with strings, flutes, trumpets, woodwinds, light percussions, and vocal ranges from alto to tenor and soprano.

If your movements are to be slow, strong, and of great anaerobic strength (such as in weight lifting), music that resonates in the lowest energy center (below the navel) would be appropriate. Music with strong brass instruments, heavy percussions, bass notes, and vocal ranges of alto, baritone, and bass.

But choosing the right music becomes more complex than having the pitch or frequency levels correspond to the swiftness or slowness of your movements. Other factors to be considered are the amount of concentration, grace, and skill your sport or exercise requires, the level of self-awareness and self-esteem needed on your part to perform well, and whether or not you need to avoid high-intensity stress or be motivated by its presence.

All sports impose a stress factor which can reduce one's ability to perform. This stress interferes with the symmetry and balance of the two brain hemispheres, with the left hemisphere becoming dominant over the right. In his own studies, Dr. John Diamond has found that mental and physical performance is always more satisfactory when both hemispheres are balanced. Since music is primarily a property of the right brain, Diamond suggests that one of the simplest ways to achieve equal balance is to hum or sing a song quietly to yourself while you are playing.

Stress and tension also lead to what Diamond calls "jamming" of the breath. When a baseball player (or tennis player, golf player, etc.) hits the ball, he must not hold his breath, for this cuts off the life energy in the body and hinders performance. Humming music alters the body rhythm so that the ball is hit at the very instant of breath exhalation. Exhaling at the moment of impact relieves the rigidity of the muscles and allows for better range of movement as well as a relaxed, yet alert, state of mind.

Trainers have expanded on this theory by using special music tapes that help athletes have better concentration and relieve competitive stress so that they perform better. Tennis champions Billie Jean King and Virginia Wade, and many other tennis pros, have used the "stress tapes" designed by Adam Knieste, Ph.D., a musicologist who has studied the effects of music on human behavior. Knieste's twenty-two-minute tapes consist of pieces of music by various composers that had been tested for three kinds of emotional effects: joy, neutrality, and calmness.

Still other tennis pros have used tapes with selections from Strauss and Mendelssohn that lower heart rate and body temperature, while increasing brain activity. The music helped to make the players more introspective and aware of themselves and what they were doing, which resulted in a more optimistic outlook and better performance.

At Ohio State University, studies were conducted on experienced runners who listened to music on headsets while they ran on a treadmill. In the studies, beta endorphin, a chemical produced by the body and released into the blood as a natural painkiller, was measured. Endorphins are called "nature's opiates" because they suppress pain in the same way narcotics do, and are released into the blood as a natural reaction to painful stress. The runners training with music produced fewer endorphins because the music reduced the stressful effect of the exercise, and all the runners said their exercise seemed easier with the music than without it.

Eric Miller, a doctoral candidate in exercise physiology at Ohio State at the time of the study, stated that the beta-endorphin and perceived exertion levels of the group that ran with music were lower because they perceived the workout as less intensive. The body thought it needed less painkiller (endorphin) because, even though the *physiological* stress was the same, the *psychological* stress was less.

Miller asserts that if you can't hear stressful sensory input—in this case, increased heart rate and respiration—you will perceive exercise as less stressful, and he believes that music helps tune out the body's sensitivity to this input.

With physical fitness in general—running, jogging, aerobics, etc.—reaching peak popularity in the past few years, some practitioners in the newly discovered field of the "effects of music on high performance skills" have created special tapes that sound like popular music rhythmically, but do not fall into any of the usual music categories. These tapes are primarily instrumental, or may contain some background vocals or subliminal suggestions to motivate you. Synthesizers, keyboards, woodwinds, and light percussions are used and the rhythms are appropriate for whatever exercise you may be performing. Some examples of these tapes are "Sole Music" (for running) by the Sweat Band; "Synchronized High Performance Music (SHPM)"—a series of tapes for many activities—by J. Raul Espinosa, president of Music in Motion; and "Fitness Suite" by Dr. Steven Halpern. The tapes have been designed to utilize and emphasize the most beneficial vibrational frequencies in music, as well as provide rhythms that are energizing and stimulating, instead of the fatiguing da-da-DAH thumping of most pop/ rock music.

"Sole Music" is a series of jazzy, funky songs with upbeat (but not overpowering) rhythms that invigorate you while you walk, jog, or run. The songs are pleasant and psychologically appealing enough, but show no indication that any special formula had been used to create the "magic" vibrational frequencies that stimulate various energy centers.

Espinosa and a group of sports psychologists, musicologists, and fitness experts created the SHPM tapes, with the help of music computer systems. According to Espinosa, several psychological factors are plotted into each composition to help the listener "tap that 90 percent of the unused brain which helps produce results." When planning the tapes, Espinosa and his panel considered such factors as the body's muscle and respiratory reactions, brain activity, pulse rate, and sensory mode. Thus, the tapes are supposed to block tension, regulate muscular coordination, and assist in focusing awareness.

Halpern's tape, very creatively composed, takes you strategically through a complete workout from warm-up, stretch, aerobics, and cool-down, to relaxation and meditation, while positive, subaural affirmations subliminally inspire you on. Halpern's concern, in all of his compositions, is for the effect of music on the total human organism. In "Fitness Suite," by using specific frequency levels in the music, Halpern asserts that the tape stimulates the appropriate energy centers in the body, allowing for maximum effectiveness. The subliminal suggestions are simple ("You enjoy exercising") as well as profound ("As you breathe in, you draw in life-giving oxygen and energy known as prana," and "You reach new levels of physical well-being and proper functioning of your human instrument, the physical vehicle").

While such tapes are a welcome respite from, and viable alternative to, hard-driving rock sounds, and are certainly health *enhancing* instead of health *hindering,* their sameness may tend to lose their appeal after a while. The psychological motivators, while positive, are somewhat limited. The human psyche, being very complicated and demanding in its need for constant change and new experiences, is rarely satisfied with the same set of musical sounds for very long.

There is no one mode of music that will inspire everybody, and no set rhythmical pattern that can serve as the impetus for movement for all sports or activities. The emotions, the dynamics, the power, the creativity of the music are what people spark to, and that spark will depend upon the age, environment, cultural background, and personal tastes and experiences of the individual. As discussed in Chapter 2, we know that many people are moved in similar ways to the same piece of music—they all feel joy or sorrow, nostalgia, sensuality, etc.—albeit in varying degrees.

We may compose, create, and design technically perfect pieces of music (vibrationally and harmonically speaking) to give people optimal life and health energy, but in the end, it is the individual who is the quintessential monitor of his own mind, body, and spirit responses.

But this is what makes the entire subject of music and exercise (indeed, music and the "Circle of Health") so exciting. Because there is a wellspring of music available to use—from classical to jazz to new age—and you need never be in a quandary about finding suitable music for any activity.

Moving and breathing with controlled but natural rhythm is vital to runner, swimmer, dancer, or any athlete. Even the fundamental exercise of walking is more effective when done in a constant, brisk rhythm. Whether you are maintaining a moderate, steady pace on the jogging path, dashing about with agility and alertness on the tennis court, or creating a visual drama on ice to win an Olympic gold medal, you can find the right music and lyrics that will allow you to "get into" yourself and bring out your best performance. Exercise should be an emotionally fulfilling experience as well as a physical one. Long after your workout is finished, the effects of the music will stay with you, complementing all the aspects of your life and strengthening your "Circle of Health."

(Because aerobics classes have become an exercise phenomenon unto themselves, I have devoted a special section to this topic alone.)

MUSIC AND STRESS MANAGEMENT

We hear a lot about stress management these days. In fact, "stress" is the big buzzword of the eighties. But it is not *stress* we want to avoid, it is *distress*. In its positive context, stress means to "emphasize and focus attention on." But most of us do not stress our bodies or our minds enough, except in negative ways. This leads to distress, making us vulnerable to a myriad of ills and disabilities. Stress Management means to control your own environment, your thoughts, actions, feelings, and attitudes, before they control *you*.

But you can't manage anything, including stress, unless you know what it is you have to manage. Looking at our complicated, overwhelming world, most of us would say, "Everything!" Job, marriage, kids, finances, relationships, the economy, the state of the world, the pressure to succeed and achieve; conflicts of goals, principles and ethics; religious convictions—add your own list to this list. Any of the above can be exhilarating, challenging, and motivating, can give us the opportunity to grow and realize our full potential. This is positive stress.

Or, they can be negative forces—distress—causing physical maladies, irritability, anger, depression, fear, boredom, inability to cope or think clearly. If these symptoms become severe and long-lasting, professional help is in order. But if, like most of us, you merely need a temporary release from these aggravating feelings, music can be a very effective means to manage the negative stress of everyday life and help prevent the escalation of symptoms before professional help is needed.

We know that physical exercise is one of the most effective ways to combat emotional distress. It is true that no two things can occupy the same space at the same time. This applies also to the brain. It is not possible to think and feel depressed while thinking and feeling good. Exercise makes you feel good. While your body is moving, you are increasing oxygen and blood flow to the brain, releasing toxins from the system, and creating chemical changes that are positive in nature. If you truly concentrate on your sport or exercise, focus in on the movements, the music, and the results you hope to achieve, all these good feelings squeeze depression right out of that "space" in your head. And even if it is only temporary, it is a "high" that cannot be achieved by any drug known to man.

But we cannot exercise twenty-four hours a day. Nor can we work or interact with other people all day. Sooner or later we have to come face to face with ourselves, our thoughts and feelings, and try to understand what our personality traits are and why we react the way we do to certain situations. If our reactions are counterproductive, we must take steps to change them. If they are beneficial to us, then we should learn how to strengthen these positive traits. Psychologists and behaviorists have developed a rating system for personality types: A, B, C, or D personalities. But a less clinical and perhaps more intriguing way to pinpoint our strengths and weaknesses is by knowing which of the following "Universal Energies" you resemble: Fire, Earth, Air, or Water.

These elements have been recognized throughout the ages by spiritualists as the four modes for life expression. While all four are present in all of us to varying degrees, one or two of them is usually dominant, while the others are recessive or dormant. The unique blending of these energies is what makes each of us the very special individuals that we are.

By defining Fire, Earth, Air, and Water energies astrologically, we can also learn to choose corresponding music that will bring out the positive forces in our nature while balancing out the negative.

Fire

I can personally vouch for the intensity and incendiary spark of this energy force. In astrology, the Fire signs are Aries, Leo, and Sagittarius (that's me). When this force is dominant in the personality, our polarities stretch from the ridiculous to the sublime. We are domineering, stubborn, egotistical, and judgmental. We are the fools that rush in where angels fear to tread, and often we suffer foot-in-mouth disease. That's the negative side. On the positive side, we can be courageous, innovative, decisive, tolerant, great teachers, sensitive, and eloquent in our feelings toward others. Fire responds to strong, powerful music with stimulating rhythms, and great surges and swells of emotions—such as symphonies and epic movie themes. We are also moved deeply by romantic melodies that touch the heart, and gentle music that is transcendental in nature.

Earth

The Earth energy brings our cautious nature to the fore. It is steadfast and perseverant in its pursuit of a personal goal. People born with their Sun sign in Taurus, Virgo, or Capricorn are strong Earth energies and have wonderful endurance and patience. But when the energy is out of balance, they can be manipulative, melancholy, and introverted. Artistic, with an aura of the occult, the Earth energy is also the rock and foundation that holds us together. But at rock bottom, Earth can be nit-picky, resistant to new ideas and change, overcritical, and hypchondriacal. To bring out the positive force of Earth, warm melodic music is very appealing. Ballads that tell stories of hearth and home, music that celebrates the beauty of nature, music that is restful, comforting and contemplative.

Air

This is a perfect designation for this energy, because that is often where it leaves us: up in the Air. If you know a Gemini, Libra, or Aquarius (or are one yourself), you might have noticed the tendencies toward indecision, restlessness, procrastination, and the inability to pay attention to—or even care about—what you are saying for long periods of time. On the up side, the Air temperament is very companionable, seeks peace, beauty, justice, and great harmony in all aspects of life. Air music is preferably very simple and clear, not too emotional, but it can be avant-garde, experimental, and extroverted. New sounds and tone colors intrigue the Air in us, until we become bored. Then it's on to a new musical excitation.

Water

The deep, brooding, and introspective Water energy is very apparent in people born under the Sun signs of Cancer, Scorpio, and Pisces. Let the negative side of this energy take control and it becomes fanatical, self-pitying, and indolent. But strike the right chord and Water becomes nurturing, vigorous, intuitive, and sharply in touch with people's needs. Music that evokes strong emotional responses and lifts this energy out of the murky depths and into the Light is very appropriate. Music of great joy and great love, of dreams and wishes fulfilled. Let's give a little happiness and hope to the Water energy (even though deep down it relishes the joy of suffering!).

With these four major elements—Fire, Earth, Air, and Water—intermingling in our beings, it is no wonder that we have so many different moods and shades of personality. By listening very carefully to music and monitoring our responses, we can eliminate, or at least diminish considerably, our destructive traits and enhance those characteristics that help us control our overreactions to stress so that we do not get into *distress*. We can find the music that lifts a heavy heart, that gives us courage in the face of adversity, that provides us with serenity when all else is chaos around us. With music we can turn frustration into hope, relieve our loneliness, live out our fantasies and wildest dreams—and make life immeasurably more enjoyable for ourselves and those we love.

MUSIC AND CONSCIOUSNESS/SPIRITUALITY

Just as the circle is a perfect symbol representing Life, it also aptly represents Consciousness. Consciousness is the complete spectrum of our awareness: our thoughts, feelings, attitudes, beliefs, knowingness, perceptions, and experiences. Like the circle, it is complete and all inclusive.

From the moment we were created as an entity of Light in the Universe, our consciousness began creating, absorbing, assimilating, and recording all of our experiences, all of our emotions and responses. If you believe in the ongoingness of the soul, you know that these experiences are innumerable and timeless, stretching through eons of the past to the present. But even if your belief system will only allow you to recognize *this* lifetime as your *only* lifetime, you still know that many bits and pieces of data, memories, feelings, and experiences are housed in your subconscious and conscious mind.

These thought patterns operate on a vibratory level that we cannot see or hear, but we can feel them as they travel into and out of our being. Everything that flows in and out of every human mind is part of the Collective Consciousness of the Universe. Thoughts and emotions created by others emanate from them and are received by us as "messages" to use—or *not* use—as we will. In turn, everything we think and feel emanates forth for others to receive into their consciousness and create from or reject.

Music is a very effective tool to help open our minds to the creative thought vibrations of the universe that will expand and raise our level of awareness of all things. And by doing so, we can attain the highest form of consciousness: self-awareness.

There are two types of consciousness: *social consciousness,* which is occupied with such things as survival, personal and professional goals, acceptance by our peers, status in the world, health, death, and other restrictive thoughts on the third-dimensional (physical) plane of existence. Then there is the *super consciousness,* a higher frequency level of thought (spirit energy) that concerns itself with life, harmony, ongoingness, love, joy, and oneness with the universe. These are the flowing, unrestricted, unlimited thoughts we create and receive that often defy description in mere words.

On this earthly plane, we bop around in our social consciousness, sometimes unaware of why we are doing what we do. But others are aware, and in fact know how to pigeonhole us and, through the use of music, push our buttons so we perform to *their* benefit.

Years ago, the radio industry realized that the medium was not just an entertainment vehicle, but a powerful marketing device (for advertisers), and a unique means through which to identify and reach people of varying demographic segments who lived specific life-styles. As popular music became more and more subdivided (rock, R&B, pop, contemporary country, fusion, new wave, soul, etc.), audiences became very fragmented, with each demographic group gravitating toward the type of music they could relate to because of their own socioeconomic and intellectual level, as well as their age and sex. This fragmentation became so complex that market research groups burgeoned forth offering their services to radio stations so the latter could target the type of audience most desirable to their advertisers.

This research analysis has become so sophisticated that consulting firms have been able to categorize listeners on attitudes, needs, wants, and beliefs. A report in *American Demographics* (1986) illustrated the four major categories of radio listeners and, while it is rather simplistic, it is quite revealing:

1. ***Need Drivens:***   these people are very limited in finances and their lives are driven more by needs (food, shelter, etc.) than choice. Subcategories in this group are *Survivors* and *Sustainers.*
2. ***Outer-Directeds***   live their lives greatly influenced by what others think and do. The life-style of this group is a major step above the

Need Drivens, for they have broadened their perspective to include other people and a host of institutions. They are further categorized as *Belongers, Emulators,* and *Achievers.*

3. **Inner-Directeds** are concerned with inner values and those personal and private needs of the individual. They are very concerned with inner growth and are broken into three subgroups: *I-am-me, Experiential,* and *Society Conscious.*

4. **Integrateds** are a small group of people who have it "all together." They combine the power of Outer-Direction with the sensitivity of Inner-Direction; they are mature, open-minded, display leadership qualities, and will yield graciously to another's leadership if necessary.

Along with their diverse character traits, all of these groups have their own music preferences...or none at all.

Since the *Sustainers* are struggling financially—but still hopeful—they listen to radio stations that offer cash contests, regardless of the music that is played. They like to be up on current issues, but want two-way communication; therefore, they are heavy listeners of call-in talk shows.

Belongers love country music—its down-home quality, the patriotic feel of Americana, the familiarity of the artists (as well as the topics of their songs). They enjoy the feeling of belonging to a group of high-spirited people. Middle-age belongers are very loyal to their music, their radio station, and the disc jockey. Often, they have bumper stickers on their vehicles that boast, "We love our Country, K _____."

Emulators favor the music of the superstars, the contemporary and pop music hits. This group goes with what and who is hot at the moment. Ten years ago they latched on to the John Travolta-*Saturday Night Fever*—disco image. Until John became the "Urban Cowboy." Then the likes of Kenny Rogers, Eddie Rabbit, and Crystal Gale struck their fancy. Now the *Emulators* have gravitated to adult contemporary music—Chicago, Billy Joel, Phil Collins, Anita Baker, Elton John, etc.—the classy and flashy music they perceive to be favored by the *Achievers.*

However, the *Achievers* prefer to listen to background music stations—anything from light, soft pop to Beautiful Music (aka Easy Listening)—as long as it stays in its place, the *Achievers* need no radio station (or its music) to tell them who to be or what to do. Some *Achievers* listen to Public Radio stations, not for the classical, jazz, or folk music on the programs (for they tend not to be too interested in the arts), but for the stimulation they receive from the news and public affairs programs.

The *I-am-me's* love contemporary hits, the Top 40, and urban contemporary music (black soul, R&B, fusion, etc.). They have a need to be innovators, so no oldies-but-goodies for them. The world view—and music view—of this group is present and forward; the past doesn't interest them.

Experientials pop buttons from station to station till they find what they like—for the moment. These "radio browsers" don't limit their intake of music to classical, jazz, rock, or folk—they listen to anything and everything. Hooray for the *Experientials.*

Are *you* an *Experiential?* Are you concerned with your inner growth and your inner values? Do you seek to understand yourself and, in your quest, open yourself to new experiences, and new music? The first step toward that self-awareness might be that you are now reading this book. However you may have acquired it (by choice, as a gift, by accident, under duress), you apparently are intrigued, curious, and open to the experience of what is written on these pages. Of course, it's possible you may be an *Emulator,* doing what others are doing, responding to someone else's suggestions. Or perhaps you are an *Achiever* merely looking to stimulate your intellect. But more than likely you are (or aspire to be) an *Inner-Directed* on your way to becoming an *Integrated:* one who has reached full emotional and psychological maturity, has great sensitivity and an ability to see and experience the overall picture of life.

Self-awareness, that highest form of consciousness, is achieved not only by gaining insight about ourselves, but by learning about other people—their thoughts, fears, hopes, desires, attitudes, and life-styles. We can achieve this by reading about other people, poring over biographies, looking at photographs, even visiting museums. And while these experiences are thought-provoking, they are only second to *living* and *feeling* them.

Short of traveling nomadically around the world and infiltrating various ethnic groups, cultures, and civilizations, one of the most effective paths to knowledge and self-knowledge is through the sensory experience of music. The lushness and richness of the melodies, the harmonies, the various instruments and their palette of tone colors, bring forth an almost indescribable landscape of feelings. All your senses are stimulated, exposed, vulnerable, touched, aroused. It is at these moments our potential for complete self-awareness is heightened, but unless we recognize and seize the opportunity, it can slip through our fingers.

There is a vast pool of music through which we can connect to other people, other places, and other points in time. Soundtracks of films and stage plays are a complete exercise in consciousness-raising unto themselves. Even without the visual impact of the film or stage sets, they provide us with a tapestry of life we might never be able to see or feel. Through certain basic themes (love, death, personal triumph over injustice, tragedy, social issues, cultural traditions and taboos, etc.), the words and music express the entire spectrum of feelings encountered by the characters that are either universal (you have experienced) or enlightening (you have learned something new). We can empathize and sympathize when engrossed in the sounds, the rhythms, the meaning of the music. The more we respond and the more intensely we feel, the more we come to know ourselves.

You can enhance your own awareness by knowing more about the music itself—who the composer is, when it was written, under what circumstances it was created, what the significance of the theme is, and so forth. Reading the album jackets can be a fascinating education in itself. Classical music albums invariably give a detailed history of the music, the composer, the response from critics and audiences when it was first introduced.

The soundtrack album of *The Color Purple* includes very eloquent reminiscences by author Alice Walker and music producer Quincy Jones, detailing the moving and enriching experiences they both encountered during the filming and music production processes. Many other soundtracks provide similar background information that gives you a feeling of being personally connected to the creation of the music.

By discovering what a particular piece of music means to a composer, we can understand why he (or she) is willing to give his life over to creativity, suffer the pain of creation, and know the exquisite joy of rebirth in that piece of music. In knowing, for example, the album *Powerlight* by Earth, Wind and Fire was the group's attempt to bring together the age of technology and humanitarian thought, to show us the "power of light that exists within us" adds a dimension to their music that transcends entertainment or aesthetic enjoyment.

We can also check our "inner pulse" of emotions to see if they are in tune with that of the composer, and if his or her music consistently strikes the corresponding chord in us of happiness, sadness, nostalgia, or bittersweet memories.

When we use music as the bridge to understanding ourselves in relationship to others, we operate in harmony with our environment, become a reflection of the Universal Consciousness, heighten our self-awareness, and realize our complete spiritual potential.

"The highest mission of music is to serve as a link between God and men..." said Corinne Heline, author and metaphysician. In looking at the origin of music, we find its connection to religion is irrefutable, "religion" being, not a specific denomination or sect, but the attitudes, beliefs, emotions, and behavior that constitute man's relationship with the powers and principles of the universe.

Long before there were instruments that played the "Music of the Spheres," man attuned himself with his Creator by chanting certain tones and sounds. These chants promoted physical, emotional, and spiritual health, for they released spirit and energy in an expression of man's soul. When the chants developed into songs and the songs were accompanied by instruments, man's spirit soared and he found new and more magnificent ways to express his innermost and profound feelings. The Great Master composers, regardless of their religious persuasions, were deeply dedicated to the "God-force" and were inspired by cosmic sources of power. They were touched by the gods and spoke to the gods through their music. Beethoven, Wagner, Vivaldi, Bach—all the great composers then, and their counterparts today, looked beyond their own human potential and talent and called upon the presence of the Divine Spirit to guide them as they created their immortal works.

This spirit is evident in so many pieces of music—from the great masses of Haydn and Mozart, to the gospel music and popular ballads of contemporary composers. It is easy to hear the Divine spirituality of Handel's *Messiah* (most notably, the "Hallelujah Chorus"). It is magnificent, glorious. It lifts us up on the wings of angels until we ascend to celestial heights. The rousing spirituality of "(Oh, Lord) I'm On My Way," by George Gershwin (*Porgy and Bess*) is filled with deep and abiding faith, expressed in the joyful words and music. In Neil Diamond's "Yes I Will," the human spirit is inspired and inspiring, in music that is gentle, solemn, and hymnal. And in the heart-pumping, "Jubilation" by Paul Anka and Johnny Harris, we hear the celebration of life and an invitation for all of us to join in.

Each piece of music is of a different form: one, a classic from the Baroque era; the second from a modern opera; the third a musical soliloquy; the fourth a fusion of gospel and jazz. But in all of them there is the common thread of love, unconditional love, universal love. Each song calls upon man to reach beyond the here and now to a higher power, to be more than he ever dreamed of being, and to give thanks for allowing the power of the spirit to flow through him.

Spirit is in all of us, not just those who are blessed with the talent to create great music. Spirit is the vital essence or animating force in all of us that is divine in origin. It is incorporeal and invisible and is manifested through our intelligence, personality, self-consciousness, and our will. It is, deep within us, our soul. Our spirituality is the sum and substance of our religious beliefs and, above all, our belief in ourselves. It represents our ability to tap into those higher powers that elevate us in thought and deed, and give us the inspiration we desire to create a more meaningful and higher quality of life for ourselves and those around us.

Music is a gift to us, to create, to hear, to feel, to use. Through it, we unite with that higher Source that gives us strength, courage, and faith. Whether we use quiet, gentle music during moments of meditation to achieve an-out-of body spiritual experience, or use rich vibrant music that makes us lift our heart and voice in song, through the music we can reach beyond the limits of time and space to the vast, unboundless heavens of the universal spirit.

When we look at all of the elements in our "Circle of Health"— diet, exercise, stress management, consciousness, spirituality—we can see how music provides a cohesiveness and connecting link that makes it all work. Music is pervasive and so much a part of our lives, one cannot assume it is a mere accident of society. Music's purpose and relation to life and health is as vital as the air we breathe and the water we drink. And when we recognize it, respect it, enjoy it, and use it well, life—like the Circle—continues, perpetuates, and never ends.

CLOSE-UP: **Gilda Marx**

The "Grande Dame" of Aerobics Speaks Out on Music

"THE reason there is an aerobic dance industry today is because of the music," declares Gilda Marx. "It is the motivating force that inspires you to move and to keep moving all through the class."

Marx speaks from more than twenty years of experience in the fitness industry. She was a pioneer choreographer of aerobic dancing to music in the early 1960's when it was labeled "exercise to music," and is now referred to with admiration and respect as the "Grande Dame" of aerobics.

Her career began in Los Angeles with ten housewives who wanted to shape up for a charity show at the famed Coconut Grove. Incorporating her dancing acumen with some exercise movements, she created techniques that toned the women up so well and so enjoyably that they spread the word around about her. Soon after, Marx opened a small studio in the back of a store in Encino.

Today, Marx is owner of the chain of Body Design by Gilda exercise studios, and is designer and founder of the famous FLEXATARD bodywear line and GILDA MARX SWIMWEAR. She has also authored the fitness book, *Body by Gilda* (G.P. Putman's Sons), and serves on the board of the Aerobics and Fitness Association of America (AFAA).

103

Marx's studios are considered to be one of the top ten studios nationally, as selected by Shape Magazine, out of a survey of 55,000 studios. They boast an enviable list of celebrity clients including Barbra Streisand, Priscilla Presley, Britt Eklund, Stephanie Zimbalist, Brooke Shields and Mary Tyler Moore, to name a few. Shirley MacLaine was Marx's first privately-coached celebrity client, and two other students went on to achieve their own fame in the fitness industry: Jane Fonda and Richard Simmons.

Marx's longevity, talent, success and popularity in the fitness field are due to her drive, her dynamic personality, her caring as a teacher, her highly effective workout programs, and her meticulous attention to the music she chooses for her classes.

"Joining exercise to music is a natural marriage," says Marx. "For centuries, the military forces have been getting people to move in cadence to the rhythm of music. It's almost a hypnotic stimulus, similar to the beat of the drum that drives the natives to move and dance. Popular music has that mesmerizing effect. It urges the body to move and exercise in class, and yet it puts the mind in another place."

Marx has spent thousands of hours researching music tapes. Her choices of music are wide and varied, and she declines the use of music services that provide ready-made tapes:

"I pick my music to fit my program, not the other way around. With a pre-programmed tape you are locked into what someone else thinks you should do musically and choreographically."

When Marx selects music for a class, she is in essence creating a Broadway show, a production that flows from beginning to end, that will have people humming and singing and remembering what they experienced for the hour or so of exercise.

"I try to find music that will create pictures in my mind that will say to people, 'move your arms, stretch your legs, move this way and that way.' The music has to be interesting and exciting enough to motivate people to increase their endurance while maintaining correct technique to achieve training results. With the appropriate musical accompaniment, the principles of correct (body) alignment are easier to uphold."

"Music with 'cuts' and stops is very disconcerting," she says. "It disrupts the momentum of the workout and scatters the students' attention. The music should have a continuity of theme but various types of music can be mixed, as long as they blend well with the choreography."

Marx constantly researches to find new music and approves all the tapes used in classes at her studios. In some studios, if someone programs a good tape, "it is played to death. People get very bored with it and it ceases to motivate them. If you want to stay in this business and be successful, you have to continually challenge yourself," she says. "You have to be aware of trends and new aspects of your work, including new music."

Marx trains her people thoroughly and they are usually required to have a strong dance or exercise background. But while you can train people in the techniques of safety and the physiology of exercise, Marx maintains "You cannot teach creativity. Many people are technically good at exercise, but they don't know how to *teach,* how to creatively get the elements of the class across to the students in an entertaining and effective way. You can't teach someone the artistic end of it—including how to choose music—if it is not in them. And yet, this aspect of it is just as important as the physiology and safety of the program. When it comes to music, there is a real finesse to knowing what music is right for the fitness level and the age group of the class."

Marx is critical of the painful volumes at which music is played in studios because it competes with the teacher's job of teaching.

"They wind up screaming—which is so hazardous to the vocal chords—and everyone in the room is in agony. I emphasize very strongly that if they must play music loud, it must also be tolerable."

This means no heavy metal, punk or hard rock music with screeching guitars and excessively low bass vibrations.

"At age 50, I have an entirely different feeling about music," Marx says. "If a piece makes you want to sing, it's good. But most of the music today you cannot sing to. Music is a release of emotions. In my classes, I want people to enjoy and remember the experience, and I pick music to enlighten, excite, involve and entertain. And yes, music that makes you laugh and feel good."

8

The Key to the Perfect Exercise Class

I think of exercise as spanning two distinct eras: P.M. (premusic) and
A.M. (after music). The difference in the forms of, participation in,
and enjoyment of exercise during these two eras is like the difference
between night and day. P.M. exercise was nothing but boring cal-
isthenics and tumble rolls on the mat in gym class. It was pure torture.
The only people who seemed to reap any benefits—or derive any
enjoyment—from exercise were athletes or movie stars. Only people
whose livelihood depended upon having the perfect body seemed to find
the time and energy for regular workouts. And the wealthy more than
likely hired someone to do it *for* them. People who worked out regularly
and methodically to music were dancers. But that was *dancing*, something
you did as a career, not *exercise*.

But suddenly a new day dawned (A.M.), and millions of men and
women began hopping, jogging, stretching, and going for the "burn" in
choreographed exercise classes to the driving beat of popular music.

Although "aerobics" classes were being taught in the early sixties,
their popularity actually skyrocketed when Jane Fonda introduced her

first "Workout" video tape in 1980. While the workout itself was the primary focus, *music* was the driving force behind the classes. The exercises were stylized, sequentialized (warm up, cardiovascular, floor work, stretch, relax) and strung together in sets of repetitions (8, 16, 20, etc.) that resembled a dance routine more than a physical fitness routine. And everyone who ever wished they could dance, could say, "Look Ma! I'm (almost) dancin'!" And they hardly knew it was exercise at all. Well, almost hardly.

Along came Judi Sheppard Misset and "Jazzercise," Jackie Sorensen's "Aerobic Dance," Debbie Reynolds doing it *her* way, Richard Simmons doing it *his* way, and even Ray "Boom Boom" Mancini dazzling us with "Boxercise" (and a dizzying display of rope jumping in place of jogging). Fonda continues to "Workout" every demographic group from pregnant women to seniors, and there are a variety of hybrids: Fluid Aerobics, Rebound Aerobics, Balletrobics and (my own) Body and Soul Aerobics.

Whatever the style or theme of the choreography, the one element that holds it all together is the music, specifically chosen to stimulate the mind and body into higher peaks of physical activity. The music and choreography have also helped aerobics transcend from purely a physical fitness phenomenon to a highly commercialized (and profitable) entertainment phenomenon, spawning exhibitions and competitions such as the Crystal Light National Aerobics Championships, a Dance-Feverlike event that has produced aerobics-Olympics superstars around the globe. (Bess Motta, et al.).

Aerobics classes are pervasive. Almost everyone you meet is either taking classes or teaching them. If you are a teacher, then you know that music is an integral part of your class. Know also, that your *choice* of music is vital to its success. Even if you are not an aerobics instructor, but are a student who wishes to experience a motivating and effective class, you should read on. It will help you evaluate your teacher, or even assist you in making your own workout tapes at home.

Music can make or break an exercise class. It can spell the difference between optimal performance and a half-hearted effort on the part of students. Yet, music is often an afterthought: haphazardly chosen, poorly programmed, or inappropriate for the level of energy needed to perform a specific exercise well.

Music does more than stimulate the body to move. It inspires a total mind-body connection that makes exercise an emotionally uplifting experience as well as a physically energizing one. Music can take your mind to another place, but it had better not take it too far. For, in exercise just as in any other endeavor, you must visualize the end result if you expect to succeed. Music helps you focus more intently on your workout, helps you concentrate on the muscle to be strengthened or stretched, and aids you in achieving cardiovascular endurance.

From a purely physical standpoint, the right music can help the body move with greater ease, strength, and fluidity, while the wrong music can confuse body rhythms, disturb concentration and inhibit energy flow. There is a fountainhead of wonderful music available that can be creatively applied to exercise: Jazz, pop, country, rock, classical, new age, etc. But since rock is the most popular music of the day, and contains that constant, driving rhythm needed for continual movement, it is also the most widely used. Unfortunately, it also contains some harmful elements that are counterproductive to the exercise experience, such as the anapestic (or "stopped" beat), heavy metal guitars, extreme low bass frequencies, etc.

We discussed in Chapter Three how these musical "negatives" can cause undue stress on the nervous system, and also noted that the excessive volume at which rock is usually played (especially in health clubs) has a further deleterious effect on the body's energy supply. Attention to the finer points of music selection, therefore, is even more important when you are trying to achieve a desired result, such as strengthening and toning the muscles and organs of the body.

When you are isolating body parts for exercise (such as leg exercises), it is important that you do not use music that undermines your efforts. For example, low bass frequencies (such as in heavy computerized soul or rapping music) resonate in the body's lowest energy center (hips down) and can actually put a drag on the leg muscles, making them feel like one hundred pound weights. Instead of drawing forth the energy to lift that leg with proper form and strength, the entire body feels dragged down and the exercise becomes an exhausting experience.

Hard driving drum beats that sound like a shot to the heart and feel like a fist in the stomach ("Born in the USA") and dominate the other elements of the music (lyrics, melody, instruments), give your internal organs a brutal punishment. These pounding sounds are physically and psychologically annoying and, as the body tries to instinctively protect itself from this sound assault, it uses up valuable energy that should be used for the exercise it needs to perform.

Synth-pop, techno-pop, and computerized funk (Prince, Janet Jackson, Klymaxx, Madonna, etc.) are not very exciting or motivating to exercise to, for most of it is created by machines that simulate the sounds of instruments, and the rhythms are controlled by computers. Consequently, the techno-pop beat is monotonously constant, the musical and lyrical phrases are boringly repetitive, and there are no emotions or dynamics in the performance. I find this music stimulates no energy whatsoever.

(Please note once again that pregnant women should never be exposed to hard rock, disco beats, and abrasive heavy metal sounds, for what affects the mother also affects the fetus. It is hazardous to subject mother and baby to music that disrupts their natural heartbeat and body rhythms, or that can damage delicate nerve endings and internal organs.)

This is not to say that all rock music should be excluded from your music program. On the contrary, as we explained in Chapter Three, when rock music is really rockin' and rollin' it gives you a feeling of forward motion because there is no hesitation between beats, and some of the discomfort you would feel from just *listening* to rock music is alleviated when the body is actually *moving* to it. But you should eliminate any music with possible injurious elements. When you broaden the selection of your music beyond the Top 40 pop-rock tunes you not only make your class more healthful, but more creative and interesting. If you really monitor your music and your physical and psychological reactions to it, you'll find it easy to choose music that uplifts you, and creates that classic visual image that a string is attached to the top of your head, lifting you upward instead of dragging you down. Just when you feel you can't jog another step or lift your leg another inch, the dynamics and resonance of the music should give you that second wind and invigorate you instead of exhaust you.

Remember, also, that just because an artist or group is classified as heavy metal or soul or hard rock, etc., does not always mean that *all* the music they perform is harmful or inappropriate to exercise to. For example, the group Styx is primarily a heavy metal band, but a very creative and artistic one. While many of their songs contain the heavy metal sounds, still others are very exciting and work well in class. "Rockin' the Paradise" for example, is one of the band's most motivating and exciting dance songs, and very appropriate for the jogging/aerobic dance portion of a class. It is powerful, forward-moving and highly stimulating, which is what you need for a high-intensity cardiovascular workout. Programming softer sounding songs prior to and subsequent to this one will allow your body to take a break from its high-charged sounds and driving rhythms. The heavy metal sounds of Judas Priest are another story altogether.

There is obviously more to choosing the most appropriate music for exercise than listening to the radio and stringing hit songs together on a cassette tape. The type of exercise you are doing (warm up, sit ups, stretch, etc.) is the primary factor in music selection. And the age level and fitness level of your students (and yourself) is also to be considered very seriously.

Music that is too fast to allow for full range of movement can lead to improper form, poor results, and possible injury. "Dancing in the Dark" by Bruce Springsteen, "Neutron Dance" by the Pointer Sisters, and "Let's Go Crazy" by Prince were all popular jogging songs with many instructors last year, but they all have been rejected by fitness experts as being too fast to choreograph effectively or safely.

Music that is too *slow* can also be hazardous, especially in jogging segments of the class. "Jump" by Van Halen (one of the more "pleasing" songs by this heavy metal group) is too slow for jogging in place, for it makes your feet come down too hard, placing extra stress on ankles, knees and lower back. The recent "discovery" that jogging in place is injury-provoking has led to the wide-spread use of "low impact aerobics," where your feet remain close to the floor and weight is shifted equally back and forth from left to right in a gentler manner. In the old days, this was called "dance exercise," and its re-entrance into the exercise regime allow you more latitude than ever in your choices of music.

From an emotional standpoint, music can be the prime motivator or the prime detractor. No matter how qualified the instructor, if the music has no emotional excitement, class performance can lag, minds can wander, and motivation can be frustrated. When the music stimulates the brain (where all energy comes from, anyway), inhibitions to the flow of energy will vanish, and a collective energy of high spirit will fill the studio.

I have seen the difference over and over: a room filled with people "walking" their way through the exercises, and a room filled with excited people applauding and cheering their own achievements that went beyond what they thought they were capable of. And the difference has always been because of the music. What stimulated these people physically and emotionally were the fascinating, pulsating rhythms and drum flourishes; the emotional ebb and flow of the song; the colorful use of strings, percussion, brass, and woodwinds; the meaningful, uplifting words; and a heartfelt vocal performance.

The age level of students often determines what motivates them musically, because each generation identifies more readily with the music of their own era. For example, seniors will react more favorably to big band, swing, and jazz than to electronic rock. Soft pop artists and fifties and sixties rock and roll are also more readily accepted because they have a carry-over flavor and style of the music they grew up with. However, *every* age group can enjoy and benefit from music of *any* era, if it is carefully chosen and creatively applied.

You can choose music *carefully* by adhering to the principles outlined previously, and by asking the advice of other trained, experienced instructors. How *creatively* you apply—or interpret—your music will depend upon your own experiences with music, and whether you have a fitness instructor's heart or a *dancer's* heart for music and movement. If you have danced, most likely you have been exposed to a wide variety of musical forms and know how to express your body through them. However, even if you have never had any formal dance training, you can certainly program an effective music tape by being aware of the basic principles behind rhythm and movement as they pertain to the structured design of an exercise routine.

Choreographing your aerobics class requires the same meticulous attention as choreographing a dance. For, in essence, this is what you are doing. From the very first neck roll to the final stretch position, you should be creating a mood, inspiring an emotional give and take with your students, and designing patterns of rhythm and energy flow that give substance and meaning to the exercise experience. Just as a dancer moves with discipline, every movement you make in class should count, should be well planned and executed, and should correspond appropriately to the music you play.

Your sense of timing and rhythm is vital. You must know where the beat of the music is and never lose it. Your transitions from movement to movement should be smooth and easy for students to follow and you should avoid intricate patterns of steps that throw everyone into a state of confusion. And, finally, the energy and spirit of your music should match the energy and spirit of the exercises and steps you do, and should correspond with your style of teaching.

Let's examine each of these points in more detail:

Rhythm is a basic part of life. The earth—indeed, the universe—moves in a constant rhythm which we observe in the change of seasons, the ebb and flow of ocean tides, the cycle of day and night. Our bodies are part of this universal rhythm. Our hearts beat and our blood flows to a certain rhythm. We move in rhythm as we walk and as we breathe. Usually, we give very little, if any, thought to these natural occurences. But in dance, or in this case aerobic exercise, we must always be conscious of the rhythm and timing of the music so that our bodies are moving and breathing with a natural, health-sustaining flow.

There are several aspects of rhythm to consider when speaking of music. There is the *tempo*—the slowness or fastness of the song, and there is the *meter*—the organized pattern of *beats* found in a measure (bar) of music. A waltz meter, for example, has three beats to a measure, with the accent falling on the first beat (ONE two three). Most of the music used in exercise class is written in four/four meter, meaning it contains four quarter beats to a measure. The accents, especially in today's popular music, fall on the second and fourth beats (one TWO three FOUR). We clap our hands or emphasize a movement on the accented beats. In jumping jacks, for example, your feet and arms are *out* on the first beat and *in* on the second.

Rhythm is akin to the beat, but it goes beyond the specific cadence that sets the music's meter and tempo. Think of the *beat* as the basic black dress (sorry, guys!), the pattern from which we begin. From there, with the help of the *rhythm*, we develop style and individuality of expression in our choreography. The rhythm, therefore, is the accessories and the embellishments that add intrigue and appeal to the basic beat. It's the flash of color, the element of surprise, the swirl here, and the sweep there, that catch us up in the vividness of the design of the entire fabric we call "the song."

Picture in your mind the dances that represent Latin rhythms (cha-cha, samba, tango, etc.), or shuffle rhythms (jitterbug), or dances done to jazz or blues music. These styles can be modified and incorporated into your exercise moves to give your class a distinct flair, without sacrificing the requirements for safety and effectiveness.

While you're "getting down" to the rhythms, don't get carried away from the beat—or the *timing*—of the music. If you rush ahead of it (or if you lag behind it), you will end up moving somewhere in between the beats, thus creating a whole new rhythm pattern that doesn't belong there. This causes confusion for your students both physically and mentally, and in trying to follow your erratic rhythm, they lose the effectiveness of the workout. Therefore, it is imperative that you move in consistent, ordered time to the beat of the music and pattern your exercises to fall naturally on the proper accents.

If you are using a lot of pop and rock music in your class, the drumbeat is usually powerful and easy to feel. But in some forms of music, such as jazz or early 1970's rock, the beat is not as emphatic and is sometimes more *sensed* than heard. Also, in Latin or other ethnic rhythms, and in progressive rock or fusion (such as in the music of Chicago, Spyro Gyra, L.R.B., Toto, etc.), the rhythms are often syncopated and complex, with flourishes of percussion that give added dimension to the music. Although the four/four beat is still the basis of this music, it takes a concentrated awareness of timing and rhythm to choreograph and exercise to it.

Transitions from one exercise or set of exercises to another should be carefully planned so there will be no break in momentum. But keep in mind "less is best." Intricate patterns of movement only you can execute well do a disservice to your students. Don't try to be clever and do combinations of steps that require an annotation chart to follow.

For example, keep patterns to sets of four or eight, or sixteen, which corresponds to the music's four/four time. Don't try complicated dance routines with two steps forward, three right, one back, two left, etc. This only frustrates people. Whether you are working arms, legs, or doing aerobic dance, do a sufficient number of repetitions so the class can easily catch on to the pattern and move in coordination and unison. Nothing is more disconcerting than being in a room filled with twenty-five bodies all moving in different directions trying to get the hang of a routine. If you see that everyone is out of sync, interrupt your class long enough to get everyone moving together. As the instructor, you should try to move in the same direction as students, whether you are facing them or facing the mirror.

It is also important to keep the natural swing of the arms and legs in your choreography (right arm and left leg moving together, left arm and right leg moving together). Homolateral moves (right arm and leg, then left arm and leg moving in unison) may look nifty, but this movement is unnatural to the body and has been known to cause switching of the brain hemispheres.

Matching music energy with your exercise energy is essential to good choreography. There is much more to it than just playing a fast song to jog to or a slow song to stretch to. If you are choosing your music wisely, you will notice the varying dynamics in the songs—the emotional color that comes with the loudness and softness of the various instruments and vocal performances. These dynamics, as well as the beat and rhythm, give the body its impetus to move, inspiring heightened physical and mental energy.

Some fitness consultants recommend music based on a song's BPM (beats per minute). Since the body should be moving at a certain pace or energy level for effectiveness, matching the desired energy level with the music's tempo (measured in beats per minute) will provide the best results. The recommendations vary somewhat, but here are the low and high ranges:

Activity	Tempo (BPM)
Walking, warm up	110-140
Locomotor movements (arms, legs, etc.)	140-150
Aerobics section, jog	140-190
Cool Down	80-92
Slow Stretch	60-80

In the cardiovascular segment of the exercise class, it has been recommended that the music be about ten to fifteen beats per minute higher than the maximum target heart rate you wish to achieve. Since this rate will vary depending upon your age and level of fitness, these BPM's will also vary.

The important question to consider is, "Can you safely and effectively perform a given exercise at a specific tempo?" If so, the BPM is acceptable. If not, you are in trouble. For example, the music consulting firm of Music in Motion recommended "New Attitude" by Patti La Belle and "Tell Me" by Al Jarreau for the aerobics section at 140-190 BMP. On the other hand, "Man Eater" by Hall and Oates at *170* BPM was rejected by Gilda Marx as too fast. The contradictions point out that selecting music cannot be done by BPM alone. So, don't use the BPM criterion as your only basis for evaluating what is or isn't an appropriate tempo.

Personally, I have never chosen *any* music on the basis of its beats per minute. I have never thought to count the beats, nor do I have an instrument or device that does it for me. I choose music for exercise based on how it *feels* rhythmically; whether I can or cannot perform an exercise or dance step properly and safely, whether I can work up a sweat when I am supposed to, slow my heart rate down and stretch a muscle when I need to, or get the surge of stamina when I think it may be lagging. I prefer to say I listen to the "heartbeat."

The creativity of the music is vital to me—how interesting the melody and lyrics are, how artistically it has been produced, and whether or not it motivates me psychologically. And I also evaluate whether or not it is appropriate for my style and pace of teaching.

When you begin to choreograph your routine, first break down the exercises into body parts: neck, arms, shoulders, legs, etc. Decide carefully just how you want to work each part of the body. Do you want to relax, stretch, and elongate the muscle? Or do you want to keep it tensed isometrically? Do you prefer arm and leg movements that are free and smooth, or do you want them definitive and sharp? Are your aerobic dance steps driving and strong or light and springy?

For every movement of your body, choose the music energy that actually represents the movement to you. Practice your exercise to different songs until it feels right, and even choose several different exercises for each body part using different types of music each time. Watch yourself in the mirror, as a dancer does, and see if you can move with graceful, perfect body form to the music. If you can't, your students can't.

An interesting way to try out new movements to different rhythms is by using a rhythm box. This is a computerized device that simulates a variety of dance rhythms and beats (often used by musicians who do a single or duo act). The rhythm box allows you to slow down the tempo for demonstration purposes, then lets you speed it up gradually as students get the hang of the routine. This is especially helpful for people with "two left feet" who believe they are uncoordinated and have trouble grasping the simplest dance steps or body movements. From there you can graduate them to the real song.

Sequentialize your exercises so that you work the entire body from head to toe. But where do you begin—head or toe? This will depend on your style and method of teaching, but the most widely used and preferred way is to start from the head and neck, gently waking up the brain first, loosening tension in the neck, then moving on down the body until all the blood and oxygen are flowing freely, breathing is regulated, and there is stamina enough to do the hard and heavy portion of the class.

If your style of teaching incorporates jazz dance movements (loose shoulder and hip action, simple but stylized dance steps), your music should center on the jazz/R&B/soul genres, which are sensual and earthy. Good artists for this type of style are Teddy Pendergrass, Al Jarreau, Earth Wind and Fire, Patti La Belle, etc.

If you tend more toward an athletic style of exercise—strong, clean, fat-burning movements—your music will probably lean toward rock and pop songs to correspond with the driving force of energy you put out. Songs like "Is This Love" by Survivor, or "Jacob's Ladder" by Huey Lewis, etc.

Pop, country, folk-rock, sixties and seventies rock are good if your style of teaching is "middle of the road," so to speak. In other words, you wish to create a happy, free-spirited environment in your class with enough energy to give your students a good, but not too strenuous, workout. If you are teaching children, senior citizens or prenatal classes, this approach may work well for you.

If you have never choreographed an exercise class, or if you wish to improve your routine, attend some classes taught by highly recommended instructors. Observe not only the teacher, but the people in the class. Is everyone following the routine easily, in unison, and with good form? Is their collective spirit high? How do the exercises feel to you in relation to the music, and is the instructor playing music you have never heard before? Was it exciting and motivating? Take the best techniques from those classes and apply them to your own class.

By listening very carefully to each piece of music you are considering for your class, you will become more in tune with your body responses, as well as psychological responses. Once you put your tape together, be certain to ask your students what *they* like or don't like about your music and choreography. Take their suggestions into account so that you can vary your music often to keep your class—and you—from getting stale.

Ideally, before you teach a class anywhere you should have some formal training, either through an accredited certification program (such as the Aerobiocs and Fitness Association of America) or through the physical education department at a university, etc. Organizations such as AFAA pay special attention to the importance of sequential exercise routines and can help you tremendously with choreographing your class and with programming your music effectively.

Based on AFAA's checklist for safe and effective classes, here are some basic music programming guidelines:

WARM-UP

Just as the body must be gradually warmed up to exercise, it must also warm up to music. Don't soundblast your class with the first song on your tape. Ease the music into the atmosphere with gentle rhythms, flowing melodies, and mellow sounds. Each successive song can then be brighter, livelier, and upbeat. A mellow beginning also relaxes the body enough so that it can develop a natural breathing rhythm and avoid "jamming" of the breath. Some excellent warm-up songs are:

"Mornin"—Al Jarreau

"American Music"—Pointer Sisters

"To the Unknown Man"—Vangelis

CARDIOVASCULAR

Whether you jog during this period or do aerobic dance (and more people are opting for low impact aerobics for safety reasons), you'll want to choose tempos and rhythms that are constant and forward moving, with dynamics that swell and subside as you pace the class. Vintage through it may be, one of the best examples of a perfect song for this portion of the class is the long-playing version of "The Main Event" by Barbra Streisand. It eases you into the jog, urges you on with high explosions of energy, and gentles you back down slightly so you don't overwork, but still keep the heart rate going. The lyrics are motivating and the entire song ends on a positive emotional and physical high.

Your music in this portion of the class should be swift enough to keep you light on your feet, landing with controlled "soft feet." If the music is too slow, you come down too hard, putting undue stress on leg joints, lower back, and internal organs. Keep that music forward moving so there is a spring in your step. Some good selections of music are:

"Africano"—Earth Wind and Fire

"Far From Over"—*Staying' Alive* soundtrack

"Take Me In Your Arms"—Doobie Brothers

"You, Baby"—Neil Diamond—*Jazz Singer* soundtrack

MUSCLE TONING

Exercises for arms, legs, and stomach all require high energy output, but also need intense concentration on the muscle at work. The tempo of the music should allow for fully controlled movements—not too fast or too slow—to prevent injury and sloppy form. Keep physical and mental energy high by avoiding songs with heavy, low bass vibrations, chaotic instrumentation, and screaming vocals. Some good choices are:

"Only the Good Die Young"—Billy Joel

"Woman in You"—Bee Gees—*Stayin' Alive* soundtrack

"Hands Down"—Dan Hartman

COOL-DOWN/STRETCH

Bring the class energy back down to a normal state by using tempos that are light and smooth, similar to the warm-up segment. Then move into the stretching exercises with music that actually feels as though it is stretching with you and encourages you to sink into that stretch position. Such as:

"Kokoro"—Hiroshima

"Time"—Alan Parsons Project

"Breezin'"—George Benson

RELAX/MEDITATE

Now is not the time to stimulate the heartbeat, but to let the spirit energy take over. So pulsating rhythms are out. Choose music with strings, light percussions (bells, chimes, etc.), woodwinds, and so forth. Classical, meditation, and new age music should be your choices here.

Some exercise classes are more structured than others, perhaps because of the time factor (classes are scheduled hour by hour, back to back), or because the class is advanced and little verbal instruction is needed for the students. In these situations, the instructor turns on the tape and for about an hour the class is led through a series of exercises with little or no stopping between exercise segments. Other classes are looser, perhaps because the class is smaller and more interaction goes on between instructor and student, or because the people in the class are older or at a beginner's fitness level.

Whatever way you have to design your class time, look to the music to give you opportunities to enhance the workout for students, as well as yourself. For example, music can be used to help people develop a better self-image or higher self-esteem, as a channel for the release of positive emotions, and as a motivational factor for continuing with their exercise program. This is when you must really be aware of the lyrics and theme (meaning) of a song and be certain that they are uplifting. Inspirational songs will have more of an effect during stretching or meditation segments when everyone is cooling down both physically and emotionally, and can concentrate on the message of the music.

Lest we forget: The greatest music in the world is rendered rotten when the equipment it is played on is of poor quality. A turntable with an old, worn out needle or stylus, a cassette deck with dirty heads, and speakers that are distorted and muffled, can be the ruination of a music experience, and psychologically demotivating to the class members. Take care of your records and tapes as though they were gold. Don't leave them in the car when it is hot, or out of their jackets to collect dust. Speakers, and all recording and stereo equipment, should be installed and maintained by professionals (if you are teaching in a studio at a professional health club or spa). Volume of the music should be at medium levels so the room doesn't sound—and *feel*—as though it is vibrating under you.

Speaker placement can also make a very big difference in the quality of sound. To help eliminate excessive low bass vibrations, keep speakers off the floor. Mount them on walls or suspend them from the ceiling if possible. Placing speakers in both the front and back of the studio gives a better balance to the sound, especially in large studios where the classes are large, and eliminates the need for excessive volume.

Above all, don't take chances in choosing and programming your music. If you feel you have no "music sense" and are uncertain about being able to recognize positive and negative elements in music, ask someone with a music or dance background to assist you. Don't leave it to chance. And don't lazily throw on a preprogrammed dance or exercise tape that may not be appropriate to your style of teaching or your class's fitness level. Learn to take control of your own music. Vary your selections often, trying out new forms, rhythms, and tempos of music. You are the teacher and it is your responsibility to be educated about all aspects of your class, especially something as important to your health and well-being—and enjoyment!—as music.

(A wide variety of music suggestions for exercise classes, dance exercise, stretch classes, and weight training, appear in the suggested music lists at the back of the book. Some hints on children's exercise music appear under the heading "Children" in the music lists.

Selections from the "Meditation" list can be used for stretch, yoga, and a period of meditation at the very end of your class. To further enhance your exercise experience, see "Music and Color" for suggestions on using color to open the body's various chakras during your workout.)

CLOSE-UP: **Vassili Sulich**

Children Come to Life Through Dance and Music

"A child is very unspoiled in many ways, and very receptive to anything he sees, touches, smells, and hears," says Vassili Sulich. "With music, children respond in ways similar to grown-ups, depending upon their cultural background, early education, and natural talents."

Music and dance have been integral parts of Sulich's life since he was six years old. One of his earliest endeavors was the organizing of a children's theater in Egypt during World War II, where he lived as a refugee with his parents. When he returned to his homeland of Yugoslavia, Sulich brought the children's theater of refugees with him, entertaining delighted audiences that included President Tito of Japan and President Benes of Czechoslovakia.

Subsequently, Sulich was discovered by Ana Roja, prima ballerina of the Zagreb Opera Company, and an illustrious career followed as a

123

principal dancer in Europe, and finally as premiere dancer in the "Folies Bergere" at the Tropicana Hotel in Las Vegas. In 1972, Sulich left the show to form the Nevada Dance Theatre, bringing artistic enlightenment to the culturally barren desert landscape. Not only was the company's presence a delight for adults, but local children could now enjoy a live ballet for the first time, and could participate in it as members of the Nevada Dance Theatre Youth Company. During the past sixteen years, the children have become important to the success of such productions as *Nutcracker, Peter and the Wolf, Coppelia,* and *Cinderella.*

As a choreographer, Sulich works from the "inside out." That is, he uses the music to guide his dancers through the emotions and meaning of the ballet while he teaches them the choreography, instead of drilling them to the count of the steps and *then* adding the music.

"The music has to inspire the movement," he states. "When the movement of the body marries that musical line, intensity, rhythm, and feeling, then you succeed. These are the greatest moments of your choreography."

Dancing requires role-playing and acting as much as it requires the technical mastering of body movements. How well the dancers emote and project the ballet's meaning and emotion depend on how well the dancers themselves can readily express their own feelings, and respond in kind to the feelings of others.

"Children respond the same way the adults do," Sulich says. "There are some who are very open-minded, while others are very into themselves and shy. Some kids open up to you naturally, they will run to you and hug you. Others will stand in the corner by themselves and you have to go hug *them.* When some of the children hear the music, you can say, 'This is your doll. Hold him and lullaby him to sleep,' and they will react instantly. Other kids take longer. You have to be very sensitive to these differences."

Sulich believes, through his own experience and working with young dancers, that music can aid greatly in the social and psychological development of a child.

"If a child has music from his early stages, that child has all the chances to grow up and appreciate it, so it becomes a part of his life; it becomes a *need.* How can a child who has never heard a Mozart symphony suddenly be expected, at age fifteen or twenty, to fall in love with Mozart?"

Sulich recalls his days at the Tropicana Hotel where, between shows, he played operas and great classics to relieve the boredom of performing the same show fifteen times a week.

"I worried about the juggler who was to share my dressing room," he remembers. "I thought, 'If this guy hates music, he is going to kill me!' But fortunately, he had been introduced to opera at a very young age. When he was about four years old, his parents took him to see *The Marriage of Figaro,* and he hated it. But his parents were determined to guide him to good music.

"So, the following Sunday they took him to the opera again—and probably had to coax him with the promise of an ice cream after the show. But this time, he saw *Carmen,* which is a visually more attractive opera, with more action on stage, and he really enjoyed it.

"Living in Vienna in those days, in the heartland of music, his parents had a different attitude than they might have today. Their philosophy was, 'When the child grows up, he can decide what he wants to do. But I will be the guiding force in the early stages of his development.'

"The presence of music in a child's life goes back to the parents," Sulich believes. "Are they uneducated about and insensitive to music? If so, they are going to pass these traits on to the child. If the parents love and respect music, and make it an essential part of their lives, then the child, too, is the lucky one."

9

All God's Children Have Music

THE answer to the question, "When does life begin?" has been debated to almost no one's complete satisfaction, for everyone has his own theories and beliefs. For our purposes in the context of this book, the question might be, "When does *music* begin in life?" Knowing that the universe, the earth, and all gross matter (including us humans) are vibrating masses of light and color, rhythm and harmony, the answer might be, "Music begins in life at the instant the soul makes its prenatal journey through time and space, and is created in physical form by man and woman."

Long before a child takes his (or her) first breath, he lives in an environment of "womb music"—the comforting sounds and rhythms of his mother's heartbeat and blood pulsing inside her uterus. All though prenatal development, the fetus is affected by the same activities and experiences that affect the mother, and there is increasing evidence that outside activities shape the personality and affect the health of a baby in the last few months of pregnancy. If the activities of the mother are healthful, joyful, creative, and inspired, the stage is then set for

127

similar prenatal and postnatal experiences for the child. When music is part of a baby's life, and if it continues to play an active role throughout the years, the healthier and richer the child's life will be.

Pregnant women often joke they are eating for two when they partake of that second helping of food. They should also remember that they are breathing, seeing, hearing, and feeling for two, and be doubly aware of their environment and the music that is played in their presence at all times.

When a mother-to-be rocks herself and listens to pleasant music, the baby-to-be is also soothed. Conversely, raucous musical sounds that overstimulate and agitate the mother have a decidedly evident effect on the baby as well. At a concert, when high-energy music is played, the kicking and bouncing fetus often forces the mother to leave the theater. One woman at a rock music concert suffered a broken rib when her unborn baby kicked her strenuously. Just imagine what the baby must feel when Mother attends an exercise class where hard rock is playing at painfully high volumes.

Lovely, joyful music can make the baby's transition from his womb-world to his new world one of spiritual beauty and celebration. Hospitals and birthing centers encourage the use of relaxing music during the labor stage to facilitate proper breathing and relieve tension, and anything from "Chariots of Fire" to "Isn't She Lovely" (by Stevie Wonder) during the actual delivery. Any music that is a favorite of the parents played during childbirth can make it an especially memorable moment: it's the first concert parents and child ever attended together!

When Baby is taken home, music can be a security blanket by re-creating the comforting sounds and rhythms he was accustomed to in the womb. As Mom and Dad rock Baby in their arms and in the cradle, humming or singing softly creates a bond of love between parent and child, and it introduces Baby to the positive emotional and psychological benefits of music, benefits that will last a lifetime.

Creating a musical environment for your child does more than provide moments of contentment and affection. It aids greatly in his physical and intellectual development by stimulating his brain and senses. Watch your infant's eyes as he focuses on the musical mobile or wind chimes hanging over his crib or playpen. He sees the colors and shapes; he hears the tinkling sounds and musical tones; he is fascinated, alert, and beginning to experience the wonders of his little world.

Babies have a great sensitivity to sound and they love to hear their mommies' and daddies' voices (as young as one month of age, children can distinguish family members by their voices). Parents can use this sound sensitivity to their advantage by making mealtime, bathtime, and diaper-changing time pleasant moments instead of moments of tears and tantrums. Sing to Baby while you tend to him, and sing *about* him—sing about toes and noses, fingers and feet. And listen to him gurgle and goo back at you.

A child is never too young to enjoy and respond to music. Infants can take an active part in music making, as well as listening, by shaking a rattle or other musical–like toy. Music helps Baby learn to release emotions: tense babies relax when you sing a lullaby or play soft music; angry babies may shake their rattle furiously (older babies may stamp their feet or bang a drum), and then become cheerful when you play happy music.

When you communicate with your baby by talking and singing, you are helping him develop proper speech patterns and techniques, and possibly avoid speech problems. Children have to hear a lot of language before they can articulate it themselves correctly, so anytime you coo and sing to them, they are getting an experience with language. As you sing to your baby, he watches your face and lips. This is how he develops an interest in speaking, to emulate your sounds. Singing to and with your child as he or she continues to grow up also helps with memory and learning skills. Some kids can't *say* their ABC's very well, but they can *sing* them beautifully.

Listening to, enjoying, and creating music is primarily a right-brain function. Learning is a process of the left brain. Music links the two halves together, and when there is more linking there is more learning. Now and then the hemispheres of the brain become "switched," or out of balance, and body confusion can occur. This switching can come about through a variety of circumstances, but one very common instance is when a baby is first beginning to crawl. He crawls in a homolateral fashion, moving his left arm and leg together, then his right arm and leg. Later, as he becomes more neurologically adept, he develops a cross-crawl pattern—using opposite arms and legs—which is the pattern of our normal way of walking. You can reverse or prevent switching by exercising your baby's arms and legs in the cross-crawl pattern, keeping a steady rhythm to the music as you do so.

When problems occur with a child's speech, professional therapy is in order. And therapists who use music during sessions report seeing higher levels of progress in the children than they do without music.

Sharon Deitz, a practicing speech therapist for the Clark County School District in Las Vegas, uses a series of specially programmed music tapes and finds they work well with all her little students, and are especially helpful in treating the severely handicapped children.

"The music has a soothing effect on the children," she states. "They attend to me better and it's easier for them to work with the music on."

Deitz recalls one little boy who was severely retarded and blind, and absolutely did not like the situation (therapy) he was in. He was getting ready to have a fall-on-the-floor temper tantrum when Dietz put on the theme music from *On Golden Pond.*

"He suddenly became very quiet and began to look around for the loons," she says. "I took this opportunity to say, 'Do you want to find the birds? They're in the tape recorder.' I rewound the tape and played the song again so he could listen for the loons. He loved it. After that, he liked coming to the sessions and I always made sure I had music playing. Even if it wasn't the same song, he felt safe and comfortable."

Deitz is careful not to play any moody music, or anything too peppy, for she herself responds to the emotions of the music and the kids in turn pick up on *her* moods. This interferes with their therapy. Her tapes are primarily new age and meditation music, as well as some selections from films such as *The Black Stallion.* The music plays softly in the background and is not distracting, mainly because the melodies are unfamiliar and not readily singable. However, she does recall some amusing instances where her older students became concerned about her and asked, "Is that the only kind of music you have?"

"I assured them that I had a wider repertoire," she laughs, "and once they knew I was also familiar with Aretha Franklin and Eurythmics, they didn't worry about me anymore."

Young children can learn a great many things from music and songs. They can learn concepts such as big and small, hard and soft, numbers, how to put on shoes and other clothing. By watching such programs as *Sesame Street* or music videos specially created to teach children concepts and motor skills through musical songs and dances, they develop mental and physical coordination as well as self-confidence in their abilities.

A child is never too young to enjoy the benefits of physical fitness. Even newborn babies should be lovingly exercised. Moving their little arms and legs to music strengthens their muscles and gives them a feeling of well-being. When children are old enough to perform simple exercises or dance steps on their own in a class situation, the metered flow of the movements performed to the music's rhythm helps develop coordination and concentration. It also reinforces the beneficial coexistence of music and physical fitness. Also, it is important for your child to express himself or herself in "free form." Turn on some music and encourage your child to move and dance without restraint. This helps release inhibitions and develops creativity of expression. This creative expression can be enhanced and developed further with proper formal music instruction. Or it can be crushed by the wrong music training.

Dr. John Diamond, who has researched the effects of music on the mind and body writes, "Every child starts with an exuberant, open-hearted love of music. Gradually and tragically this is destroyed by the horrors of most musical training systems."

Diamond does not specify which music training systems are horrifying, but he does call for more enlightened teachers who realize first and foremost the young musician's burning love for music, a love that must always be encouraged. "This must be the sacred duty of every teacher," he adds.

There are many "institutions" for music instruction, including public and private schools, music conservatories, music camps, and private instructors. Most music teachers subscribe to the "Classicist" theories that have kids wading through pages of notations and written scores of music before they ever get around to what music is all about: the feel of the rhythm and the emotions and meaning of the song. Children are drilled on how to read the notes before they play them and often become bored and frustrated with the music-on-paper system. But a few innovative souls have broken with tradition and developed more enjoyable and desirable methods of teaching music to children, giving them physical and emotional experiences before they ever learn the notations.

One of these is the Orff-Shulwek method, developed by a German composer in the 1930's to allow music students to become directly involved in the feel of the music more quickly. The American Orff-Shulwek Association held their national conference in Las Vegas in 1984, drawing about twelve hundred teachers from across the nation. At that time, at least fifty elementary schoolteachers in Las Vegas were using the Orff-Shulwek method, and at least one of them wishes that she could have been trained this way as a child.

"I would be a better musician today, because I would feel the music first," she states. "Now, I see it, play it, and *then* I feel it."

When students "feel" music first, they can then transfer these feelings back through the musical instruments. For example, they do exercises in which they pat their knees and arms in rhythm, and chant the note patterns they are tapping out. This is done before they ever pick up the instrument to play. When the time does come for actual playing, the kids are urgently enthusiastic. They also learn how to express the dynamics of the instruments themselves through little songs like, "First come the glockenspiels, so delicate and light. Please play them gently, like stars in the night."

In the private sector, there is a wide variance in the credentials and abilities of music teachers. They range from "tragic to mediocre to occasionally excellent," as Buddy Hill describes them. Hill, a professional musician for more than thirty years, and a teacher since 1969, belongs to the Music Teachers National Association (MTNA), which is the oldest group of private teachers in America. Most private teachers do not advertise, but usually acquire students through word-of-mouth referrals. "Maverick" teachers doing high quality work often do not have teaching diplomas, but this is a plus in many ways, Hill feels, because they do not have to conform to the Classicist methods and teaching theories of an organization.

Hill, himself, straddles both fences. He is a graduate of Westlake School of Music in California, has earned several teaching degrees, and consequently is proficient in a wide range of musical languages and analysis tools. This allows him to label himself as a "jack-of-all-trades" teacher who customizes his lessons to the goals and objectives of the students. His wide cross-section of students ranges from hard-core jazz musicians to church organists, have been as young as five-and-a-half years and as "old" as 80 years of age, male and female, amateur and pro.

Amazingly, most parents and students themselves do not inquire as to the credentials of a music teacher. They presume that because someone teaches, he or she is qualified to do so. There can be a vast difference between being a consummate performer and an excellent teacher. A person can be technically skilled in music, but if he or she cannot articulate the lesson to the student—cannot relate it to them in terms they can understand—it can be disastrous. It can cause a potentially talented student to become frustrated, insecure, and quit music studies altogether. And of vital importance is a teacher's compassion for the less-than-talented, but very eager student.

"I would never tell a student he has no talent and should quit," says Hill. "That's a terrible thing to do to someone. If they have the desire to study, they should be encouraged to do so. It will have very positive effects on other aspects of the person's life even if he never achieves any status as a musician."

In seeking an instructor for your child, it makes sense to ask to see diplomas or their equivalent, and ask for a list of satisfied students so you can obtain some honest critiques on the teacher's abilities.

Music lessons can be an enriching experience for a child, opening up new vistas of sight, sound, touch, and emotion that are incomparable. But how young is too young to begin music lessons? Obviously, it depends on the child. A precocious youngster of five or six can begin a leisurely overview of music, but if the child cannot read, he cannot be expected to understand the highly structured texts that are so popular with teachers today. An eight-year-old can learn as much in three or four months as another child learned in the two years between six and eight.

In the Suzuki method of teaching, however, children learn to play violin and piano by rote, imitating the instructor's technique on the instrument. Developed by Shinichi Suzuki of Japan, the Suzuki method has children as young as three years begin by playing "Twinkle Twinkle Little Star" and gradually advancing to the music of Bach, Mozart, and other great composers. Even if a child is old enough to read, music notation is not introduced until a certain period of rote-playing is experienced. And at that time, the child generally is given his piece of music to sight-read that he has already committed to memory by rote. Thus, the Suzuki method introduces visualization techniques to children at a very young age.

The Suzuki philosophy and purpose is not to train professionals, "but to give all children the opportunity to develop their amazing potential." Parents take an active part in the child's studies, using the manuals, following the music, and teaching correct fingering and bowing, in cooperation with the teacher. Cooperation, not competition, is the child's motivation, with older students helping the younger ones, and a mutual respect given to parents, teachers, and students.

One of the most exciting aspects of this method is the ability of children, even at ten years of age, to play pieces such as Bach's "Double Concerto" and Vivaldi's "A Minor Concerto" with ease and security. And these are children with no previous aptitudes for music.

Another important element in the Suzuki method is the time spent merely listening to recordings of music. This helps them achieve an "inner image" of tone and structure. Since music is an auditory art, the child's ear for music is cultivated very early.

"This is very virtuous," Hill states. "In Western cultures we introduce the notation of music in the very first lesson and the student has to conquer this abstraction on paper in order to play the instrument. Consequently, the *eye* usurps the *ear* as the final arbitrator of what is correct or incorrect. So, now we have students who play at a very high technical level, but cannot *hear* what they play. We always speak derogatorily of playing by ear, but in reality that's the equivalent of a person learning speech by ear, which is a natural phenomenon. Of course, there is a question of what ear means here (in music)—the *physical* ear versus the *spiritual* ear."

Of course Hill emphasizes that the skill of sight-reading music must not be glossed over. As music lessons become more complex, the ability to sight-read is vital, especially in executing rhythm patterns. One of the reasons for a high drop-out rate on the part of music students is their abysmal sight-reading ability. Flash cards are often used in the teaching programs today so that students learn instantly to recognize the notes on the staff. Tapping out rhythm patterns with the hand and counting out loud as the students reads the music should be part of the lesson, for the most crucial factor in music playing is knowing how to control the rhythm.

Whether students learn to play by "ear" or by "eye," there is no question that playing an instrument is a complex neuromuscular activity. Some pediatricians are especially amazed that children can play an instrument such as the piano, because doing so contradicts all the concepts they embraced as physicians having to do with cerebral coordination, abstractions becoming concrete in the mind, and muscular development. Playing the piano (and the organ) with all ten digits is one of the most involved neuromuscular activities in the world. One must read with the eye, assimilate the score with the brain, pedal with the feet, and execute four-and five-note chords with both hands, as well as play single-digit melodies and improvisations. There is also the job of keeping the rhythm and listening with the ear. If these techniques can be conquered, the cerebral accomplishments carry over into other aspects of life.

"A child who studies music and performs moderately well," says Hill, "can do better in high school and college years than if he only performed academic studies. Through music lessons, he or she has learned to be goal oriented and work in a structured format toward achievement."

But a teacher's job can be made much easier and a child's learning experience with music can be made infinitely more rewarding if there is a strong support system in the home (not to be confused with a *coercive* system that forces or demands certain levels of achievement). Parents should take an expressed interest in the child's lessons, and an atmosphere of music and the arts should be apparent. A healthy, stimulating variety of music should be listened to, parents and children should attend concerts together and have open discussions about various musical forms, composers, the meaning and impact of the music they hear.

Psychologists have spent years devoted to the study of what actually molds our character—do we inherit all of our traits, likes, and dislikes, our intelligence, etc., or does our environment shape us? The answer, of course, is "both." The experiences we encounter and cultivate are as important to making us the defined human beings that we are, as are our genes and chromosomes. We cannot control or change the latter, but we can choose our experiences. We can make them broad and colorful and thought provoking, or narrow and stagnating. When a child is tutored by professionals who are caring and innovative, and encouraged by parents who are filled with a zest for living and a love for music, he will have a kaleidoscopic view of life and a deeper appreciation of music's role in his life. Now and then, however, that role is preordained.

Andy Anka, father of musician-entertainer-composer Paul Anka, recalls the early days of his son's passion for music, a passion he and Paul's mother found almost "scary."

"As young as nine years old, Paul's teachers recognized his writing skills and his intelligence," Anka says. "We thought he should be a journalist or a lawyer, but the teachers just could not get Paul's attention in class. All he cared about was his music. It was so consuming that we realized, after a few years, that we couldn't fight it or divert this talent into more traditional lines of work. Music was what he wanted to devote his life to, and we realized that it was a gift from God that had to be expressed."

Outside of family influences, preteens and adolescents begin to develop their musical tastes through social interaction with their peers and through exposure to music via television, radio, and films. Usually, these tastes are narrow and limited to the music of their own generation. But there was not always this chasm between the music of the young and the music of the old.

The enjoyment of music has been intertwined with the aches and pains of growing up since the beginning of this century. When the dance craze swept America, dance halls were frequented by young working men and women out for a Friday or Saturday evening of socializing. They cakewalked, bunny hugged and foxtrotted to the popular tunes of the day: "Bill Bailey Won't You Please Come Home" (1902), "By The Light of the Silvery Moon" (1909), "Down Among the Sheltering Palms" (1914).

By the 1920's music and radio had topped the list of favorite pastimes for boys and girls and dancing was the focal point of their social life (charleston, black bottom, et al.).

In the 1930's, jazz music (such as Benny Goodman's "Stompin' at the Savoy") seemed to appeal to the young as music to dance to, but it was not yet *their* music. Adults still shared a common enjoyment of the new music and attended the same dance halls and clubs as the kids. Perhaps this is why music then was more sophisticated, for it was music created by and for adults and the kids went along, because the dancing and socializing were the important things, not the form and meaning of the music. Phonographs and radios were still properties of the entire family, not just the teenagers alone. This comingling continued into the 1940's, with big band sounds (Glenn Miller, Les Brown, Tommy and Jimmy Dorsey, etc.) playing swing ("Sing, Sing, Sing"), blues ("Sentimental Journey"), and other standards ("Come Rain or Come Shine") that had an equal appeal to both the older and younger generations.

Then came rock and roll and the musical generation gap was born. Performers were now the same age as their teen audiences, came from similar cultural or socioeconomic backgrounds. And as dance halls played more and more rock and roll, the adults stayed home or went to clubs that played *their* music. Now on a roll, rock music promoters created rock and roll revues, radio and TV shows, and an entire new world of teenage consumption that flourished (clothes, magazines, cafés, musical instruments, radios, tape players, etc.). By the end of the 1950's, teenagers were the predominant purchasers of popular music, and music itself was their favorite form of entertainment.

But the music gap was not only generational, it existed among the teens themselves. This fragmentation of music tastes was then, and continues to be, relevant to the teenagers' social class, academic level, cultural philosophy, and value systems. For example, middle class kids look to music that is progressive rather than commercial ("formula"). The meaning and lyrics of a song are listened to, evaluated, rated, and praised according to their originality, truthfulness, and beauty. They tend to reject music that is trivial, banal, and repetitious. Kids who "drop out" or have limited opportunities in life are drawn more to the beat and the sounds of the music than to the meaning. This is the rebellious group who resist the adult Establishment as well as their upper-class contemporaries. They have cultish tastes (hippies, greasers, bikers, punkers, metalheads) and often a dreary perspective on life.

More and more, the type of music kids listen to dictates the clothes they wear and the people they associate with. Popular music is truly a peer-group phenomenon. Since the "Happy Days" of the 1950's, popular music has had a distinctive influence on the fads and fashions adopted by teenagers seeking to express their independence and individuality (by being like everyone else).

Recall the bobby socks, leather jackets, and poodle skirts of the "Grease" decade; the unkempt, flower child look of the sixties; the sensual disco look (girls in body-hugging Danskins, boys in three-piece white suits) of the seventies; and now the sleek "Miami Vice" look of the eighties. Lest we forget, there has also been the androgynous look: David Bowie with orange hair and heavy makeup; Michael Jackson in boyish clothes with girlish face; Annie Lennox (Eurythmics) with crew cut and unisex suits; Boy George with his mixed bag of clothes and makeup tricks.

Each of these, and other, fashion statements represents its own type of music, having its own unique appeal to different types of kids. The impact of the music and the artists performing it is overwhelmingly evident, and *very* lucrative for both the music and fashion industries. And although kids are "Knee Deep in the Hoopla" of a highly commercialized world, most of these fads and fancies are normal and healthy, and usually outgrown at the appropriate time. But there are certain other influences of the music world that are decidedly *un*healthy—even dangerous—to both a child's psychological and physical health and have come under the heavy guns of very concerned and angry adults.

"Drugs, Sex, and Rock and Roll!"

That was the hell-raising motto of the sixties and seventies when acid rock and social anarchy comingled in an atmosphere of philosophical and hedonistic expressions. Rock groups such as the Grateful Dead, the Doors, the Mothers of Invention, Pink Floyd, etc., sought to produce mind-expanding experiences similar to an LSD (acid) trip, through the use of synthesizers, high-decibel amplification, feedback, fuzztone, and Middle Eastern instruments. The lyrics of the songs had a mystical or surreal quality, and often were quite meaningful, such as in anti-Establishment and anti-Vietnam songs. Many of the artists actually did perform under the influence of drugs, and some of them—Janis Joplin, Jim Morrison, Jimi Hendrix—died from their use.

Although the acid rock label subsequently faded, the drug aura and the heavy metal sound continue on. But in place of the mind-altering disorientation of the senses provided by the music, there are sexual vulgarities and simulated physical violence performed to a mesmerizing beat that debase the art of music and insult the music fan. Before the advent of rock music videos and MTV, et al., rock groups who acted in a depraved manner on stage were witnessed by mere *thousands* of fans at any given time. Now, *millions* of youngsters, as young as five years old, can flip on a switch and watch—what?

In the past couple of years, rock videos have come under the fire of such groups as Women Against Pornography, the National Coalition on TV Violence, and the Parents' Music Resource Center (led by Tipper Gore, wife of Albert Gore, Democratic Senator from Tennessee.). They and others protest the blatant emphasis on violence and degradation of women (such as the Rolling Stones' "Under Cover of the Night," which featured intense automatic weapons violence; Billy Idol's "Dancing With Myself," featuring a naked women struggling in chains behind a translucent sheet; and other similar fare from groups like Motley Crue, Ozzy Osbourne, Kiss, Judas Priest, Scorpions, etc.).

In October 1986, the editorial staff of *TV Guide* awarded "Jeers" to MTV for repeatedly telecasting "one of the most tasteless, salacious, and sexually explicit rock videos ever produced: David Lee Roth's clip for *Yankee Rose."*

Grotesque album covers; explicit lyrics; themes about drugs, suicide, murder, hate, Satanism are common in heavy metal and punk music, and some very hard-core messages are also found in "rap" music. Violent and tragic acts, such as riots at concerts, clashes between teenage gangs, and even suicide are part of the scenario.

Although the case was subsequently dismissed, the parents of nineteen-year-old Daniel McCollum filed suit against heavy metal rocker Ozzy Osbourne, charging that the young man was enticed into killing himself while listening to Osbourne's song, "Suicide Solution." Whether it was the song (which is defended as an *anti*suicide song) or the young man's own sad state of mind that pushed him to kill himself, we will never know. (Many people have committed suicide while playing "love" songs). But the concern over young people's overexposure to the grossest kind of human behavior is legitimate.

Never before in our history (except perhaps in the Dark Ages), have people gone to such extremes in pursuit of "ugly." There are bizarre costumes, painted faces, multicolored and shaved hair, metal-studded dog collars and wrist bands, and Satanic trappings—not just on stage, but on the kids as they go to school and the supermarket! There are ugly thoughts, ugly words, ugly behavior, ugly music. The ugliest part of all is that none of it is created as an expression of the love of *music.* It is strictly created as a marketable commodity by adults to seduce and manipulate young minds for the love of *money.*

Music videos are sophisticatedly and attractively produced, yet many of them have been criticized for promoting values that are worthless. Through the provocative scenarios, kids get mixed messages on love and life, and although rock music and videos are certainly not the one and only cause of such turmoil as teenage pregnancies, sexually transmitted diseases, violence, drugs, and so forth, many of them perpetuate a distorted idea as an ideal.

Dr. Joyce Brothers, psychologist and nationally syndicated columnist, states that teenagers have not fused the idea of love and sex, "so when you teach them that violence and sex are related, it is extremely dangerous for their future behavior."

The amount of damage caused by viewing destructive behavior has been disputed since 1972 when a report was released by the surgeon general on television violence. This report found only short-term consequences, but a subsequent study in 1982 by the National Institute of Mental Health found that television violence is strongly correlated with aggressive behavior. Even adults become desensitized to violence after being consistently exposed to it in films and TV shows. Imagine the impact on young minds, especially those who sit for hours on end watching degenerative behavior, whether it is disguised as musical entertainment or not. If children are not offered a counterbalance of positive, healthy experiences, their viewpoint can, indeed, become distorted and cause tremendous emotional stress.

Attempts to regulate or develop ratings systems for rock music have been met with outrage and cries of "censorship" by artists and producers who purport to be exercising their First Amendment rights of "artistic freedom." Still others in the industry pooh-pooh the idea that aggressive, violent music has the power to influence minds in a negative way. This is absurd since the bottom line of their business is accumulating billions of dollars by influencing people's moods, behavior, and buying habits. You can't have it both ways. If music has the power to evoke healthful, happy, and inspired emotions and actions (which has been an accepted fact for centuries), it is incongruous to think that it cannot work its power in ways that are maleficent. Nor is this a motive exclusive to the 1980's.

Consider some of the quotes from the past (1960's) by some very influential artists in the rock music field:

> "We are moving after the minds, and so are most of the new groups."
> *Mick Jagger (Rolling Stones)*
> "I'm just talking about changing their (teenagers') value systems, which removes them from their parents' world very effectively."
> *David Crosby (the Byrds)*
> "By carefully controlling the sequence of rhythms, any rock group can create audience hysteria."
> *John Phillips (Mamas and Papas)*

Paul McCartney, whose phenomenal music career has spanned nearly thirty years, was asked what he thought about ratings systems and regulation of popular music. His reply in a 1986 issue of *Rolling Stone* magazine:

> "I think there is a point...where you start to want to censor stuff...let's say a really great group emerged advocating killing, Satanism. And they turned a lot of people on to Satanism. There's got to be a point were you're gonna say, 'Look guys, we're all for artistic freedom, but maybe we don't want de debil trampling across America at the moment.' "

Censorship is abhorrent to all of us who create, whether it is words, music, or other art forms of inner expression. And it does nothing but bring about a backlash in that it makes the forbidden more desirable. Rather than censor offensive music or prohibit youngsters total access to it, we might, instead, "sentence" them to an hour or two of classical, jazz, or new age music every day for a month. Instead of grounding a kid to his room (where he has access to his ghetto blaster and MTV), ground him to so many mandatory hours of Mozart, Gershwin, Keith Jarrett, Mannheim Steamroller, or Paul Winter.

For every energy there is a polarity. For every negative there is a positive. And for every dark side of music, there is a gleaming, bright light. Most composers and musicians use their art to create good, to make people happy, and to contribute something meaningful to the world. There are artists who raise money through their concerts to provide education to kids on the dangers of drugs ("Crack Down Concerts"), and to protect the environment ("Get Tough on Toxics" concerts). Others are singing inspirational messages via Christian rock, or by giving rap music a good rap with fun-type party lyrics and antidrug songs.

As for parents, they can provide that vital balancing energy by being aware of their children's music experiences and by affording kids the opportunity to hear and enjoy many different types of music. And by encouraging them to study music in school or with a private teacher.

Even if we were able to do away with all the worthless, meaningless popular music that poses a threat to our children's welfare, there is one other aspect that we cannot ignore: musical illiteracy.

Music is omnipresent in our lives and in our children's lives. But our awareness of it—its ingredients, how it is created, its powers, its meaning—is at an all-time low. Unless we are music professionals or scholars, we tend to passively accept what is foisted upon us by producers and distributors of music who are only in it for the cash flow. We have a Pop culture in which we pander to the lowest common denominator in music tastes because so few of us are ever educated in the aesthetic appreciation or art of playing "real" music. Therefore, we are more willing to accept musical drivel packaged in a mezmerizing beat and mind-boggling visual effects.

Just as we have an entire generation of kids who have probably never tasted a morsel of natural, unadulterated food, we are also, in this age of high technology, producing generations of children who have never heard a note of live, unaugmented music. Instead of learning about the art of music so they may make more intellectual choices, they are being indoctrinated into the science of sound, and anything less than dazzling special effects created by synthesizers, samplers, computers, etc., leaves them bored and indifferent.

"I regret the passing of tradition," comments Buddy Hill. "We worship the contemporary world and youth, and it is pathetic that this generation knows little of music that is more than two or three years old. There is so much time to fill in the media that artists are not encouraged to achieve the technical proficiency of a Mozart or a George Gershwin. I think people, even youngsters, were more hip in 1945. A song then could be much more elegant and sophisticated musically and lyrically and still be accepted by the masses. A century from now, the past fifteen or twenty years may be known as the Age of Mediocrity in the arts in America."

We cannot, singlehandedly, change an entire industry or its music trends. But we can all bring more music and music education to our children and enrich their lives, not just aesthetically but physically and psychologically.

Research has shown that the study and practice of music is beneficial to the central nervous system, including the brain. Animals placed in enriched environments actually show physical changes in their brains, in an increase in neural connections. A person who remains mentally active through music study may reap benefits in increased mental acuity, even at a very advanced age.

But these benefits should be spread to the population at large, through music education in the schools and through increased encouragement to children who will never become professional or virtuoso performers. Let us not forget music training, also, for nonprofessional *adults.* You are never too young, nor are you too old to benefit by music study. You may not become a concert musician, but then again, if you are willing to make the arduous commitment, who knows?

It has been estimated that it takes about ten thousand hours of practice to become a virtuoso pianist, or something like fifteen years. Noting that I would be about sixty years old by that time, I asked my teacher, "How long would it take to become a *mediocre* pianist?"

Perhaps I should ask how long would it take to become mediocre on the keyboard—the computer keyboard, that is. Children today have an edge on my generation. They are growing up with computers as their little friends. Today, there are computers that teach music by creating visual images on the screen that signal when you have hit a wrong note or are playing out of meter or have an imbalance of touch, etc. Learning music this way is both a step forward and a step sideways.

In learning one mechanical skill, we give up one natural skill. For example, constant use of a calculator relieves us of the necessity and ability to do math in our head. Video and audio "books" have lessened our desire to read; hence we see an increase in illiteracy rates. Learning music theory, composition, and playing through the use of computers may well diminish the acuity of the "spiritual ear" that is so important in composing and improvisational playing of an acoustic instrument. We won't need (or be able) to hear music in our head. The computer will do it for us. Infinitely easier? Infinitely less human. It's a trade-off.

If it takes five, ten, or fifteen years to become an accomplished pianist, I'll stick it out. Perhaps if all music becomes computerized, the player of an acoustic instrument will be quite a novelty and highly in demand. And when I am sixty or seventy and they wheel me and my grand piano on stage, thousands of children may just discover something wonderfully "new" and exciting: pure, unadulterated, natural music. And the cycle will begin again.

Music is a part of our lives long before we ever take a breath. It is a part of the exquisite universal harmony. It is there—created for us and created by us—to feel, to hear, to enjoy, to treasure through all the moments, hours, days, and years of our lives. Our only hope in keeping the beauty and splendor of music alive is in the legacy we leave our children.

10

Life's Song

From the moment you arise in the morning until you at last drift over from your wakeful state to a peaceful sleep at night, your day can be made more exciting, fun, and inspiring by the use of music. Whether you face the mad rat race of the working world each day, or stay home and raise kids, roses, or chickens, music can be your motivator, companion, and energizing force.

To illustrate, I have outlined a day of activities and suggested ways to apply music to each situation. It is a brief overview of what we have covered in previous chapters and, once you begin to incorporate some of these suggestions into your life, you'll discover many other ways to use music to your benefit.

Morning, 7:00: If you have fallen asleep to soothing, relaxing music, you will awake fresh and alert. If you are feeling sluggish and lethargic, try this. While you are still lying down, stretch to your full height to reverse your sleep position (usually fetal). Exhale all of your breath to clear your head and lungs and relax all your muscles.

Get out of bed and turn on your stereo or cassette player to music that is light, uplifting, and energy stimulating. Perhaps you favor harpsichord concertos, Strauss waltzes, country music, the Boston Pops, or bluegrass. Choose whatever pleases you, that lifts your spirits and lets you welcome the new day with joy and eagerness. Do some light stretching and warm-up movements to get the oxygen and blood circulating throughout your body until you feel totally awake and vitally alive. Look out world, here you come!

7:15:   Get into the shower and feel the flow of the water on your body (negative ions at work). Do some easy neck circles as the warm water loosens up any tension in your neck. Sing! The worst voice in the world sounds great in the shower—the acoustics are fantastic. You are at the Met, in Carnegie Hall, Live at the Greek. Throngs of people shower you with adulation as you let your voice ring out and resonate with health and life. Every note you sing will reverberate, embracing you in the positive vibrations that you "tone." Climb out of the shower and rub yourself dry to the rhythm of the music, stimulating more life and energy through your body. Take a deep breath, exhale. You are ready to face the day. You can handle anything that comes your way.

7:30:   Have a breakfast that is as nourishing and healthful as the music you are playing. Forget the coffee and doughnut, or the fatty bacon and eggs. Choose some fruit, juice, whole-grain breads, and cereals. Keep those electrolytes in balance and those brain cells working. Be sure to keep calm while you eat, savor the moment as well as the food, tune in to the music—gentle and easy—so that you digest and assimilate your food properly. You have just fueled your engine (with good nutrition) and overhauled your spirit (with music).

8:00:   As you prepare to drive to work, turn on your cassette deck, if you have one, or your radio to music that does not assault and jangle your nerves. Even short drives around town are no pleasure anymore, with more and more cars on the streets, construction causing traffic slow-downs, bicyclists, moped riders, and motorcyclists all vying for the same traffic lanes. Driving defensively means to drive safely, and you need a keen eye and nerves of steel to maneuver your car without mishaps. If hard rock music is blaring away, it can agitate you without your being aware of it. If you don't have an accident, your attitude while you drive can still be affected. There are special "drive the car" programmed tapes (such as Steven Halpern's "Driving Suite") that provide soothing music and subliminal suggestions to keep you alert and alive on the road. If you have tapes or a public radio station that plays classical, jazz, new age, or easy listening popular music, so much the better.

If you have a long drive ahead of you, be sure your music is not *too* slow or *too* relaxing or you may lose concentration on your driving. A friend of mine loved the music "Seapeace" by Georgia Kelly so much that he would play the tape while driving the Los Angeles freeway. He soon found himself nodding off to sleep and off the road. So, meditation music, with its transcendental tones are not ideal for driving. Also, you should never wear earphones while driving your car, even if you are playing the most health-enhancing, enjoyable music ever created. That ambulance that you did not hear racing down the highway might just be coming to rescue *you*—and some other innocent victim.

If you get caught in a traffic jam and must sit there, try to keep your agitation under control. If you feel your nerves starting to jump, *now* is the time to punch up some slower-than-heartbeat rhythms on your radio or tape player. Use this time to meditate, do some visualization exercises (visualize the end of the traffic jam!). Put yourself in that special imaginary place of yours that gives you inner peace and harmony, and takes you out of this physical consciousness of angry horns blaring and tempers flaring. Some baroque melodies, Mozart piano concertos, flute solos, and so forth are perfect now. Or you could take the time to let your imagination soar and play some Aaron Copland (*Appalachian Spring*) or Jean Michel-Jarre (*Rendezvous*), or soundtracks from your favorite Broadway plays, and even music from other cultures.

8:30, At Work: Be aware of the vibrations around you. Are they positive? Are the people smiling, pleasant, of good attitude? If so, drink it in. Take a deep breath, exhale the toxic air, and feel the positive energy flow. If your environment is negative—noisy machines, grumpy people, sad colors—tune it out. This is difficult, but you can develop your own higher state of consciousness by softly humming some pleasing tones. If there is no music in the office, ask for some. And suggest what you believe is the most healthful and positive music for the office. If possible, open up the subject of music to discussion among coworkers and your boss. Don't let hard rock music be foisted upon you by the musically "unenlightened." And if you can put a nix on the blandness of Muzak or other background music systems, speak out. Just as employees today have the right to demand a smoke-free workplace, they should also have the right to an atmosphere of "sound health."

If no music is available in your workplace, bring your own tapes or small radio if you are allowed. If not, try bringing a little music box to work and play it every so often, being certain to focus in on the pure clean tones and sweet melody. If the music-box melody has a certain sentimental value to you, it can lift your spirits immeasurably. Sitting on top of my beautiful piano is a miniature piano music box, given to me one Mother's Day by my son. It plays the lovely, "Edelweis" from *Sound of Music.* Whenever I play it, I feel a rush of warmth, love, and affection from—and for—my son, even when he is far away on tour.

At Home: If you work around the house in any capacity, use music as a stimulator to your creative energies, or to clear your mind for any mental tasks. If you are doing work that requires a steady hand (such as some sort of craftwork, art work, sewing, etc.), it also requires calm nerves. Choose music that is lilting and pleasant and light, with strings, woodwinds, light percussions. William Ackerman's *Past Light* is a refreshing, mind-centering blend of neoclassical and impressionistic music, using acoustic guitar, fretless bass, cello, piano, English horn, and oboe. Gentle, but never lethargic, it is one of many album selections from Windham Hill records that transcends the bounds of traditional music and is in a category unto itself.

If your "home work" is very physical, such as housecleaning, ironing, carpentry, etc., then it is music to stimulate the heart, lungs, and lower chakras that is in order. Try some brisk Sousa marches, rousing gospel songs, Broadway melodies, even martial music (to declare war on housework!)—whatever uplifts you psychologically as well as physically to get you through those chores. As Edgar Cayce stated: "The housework flies to a fast-moving full symphony playing the *William Tell Overture.* This can produce the stimulation to accomplish twice as much housework as if we work under our own steam. Music can also aid our attitude about the job we must do, and the very attitude we hold while working contributes to the overall vibrations of our home."

10:00:   If you have children at home, buy them their own little phonograph with wonderful children's songs that are creative, as well as educational and fun. Reserve an hour each day to sing with your children, dance with them, help develop their imagination by asking them what the music "looks" like. Have them draw to the music, inspired by the melodies, rhythms, and lyrics of wonderful songs. Children love classical music, such as *Peter and the Wolf, The Nutcracker Suite,* and *Fantasia,* as well as the songs of Hans Christian Andersen, Disney fantasies, and so forth.

If the children are in a room playing and start to bicker or get too hyperactive, play some mellow music—even meditational music—anything that will bring their body rhythms back to a normal, quiet pace. Or better yet, have the music on *before* they begin to play and circumvent any problems.

If you have an infant at home, a musical mobile is a wonderful companion and stimulator to the senses. And it keeps Baby occupied, diverting his attention from an already overburdened mom, at least for a while. At naptime or bedtime in the evening, play soft "angelic" music (hymns, lullabys, new age music) to seranade Baby to sleep. Sing to Baby while holding him (or her) close enough to feel your heartbeat and the soothing vibrations of your own crooning voice.

If you are an expectant mom, serenade your unborn babe with the "Music of the Spheres." Set aside a quiet half hour or so to specifically concentrate on health and well-being for you and your child. Allow yourself the feelings of contentment, pride, and joy that come with the creation of a new life. Shower yourself and your baby with visualizations of peace, harmony, and unbridled love. Settle yourself down in that comfortable rocking chair, and rock Baby gently back and forth, letting both of you enjoy a natural, health-sustaining universal rhythm, while beautiful music plays in the background. Treat both of you to a concert of cosmic sounds, wonderful glorious music inspired by the Universal Life Force and created by the Great Masters. Listen to the great operas, symphonies, and film scores that are thrilling and mind-expanding. Or lift yourself spiritually with music that takes you to a higher dimension and state of consciousness. And when labor and delivery time come around, introduce Baby to his new world—a world of love, life, joy, and music.

12 Noon Lunch Out: Avoid places that are overly noisy and have annoying raucous music on top of it. That nervous edge that you feel from the noise pollution will detract from the pleasure that mealtime should be, and hinder digestion as well. Choose quiet places, eat outside in the sunshine, go where there is pleasant music or none at all. Don't forget a few well-chosen words of complaint to the management—as you leave without ordering lunch—will work wonders in getting rotten music replaced with pleasant music. (Even if it doesn't work, it will make *you* feel better.)

Lunch In: Now is your chance to set the mood and create the atmosphere for dining that you want. Try a little Mozart, Mendelssohn violin concertos, or *Opera Sauvage* by Vangelis. Soft vocals are not out of line at mealtime. Choose some of Seals & Crofts' greatest hits, or Simon and Garfunkel. Eat slowly, relax, enjoy the food, the company (if you are eating with a friend or mate), and the musical experience. Many of life's greatest pleasures can be experienced during one enjoyable meal.

1:30 p.m.:   If you have a meeting to conduct back at work, and it looks like there may be some conflict between parties, play some new age or meditation music in the background. Don't call attention to it, but monitor the effects and see if it helps to keep some decorum. It will also help *your* mood, keep you controlled, mellow, and laid back. Your serene attitude, aided by the tranquil music, can set the tone for the entire meeting. Just as a high-spirited concert can bring everyone's collective energy to a peak of exhilaration, a tranquil atmosphere and a calm group leader can help to balance out frenzied emotions and hot tempers. Thus, meetings are far more constructive and productive.

So you have to give a speech and motivate a room filled with about four hundred businessmen and women to think, act, and be successful? I know a highly successful speaker who "psyches" himself up for sales presentations by listening to Neil Diamond music ("Holly Holy," "America," etc.). He needs to be inspired and inspir*ing*, and listening to strong, uplifting music strengthens both his mental and spiritual energies. This vigor charges up his personality and the enthusiasm spills over to his audience. Whether you choose Neil Diamond or the theme from *Superman*, your dynamic quality will shine through, giving you poise, confidence, and powers of persuasion.

6:00:   Whether you dine with family or with friends, this should be a happy social experience where you unwind after a busy day. Mood music in the background provides a pleasant atmosphere and promotes good conversation of positive subjects. Try using some music to coincide with your menu. For example, if you are eating lasagna, play some Italian favorites ("O Sole Mio," "Come Back to Sorrento", etc.) or some light Italian operas. Whether you are having crepes, enchiladas, or hot dogs and beans, choose some music that gives you the ambience of the native country associated with the food. Have fun, enjoy your meal, eat slowly, and digest properly. And remember, now is not the time to chastise the kids about their school grades, or vent your spleen over the day's aggravations. There is a time and place for everything, and anger has no place at the dinner table.

8:00:   If you wish to ventilate your hostilities, or lift yourself up out of the doldrums, do it during your exercise or work-out session.

Whack a few tennis balls, run yourself into a healthy sweat, dance yourself out of the blues, swim into tranquility. But don't forget the music. The right music for exercise will aid concentration, ease the stress of physical activity, and motivate you to peak performance.

If you have an aerobics instructor who is in a hard rock rut, diplomatically suggest that he or she soften and vary the music. Don't be afraid to express your opinion and make some suggestions as to what kind of music you would like to exercise to. You are paying for the class and/or your membership to the gym, so you have every right to have an enjoyable, healthful, beneficial experience. And if the instructor does not end the class with a brief meditation exercise, why not suggest it? The meditation was one of the most popular segments of my classes. I did not ask my students if they wanted to do it, I just gently thrust it upon them and, believe me, not one person objected. After stretching and working and sweating to get their bodies in tune, they welcomed the five minutes or so that I provided for them to get their spirit in tune. Just this brief amount of time sitting in a yoga position or lying flat on the floor, breathing slowly, visualizing themselves surrounded in a warm golden light, did as much for their mental and physical well-being as the hour of exercise. Most of the people didn't even want to get up off the floor after the meditation. It was wonderful to see how easily they learned how to drift off in a peaceful state of consciousness. Of course, it helped to have such music as "Ancient Echoes" by Georgia Kelly and Steven Halpern playing softly in the background.

10:00:   While you were gone, I do hope you remembered to leave some music playing for the dogs, cats, and plants. Animals have as much need for a harmonious environment as people do. It might even keep the dog from dragging the trash can around the kitchen in a fit of loneliness and keep the cat from climbing the drapes. And it will certainly help your plants grow luxuriously as long as the music you play is luxuriously life-giving.

Music playing in an empty house will also clean your home of negative vibrations, giving the room a feeling of serenity and balance. Play classical, or new age music such as Jean-Michel Jarre's *Oxygene,* or perhaps *Fresh Aire* by Mannheim Steamroller, gospel or inspirational songs, or Mozart's *Mass in C Minor.* The choices are gloriously endless. And speaking of endless, many dual cassette players have a "continuous play" feature that will allow two cassettes to play alternately up to fifteen times before turning off. That's more than a full day's worth of music (if you're inclined to having the same two tapes play over and over again).

10:30:   At this time, you may want to settle yourself down and do some affirmations, visualizations, and guided imagery, to put your life in perspective, your priorities in order, and allow problems to be solved by creative thinking. All of these techniques are enhanced by music that helps you relax, focus your mind, and receive the wondrous pictures and messages from the Universal Consciousness. Music? Try *Crystal Cave* by Upper Astral.

When lovemaking time rolls around, you'll be free of anxiety and more in tune with yourself and your lover's needs. Of course, Johnny Mathis and *Open Fire, Two Guitars* wouldn't hurt at a time like this (am I dating myself?).

Time for sleep. Ethereal and celestial music is what you need now. Selections from Neil Diamond's classic *Jonathan Livingston Seagull* soundtrack (especially "Dear Father" and "Be") lulled my son and I to sleep every night for months. Now is the time to count your blessings, and vow to live each new day with a renewed awareness of all the wonders and joys of life. Let the music lift you skyward as you drift into the gentle arms of Morpheus. Pleasant dreams.

Suggested Music Lists

The following music lists are certainly not meant to be all inclusive, or representative of the entire musical spectrum. They are samples—appetizers, if you will—in the magnificent smorgasbord of music with which to satisfy your palate. Ideally, these suggestions will whet your appetite and make you hunger for more.

Walk into your local record store and glance at the rows and rows of records and tapes. It is overwhelming. How do you decide which piece of classical music is better (or more appropriate) than another? Or which jazz album is the most romantic, which new age album is more healing, which pop-music album will give you more energy and enjoyment than another? How do you know which opera, film or stage soundtrack will be the key to unlock your emotions or stimulate creative thought? You don't know, until you yourself have experienced that particular piece of music which strikes a harmonious chord in your internal knowingness. But where do you begin?

In going through my own personal music collection, I have categorized some of my favorites and illustrated how to use the different types of music for a desired effect. I hope my suggestions will be the beginning of some new musical experiences for you, and that they will help you listen to and evaluate music in a non-judgmental way—that is, not deem it good or bad, but decide for yourself if it is good or bad for *you* in a specific situation, to achieve a desired result. And when you do evaluate a piece of music, examine its *purpose* (the motive behind its creation) and not merely criticize its form (rock, jazz, classical, etc.) Ask whether the music is meant to manipulate or exploit human emotions for profit, or whether it was created to help elevate our consciousness, uplift our spirit, express our innermost feelings in a positive and constructive way. Then choose to keep it as part of your life experience, or dismiss it and move on to other music more to your benefit.

While listening, keep in mind the principles and points of information from previous chapters about the effects of music on your spiritual, emotional, or physical body. Allow yourself time to focus in on the sounds and tones you are hearing—whether it's a simple piano solo or a full blown orchestral overture. Feel, see, and fully experience what is happening to you. Do the brass instruments give you a rush of excitement and exhilaration? Do the woodwinds make you feel melancholy? Do the percussion instruments inspire you to move without inhibition? Notice which instruments are dominant in the song. Listen to their tone color. Is it vibrant, mellow, delicate, brilliant? What of the tone color in the singer's voice? Is it pleasant, appealing, soul-stirring?

Notice where the musical vibrations resonate in your various energy centers: your head, solar plexus, heart, groin, throat, etc. Ask yourself if the feeling is good, if you feel balanced physically and emotionally, or if it annoys that part of the body and agitates your entire mood and state of being. Remember that the *tempo*—the quickness or slowness of the music—has a direct bearing on your ability to relax, concentrate, and learn, or facilitate healing. Listen to the rhythms and note which ones inspire your body to move with vibrancy and energy, giving you strength and motivation for exercise or other physical activities. Close your eyes and envelop yourself in the entire essence of the music and note the kind and quality of images that appear in your mind. Are they uplifting, creative, expanding beyond the images of your everyday reality?

Practice the self awareness exercises so that you will be more in touch with your emotions and senses. By listening to the lyrics of a song, you can unlock your emotions and express your innermost feelings. People who respond deeply and sensitively to music are more in tune with themselves and the forces of the universe, and can achieve a better grasp on their lives. If you are in psychological therapy, ask your doctor to explore the possibility of including music in your therapy sessions. Music therapy for emotional and psychological problems is a widely accepted and utilized practice, providing astounding results.

The key is to make that total mind-body-spirit connection that is unique unto you. This may take time and practice, but it's well worth it, for there is no transcendental experience as complete and spiritually enriching as one accompanied by pure, ethereal tonal vibrations. And there are few physical and emotional experiences that can match the rush of exhilaration, passion and sensuality that music provides.

Some of the selections I have listed can cross over from one category to another and work equally as well. For example, relaxation and meditation music can be used for stretching exercises, sensuality, or mental concentration. The largo movements from Baroque music can be used for sleep and healing as well as for learning. Music for mental clarity can also be creatively inspiring, romantic, or provide moments of relaxation as well as pleasant listening. Any music that makes you feel "whole" balances your energy and provides a "healing" experience. In other words, music can give you a host of options and opportunities for enriching your life and your health.

Little by little add some of these selections to your own music collection. Or experiment with the music you have and see what category it fits into. Visiting your record store and chatting with the resident jazz buff or popular music expert is another way of taking the chance out of your music experiments. Your local public library should have a collection of records that you can check out and listen to, free! Do you have a public radio station in town? The "dee jay's" are usually volunteers and are very well versed in their chosen music genre. And don't forget to attend concerts, ballets and community music performances with your children and friends so you may converse later about the music you heard and how it made you feel. Most composers are serious about their art and give a great deal of time, effort, heart, and soul to creating a piece of music. As a listener, respect this and give music more than just cursory attention. Don't let it thump mindlessly in the background, unheard and unappreciated. You'll be surprised at what you'll discover, even in the simplest pop ballad, if you truly listen.

Your environment for listening should be appropriate. Set aside some undisturbed moments for relaxing, meditation, or self awareness sessions so you may involve yourself totally in the experience. This means turn off the TV, unplug the phone, lock the door, hang a "Do Not Disturb" sign on the door if you have to. These are your precious moments for self exploration.

And remember, the quality of your equipment should be good. You needn't have state of the art equipment, but take care that the reproduction of the sound on your stereo or cassette deck is clear and sharp. Speakers should be free of distortion, the stylus on your turntable should be as new as possible (never play old scratched records on a new stylus), and cassette deck heads should be cleaned regularly. Compact disc players, and the CD's themselves, provide the optimum in sound quality. But if you haven't yet treated yourself to this luxury, be sure to keep your records and tapes in their covers, free of dust and possible damage, thus maintaining their quality and extending their shelf life.

Music is a treasure, one of the few immortal treasures that anyone, rich or poor, young or old, educated or disadvantaged, can acquire and enjoy. Treat it as a treasure, respect its creation, give it your time and attention, and in return it will give you its power, its strength, and its beauty forever.

Oh...one more thing. Don't forget the power of your own voice. When you listen to the music and the impulse comes over you to sing...do it. Sing softly, loudly, proudly, liltingly, happily, joyfully. You, too, are a musical instrument, and the making of music with your own voice brings you in total alignment with the music power of the universe.

Mental Clarity

Sometimes you need to clear your head from "information overload," all those thoughts and worries and pieces of data that whirl around a mile a minute. This is when you should take time to reenergize and refresh your mind, to give it a respite from the tensions and pressures that alter your moods and cloud your thinking.

When listening to music for mental clarity, your brain feels like it is receiving a good spring cleaning. It opens up all the windows of your mind and lets the stuffiness out, while bringing in fresh "air" energy in the form of fresh new thoughts. The music listed below will stimulate the heart chakra, resonate "green" to provide balance, harmony, and tranquility to your mind and body. The instrumentation is simple, the music uncluttered. It will soothe you, then gently stimulate the receptors in your brain so you will be able to plan and execute the things that you desire to do.

It is wonderful music to use as background for reading, writing, or light mental tasks such as balancing the checkbook. You might try playing some of the selections while practicing tennis serves, or some other activity that requires a clear head and focused concentration.

Mendelssohn violin concertos

Tchaikovsky violin concertos

Haydn harpsichord concertos

Bach harpsichord concertos

Mozart flute concertos

Vivaldi Concerto for Guitar, Violin, Viola, and Cello

Vivaldi Concerto in A minor for Strings and Continuo

"Four Seasons"—Vivaldi

Telemann sonatas for flute and continuo

Telemann concertos for flute and harpsichord

Windham Hills label—various artists

    Past Light—William Ackerman (guitar)

    Passage—William Ackerman

    Windham Hill sampler 1982

    Windham Hill Piano Sampler

    Ballads and Blues—George Winston (piano)

    Elements—Ira Stein (piano) and Russell Walder (oboe)

Fresh Aire I, IV, VI—Mannheim Steamroller

The Shearing Touch—George Shearing (and strings)

White Winds—Andreas Vollenweider

Down to the Moon—Andreas Vollenweider

"Arioso"—J.S. Bach

Concerto in A minor for Piano and Orchestra—Schumann

Crystal Silence—Chick Corea/Gary Burton

The Black Stallion—movie soundtrack

Hiroshima—Hiroshima

Keith Jarret—piano solos

Art Tatum—piano solos

Classical, jazz, or new age music for solo instruments

Chariots of Fire—soundtrack—Vangelis

To The Unknown Man—Vangelis

Learning

The largo movements of works by Baroque-era composers have been tested and recommended, because the slow tempo (sixty beats per minute or less) calms the body and relieves the tension associated with learning. The music occupies the right side of the brain, while keeping the left side of the brain alert to receive the data to be learned more easily. Largo movements from any music by the baroque composers may be used, including:

J.S. Bach
Concerto in G minor for Flute and Strings
Harpsichord Concerto in F minor
Handel
Concerto No. 1 in F
Concerto No. 1 in B-flat major
Telemann
Double Fantasia in G major for Harpsichord
Concerto in G major for Viola and String Orchestra
Vivaldi
"Winter" from *Four Seasons*
Flute concertos

Steven Halpern's "Comfort Zone" and "Learning Suite" are also appropriate for study sessions. Or try any of the music for relaxation or mental clarity, choosing only the slowest in tempo from the albums. The idea is to keep the mind alert and the body relaxed. The music should never be an intrusion. You should not be consciously aware that it is playing. Rather, it should provide the atmosphere most conducive to studying and learning for you.

Creative Stimulation

Now and then our ability to think creatively is blocked by tension and just plain forcing the brain to think, think, think. This is when we need to divert our attention away from the situation at hand and reinspire the mind so creative juices start flowing again.

Whether you are inventing a new wheel, writing a book, preparing a business presentation, need to solve a personal problem, or wish to change the direction your life is going, listening to music that paints pictures in your mind of far-off places or exciting romantic adventures will fill you with new inspiration.

An onrush of creativity can come at the most intriguing times: walking the dog, cleaning closets, working in the garden, washing the car. While our hands and body are occupied in some other activity, listening to music with sweeping landscapes of emotions can bring magical resolutions to the problems that plague us. The art of music is also a marvelous key to unlock our creative skills in performing other forms of art, such as painting or sculpting.

Vassili Sulich, artistic director of the Nevada Dance Theatre in Las Vegas, recounts that it was music that saved his "sanity" from the monotony of performing the same show every night for years at the Tropicana Hotel. Listening to a wide selection of musical works not only gave him hours and hours of great enjoyment, it laid the foundation for his career as a choreographer, for the many new pieces of music he heard provided Sulich with the resources for creating future ballets. His music choices—mostly operas and classical works—also helped him achieve the concentration and patience he needed in order to work on his highly detailed paintings between shows.

Music takes your mind to another place and allows it to wander freely and unencumbered. Whatever the theme or mood intended by the composer, no two people will have the same visual images when they hear a piece of music. Artists use all of their senses when they create. They feel, smell, see, even taste their creation before it ever takes physical form. But the most truly inspired and inspiring works are never forced or manufactured from our conscious efforts. Rather, they are received openly as messages from the universal consciousness, then honed and shaped by the writer, the sculptor, the painter, or the composer into an interpretation of his or her own individual artistic expression.

These universal "messages" are there for all of us to receive and use to make our lives fuller, richer, more productive, and more prosperous. No matter our lifestyle, profession, or status in life, creative thinking—the visions that reach beyond our normal contrived images—can open doors to us that were heretofore closed and sealed.

Movie soundtracks, classic ballets, and music of the Great Masters are wonderful for creative stimulation because of the kaleidoscopic ranges of moods and emotions, and the diversity of the instrumentation. The music may vibrate from blue to indigo, stimulate the Fire energies of passion or the intuitive sense of the Water energy. Before you begin, be sure to relax first, with deep breathing exercises and some of the Relaxation/Healing music listed, if necessary, then choose your music selections for creative inspiration. Allow it to carry you away where it will, let whatever images that spring forth from your "super consciousness" stir up the wonder and magic that is you.

Here are a few musical suggestions:

"Scheherazade"—Rimsky Korsakov

"Appalachian Spring"—Aaron Copland

"Billy The Kid"—Aaron Copland

"Rodeo"—Aaron Copland

Gone With The Wind—soundtrack (Max Steiner)

The Turning Point—soundtrack (various classical)

Somewhere in Time—soundtrack (John Barry)

"An American in Paris"—George Gershwin

"La Boheme"—opera—Puccini

"La Mer"—Debussy

"Afternoon of A Faun"—Debussy

"Carnival of the Animals"—Saint-Saens

Fresh Aire VI—Mannheim Streamroller

Chariots of Fire—Vangelis

E.T.—The Extra Terrestrial—soundtrack (John Williams)

Born Free—soundtrack (John Barry)

Star Trek—The Motion Picture—soundtrack (Jerry Goldsmith)

On Golden Pond—sountrack (Dave Grusin)

Ravel's "Bolero"

Castelnuovo Tedesco Concerto in D for Guitar

Nutcracker Suite—Tchaikovsky

Carmen—opera or ballet suite by Bizet

Romeo and Juliet ballet—Tchaikovsky

Music of Richard Wagner

Beethoven symphonies, especially *Pastoral* (no. 6 in F major)

Fantasia—soundtrack (various classical)

Madame Butterfly—opera—Puccini

Out of Africa—soundtrack (John Barry)

Strauss Family—soundtrack

Strauss waltzes and marches

The Natural—soundtrack (Randy Newman)

Black Stallion—soundtrack (Carmine Coppola)

Superman—soundtrack (John Williams)

Amadeus—soundtrack (Mozart)

"The Planets"—Gustav Holst

Swan Lake Ballet—Tchaikovsky

"Rhapsody in Blue"—George Gershwin

December—George Winston

The Longest Day—soundtrack (Paul Anka)

The Color Purple—soundtrack (Qunicy Jones)

Jonathan Livingston Seagull—soundtrack (Neil Diamond)

Relaxation/Healing

Healing is a process that occurs through a balancing of our energy centers, when the body and mind are in complete atonement with their environment, with life, and with the universe. But what kind of healing do we need? And what kind of music will facilitate that particular healing process?

Many hospitals and therapists have found that music eases the devastating pain of serious physical disorders, especially when combined with treatment methods such as hypnosis, guided imagery, visualization, and meditation. In some cases, music is prescribed instead of tranquilizers for chronic pain. The music may vary, from new age music to more melodic types of easy listening. Still other patients may need music that matches the intensity of their pain, tension, or anxiety, music with strong emotions and tempo changes, and complex orchestration. Whatever the choice, music either helps take the patient's mind off the pain, or helps in focusing in on it to "visualize" it away. Music has even been known to reach through a patient's comatose state and elicit conscious responses.

Music has been highly successful in treating *psychogenic* diseases, where symptoms such as headaches, stomach upsets, and depression are linked to psychological problems. Persons with deep-rooted emotional and mental disorders may require highly dramatic, somber, or even aggressive music to draw out the repressed anger, fear, or hostility that is causing their disassociation from life.

While scientists, physicians, and therapists are still studying *why* it is so, most of them agree that music is a profoundly effective form of treatment and well worth applying as an alternative or conjunctive form of therapy.

For most of us, however, the *healing* process can be as simple (or as complex) as reducing the stress and strain of "normal" everyday life, and music here can serve as a preventative measure to circumvent any serious disorders. *Relaxing* seems to be the catch-all term that is used when speaking of stress reduction, and music that relaxes us, that we enjoy, and that releases the physical and emotional tensions that we experience from overwork, responsibilities, and so forth, is the key to the normal healing process.

Our choices? Music that is rhythmically gentle, without emotional crescendos and surprises, that is melodically appealing, and that brings the body down from a frenzied state to a serene one will provide relaxation. Yor choices can be anything from classical to jazz, folk to new age. Pop and rock, with heavy pulse beats and extreme high and low frequencies of sound, will stimulate your heart and respiration and therefore undermine your efforts to calm down.

Choose some music that appeals to your Earth energy and that balances the heart chakra with cool green rays of tranquility.

The following are some of my favorites:

Montavani Strings—various selections

Music of Ferrante and Teicher

Music of Roger Williams

Music of John Denver

"Claire de Lune"—Debussy

Mozart piano concertos and string quartets

Bach violin concertos

"Goldberg Variations"—Bach

Mystic Moods Orchestra—various selections (includes environmental sounds such as falling rain, ocean tides, birds, and wildlife)

Opera Sauvage—Vangelis

Songs Without Words—Dashiell Rae (Landscape series)

Touch—John Klemmer

Fresh Aire—Mannheim Steamroller

Water Colors—Pat Methany

Inside Moves—Grover Washington

Music by George Winston (Windham Hills) Autumn, December, Winter Into Spring

Pastoral Music by Ralph Vaughn Williams

Eventide—Steven Halpern

"Good Morning, Good Night Suites"—Steven Halpern

Classical Barbra—Barbra Streisand

Birds of Paradise—Georgia Kelly

Various selections performed by solo artists:

    Jean-Pierre Rampal (flute)

    James Galway (flute)

    Liona Boyd (guitar)

    John Williams and Julian Bream (guitar)

    Nancy Allen (harp)

    Zamfir (pan flute)

    Benny Goodman (jazz and classical clarinet)

    Pablo Casals (cello)

    Issac Stern (violin)

    "Edelweis" (*Sound of Music*)—Rodgers and Hammerstein

    "Arioso"—Bach

    "Akatonbo"—K. Yamada

    "Jogashima No Ame"—T. Yamada

    "Children's Prayer" (*Hansel & Gretl*)—Humperdinck

    "Lullaby"—Brahms

    "Adagio For Strings"—Samuel Barber

    "Sugar Plum Fairies," "Waltz of the Flowers," "Arabian Dance"—(*Nutcracker Suite*)—Tchaikovsky

    "Dance of the Hours"—Ponchielli

    Sundown—Gordon Lightfoot

    Harmony—Zamfir (pan flute) and orchestra

    Music of Steven Halpern, Georgia Kelly, Kitaro, Andreas Vollenweider, Paul Winter

The Shearing Touch—George Shearing and strings
Chariots of Fire—soundtrack (Vangelis)
Music of Seals and Crofts
Music of Simon & Garfunkel
Music of James Taylor
Music of Willie Nelson
Ballads by Ambrosia
Ballads by America
Music of Air Supply

Meditation

Healing of the spirit is the most profound healing of all. When we are lifted from the physical to the metaphysical plane, we become filled with Light, close to our Creator, and in touch with the life force of Eternity. Periods of meditation should be the most special—perhaps the holiest—time of our day, a time when we seek to open ourselves unconditionally to the guidance of the cosmic consciousness.

You may meditate in a purely transcendental way—lifting yourself higher and higher through the planes of consciousness while using deep breathing and visualization techniques (such as focusing on a color, or seeing yourself as an entity of light in a wide expanse of the endless universe, and so forth.)

Or you may meditate in a structured way, by focusing in on a particular object, or contemplating on an aspect of yourself that you wish to change or rediscover. This, too, employs visualization and imaging, but in a more intellectual way.

The actual techniques of meditation are complex to describe and explain, and if you desire to embark upon meditation seriously, there are many fine books available on the subject. But in choosing music for this activity, take care that it does not interfere with the imaging process. Rather, it should enhance it by placing your body in a very relaxed, receptive state of being.

Music for meditation, therefore, should be celestial and ethereal, free floating, pure in tone, and utilize instruments that resound in the soul (flute, harp, bells, chimes, high strings). It should quiet you, give you a feeling of tranquility that allows you to transcend the physical plane. As the music plays, breathe deeply and easily, let the music happen to you, until you feel weightless and unaware of your surroundings. Then begin your meditation.

Here are some of my favorites that give off lovely violet rays and open the crown chakra:

Golden Voyage—Ron Dexter

Tenku, Ki, Silk Road—Kitaro

Eastern Peace—Steven Halpern

Ancient Echoes—Steven Halpern and Georgia Kelly

Whisper on the Wind—Steven Halpern

Spectrum Suite—Steven Halpern

Birds of Paradise—Georgia Kelly

Seapeace—Georgia Kelly

Inside the Taj Mahal—Paul Horn

Crystal Cave—Upper Astral

Tibetan Bells—Henry Wolf/Nancy Hennings

"Be," "Dear Father," "Anthem,"—Neil Diamond (*Jonathan Livingston Seagull* soundtrack)

"The Island," "Campfire"—Carmine Coppola (*The Black Stallion*—soundtrack)

Music by Paul Winter Consort

Crystal Silence—Chick Corea/Gary Burton

"Ave Maria"—Schubert (*Fantasia* soundtrack)

"Sunrise at Rhodes"—(*Fresh Aire VI*)—Mannheim Steamroller

Children

Children naturally respond to happy, lively music, but the last thing they need is music to make them (even more) hyperactive. Children need to balance their energies and emotions as much as adults do, and they also need creative stimulation for those wonderful daydreams that make them the magical creatures they are.

Today's child is born into an age of high-tech stimulation through radio, television, MTV, films, video games, and computers. It is difficult to get them to sit still and pay attention to any entertainment or art form that does not emanate from an electronic box, including music. But, paradoxically, children have been unwittingly introduced to the joys of classical music via some of the most popular movies of the past decade:

Superman
Star Wars
Close Encounters of the Third Kind
E.T.—the Extra Terrestrial

They have also been exposed in subtle ways to meditative music through these films:

The Black Stallion
Jonathan Livingston Seagull

Very young children still enjoy the classic story ballets and operas such as:

Peter and the Wolf
Nutcracker
Hansel and Gretel
Sleeping Beauty

as well as the delightful tales of Hans Christian Anderson and Walt Disney set to music.

So, by catering to their penchant for fantasy and fairy tales, you can begin to acquaint them with new types of music that are healthful, positive, stimulating, and enjoyable. There are wonderful records and tapes that combine music with learning educational skills and social skills. Music videos especially made for children are also fine ways to teach them the connection between music and everyday life situations.

The specialty bookstores where you buy your meditation music will also carry some appealing music for children, such as "The Harp of Brandiswhere" by Sylvia Woods. And don't forget the Broadway musicals and films that they love so much:

Sound of Music
Fiddler on the Roof
The Sting

Born Free
Annie
Oliver

You can also play music for children that you would play for yourself for relaxation, sleep, healing, mealtime, learning, etc. If you are pregnant, please note that it is vital to surround yourself and your unborn babe with positive sounds and vibrations. Set aside a thirty-minute serenade session for you and Baby, and play the music that soothes you, stimulates creativity, and inspires you in thought and deed. While young children respond to a variety of music, be careful in choosing music with singing voices. Avoid operas with the sweeping vocal ranges of bass, tenor, and soprano singing. A soft, pleasant man or woman's voice is more appealing to infants and toddlers. *Classical Barbra* (Barbra Streisand) works beautifully at "lullaby" time.

For toddlers and youngsters who are ready to learn concepts and simple skills, there are a wide variety of excellent educational albums, tapes, and videos available, including:

Kidsongs—View-master Videos
Hap Palmer series of activity songs
The Sesame Street series
The Agapeland Library of songs and stories

And for pure enjoyment try:

Storybook Album of E.T.—narrated by
          Michael Jackson, produced by
          Quincy Jones; music by John Williams
          MCA records, 1982
The Care Bears Movie (soundtrack)
          music by Carole King and
          John Sebastian
          American Greetings Corp. 1985
Fantasia (soundtrack)
          (a collage of magnificent classical
          works from the great composers)
          Disneyland/Vista Records 1982

> *The Snowman*—soundtrack of the award-winning
>> British animated film
>> words and music by Howard Blake
>> CBS Records 1983

Exercise music for children should be less intense than the hard-driving music used for adult exercise classes. And the themes of the music should be wholesome and as "normal" as possible (no aberrant themes of violence, rebellion, drugs, etc.). Toddlers and youngsters may enjoy exercising to:

> *Mousercise*
> *Big Bird Exercise*
> *The Happy Hamsters go "Ghostbustin'"*

Preteens and Teens will enjoy working out to favorite soundtracks:

> *Beverly Hills Cop*
> *Stayin' Alive*
> *Fame* (movie and TV show)
> *Ghostbusters*
> *Jewel of the Nile*
> *Back to the Future*
> *The Big Chill*

as well as to soft rock, and "fun" rock artists like:

> Huey Lewis and the News
> Air Supply
> America
> Dire Straits
> Genesis
> Beatles
> Neil Diamond
> Billy Joel
> Elton John
> De Barge

Pointer Sisters
Hall and Oates
Eurythmics
Stevie Wonder
Wham
and almost anything country

Add to your list of soundtracks, the wonderful *Saving the Wildlife*, by Mannheim Steamroller, soundtrack for the PBS television special. This delightful music depicts our precious animals around the world, such as lions and tigers, dolphins and whales, Amanda Panda, and Wolfgang Amadeus Penguin.

Sensuality

Love's Song
It matters not how long the melody, but that it sings and is heard by someone; that its gentle strains, like morning sun, fall softly on a lover's face; that its beats and pauses intertwine, that it rises full before it wanes, and its passioned movements harmonize until two breathe as only one. And though all we have are passing themes, let the music take us, then be done.
                                        BARBARA ANNE SCARANTINO

Wherever the music takes you will depend on your own penchant for romance and your own depth of passion. But have no doubt—the music *will* take you "Somewhere," just as Leonard Bernstein and Stephen Sondheim promised Tony and Maria of *West Side Story*.

In a 1986 episode of the *Bill Cosby Show*, Cliff Huxtable (Cosby) reminisced to Clair (Phylicia Rashad) that music really "does it for you." No matter how many years go by, when a certain favorite song is played, you can still recall the memory of the first time you heard it. All the sensory experiences that you had then are relived: "you can smell, touch, feel, hear, and *be* there" once again. For Cliff and Clair, it was that old standard, "Candy."

Through the years, other famed romantic couples have responded passionately to their own love themes, and at the same time struck a universal chord for romance in all of us.

Remember Rossano Brazzi standing across a crowded room serenading "Some Enchanted Evening" to Mitzi Gaynor in *South Pacific?* For Kim Novak and William Holden in *Picnic,* it was the earthy "Moonglow" that brought them passionately together. And for Kim and Shane on *Days of Our Lives,* their romance kindled to "Friends and Lovers" (sung by Gloria Loring and Carl Anderson).

For all of them, their "passioned movements" harmonized to music and lyrics that were positive in thought, sweet, sentimental—words that expressed what they wanted to say to each other, but could not find the courage to say; music that was tender, graceful, and sensuous.

Music brings all of your feelings to the surface, and if it is slow and tender, you will be more inclined toward the tenderness and patience needed to explore your lover's emotions, and fulfill his or her physical needs as well as your own. Music that makes you feel romantic, dreamy, and inspires fantasies when you are alone will no doubt be even more arousing when you are with that special someone. Here are a list of everyone's favorites, as well as mine:

> *Mystic Moods Orchestra*
>> *Summer Moods*
>> *Erogenous*
>> *Night Tide*
>
> "Fantasia in C minor"—Mozart
> *More Late Night Guitar*—Earl Klugh
> *Round Midnight*—collection of standards sung by
>> Linda Ronstadt, Nelson Riddle Orchestra
>> Includes beautiful standards "When
>> I Fall in Love," "Someone to Watch
>> Over Me," "Round Midnight," etc.
>
> *Crystal Silence*—Chick Corea
> *Classical Barbra*—Streisand sings mellow, romantic classics
> *J'mappelle Barbra*—Streisand and French romantics
> Keith Jarret piano solos
> Songs by David Gates and Bread ("If," "Diary,"
>> "Lost Without Your Love")
>
> Music of the Mantovani Orchestra

Ballads sung by Barbra Streisand
 "The Way He Makes Me Feel"
 "Evergreen"
 "The Way We Were"
 "Lazy Afternoon"
 "If You Could Read My Mind"
 "A Taste of Honey"
 "A Sleepin' Bee"
Paradise Cafe—Barry Manilow
Guitar solos by William Ackerman (Windham Hills)
Ballads by Ronnie Milsap
Ballads by Frank Sinatra
Ballads by Tony Bennett
Touch—John Klemmer
"Nocturne in E-flat"—Chopin
"Watching You, Watching Me"—Grover Washington, Jr.
"Hold Me Till the Morning Comes"—Paul Anka, David Foster
"Here Comes the Sun"—George Benson/Collection
"If You Go Away"—Neil Diamond
"Suzanne"—Neil Diamond
"Hello, Again"—Neil Diamond
"Play Me"—Neil Diamond
"You Don't Bring Me Flowers"—Neil Diamond/Barbra Streisand
"All In Love Is Fair"—Stevie Wonder
"Summer Me, Winter Me"—Barbra Streisand
"Hello"—Lionel Ritchie
"I Want To Give It All"—Air Supply
Music of Michel LeGrand
Music of Antonio Carlos Jobim
"Nadia's Theme" (Young and the Restless)
Friends and Lovers—Gloria Loring & Carl Anderson
Ballads by Rodgers and Hart
Music of Rod McKuen
Strictly for the Birds—Yehudi Menuhin/Stephen Grappelli

"Blue Eyes"—Elton John

"Breaking Hearts"—Elton John

"I Just Fall In Love Again"—Anne Murray

"Tonight I Celebrate My Love"—Roberta Flack/Peabo Bryson

"Just Once"—Quincy Jones (sung by James Ingram)

"She's Got A Way"—Billy Joel

"Just The Way You Are"—Billy Joel

The Hollywood Musicals—Johnny Mathis/Henry Mancini

Round Midnight—soundtrack—featuring Herbie Hancock, Dexter Gordon and other jazz greats

To Amadeus With Love—Roger Williams

The Art of Excellence—Tony Bennett

Courage/Inspiration

When life becomes overwhelming—when we have major crises, decisions to make, or suffer great losses—we need courage and faith to carry on. We can find strength and inspiration in our religious beliefs or in our own spirituality. Music of great depth, that is inspiring and inspired, can lift us to new heights of courage and give our life a connective meaning to the Divine Order of the Universe.

Music that has lyrics of compassion and sensitivity, that strengthens our determination and will power, and gives our physical body the stimulation needed to pull us out of the depths into the Light, is especially beneficial in times of fear and uncertainty.

Religious music, patriotic songs, and music borne of man's quest for "The Impossible Dream" are all good choices.

In trying to gather up your courage to face the stresses and strains of everyday life, vocalizing positive affirmations (or listening to them stated to you) is very helpful. The following exercise combines the power of music and the power in *you* for a completely uplifting and strengthening experience. You can either read it aloud (with authority) to yourself with music playing in the background, or you can tape your voice over the music, lie back, and let the suggestions filter into your mind and body.

Suggested music background: "Chariots of Fire" (long version) by

Vangelis. The graphic affirmations demonstrate the power we all have within ourselves to connect with the universe, through music, if we only believe it!

I Am the Music

As I breathe slowly and smoothly, in concert with the music, my body is being renewed with pure, healing energy...creating an environment for health and total well-being.

As I hear the music, it penetrates my skin, my body; it envelops me, it bathes me in its healing and strengthening powers. The music becomes me, and I become the music. It is alive through me...and I live wholly and fully through the music. It cleanses my body and heals me when I am ill. It has the power to create me again and again...and I, through the music, have the power to heal and re-create myself...for I become the music, and its power becomes mine. I am at peace. I am at rest. I am renewed.

The energy flows through me and it is mine to use, to feel, and to become. The music is no longer outside of me—it is within me—the music from a Creative Life Force that cleanses me, heals me, pleases me, uplifts me, envelops me, and becomes me. I am at peace. I am at rest. I am renewed. I am alive.

I can do all things. As I believe and as I see, I shall become. For what I can imagine in my mind becomes my reality. And if I wish it and see it, I will become my vision. If it is health I see, if it is love I see, if it is worldly achievements I see, they are mine because there is the power within me to make it so. And through my own inner music, I am all that I imagine myself to be.

The power is within me. It has always, and will always be, within me. And through the music that caresses me, protects me, strengthens me, heals me, become me...I become my vision and my vision become me.

I am at peace. I am at rest. I am renewed. I am alive—as I wish myself to be and as I always will be. As long as I believe and see and hear the music around me and within me, life is as I vision it, as I feel it, and as I desire it to be.

I Am the Music, and the Music—in all its power and strength and beauty and energy—is Me.

Barbara Anne Scarantino

The following are some music selections that will provide courage and inspiration:

Rendevous—Jean-Michel Jarre

This album was dedicated to musician Ron McNair and the six other astronauts who died aboard the Challenger shuttle on January 28, 1986

Exodus—soundtrack (Ernest Gold)

Music highlights the inspiring story of Israeli men and women who brave death in their determination to reach Palestine.

Fiddler on the Roof—soundtrack (Jerry Bock/Sheldon Harwick)

The warmth, dignity, pathos, and humor of Jewish community life during the Russian Revolution inspired these songs:

"Tradition," "To Life," "Miracle of Miracles," "Sabbath Prayer"

Porgy and Bess—soundtrack (George Gershwin)

Brilliant folk opera includes "Oh, Lord, I'm On My Way" "I Got Plenty of Nothin' "

Sound of Music—soundtrack (Rodgers and Hammerstein)

The enchanting story of the Trapp family includes the very dramatic "Climb Every Mountain" and the soul-stirring "Sound of Music."

The Gospel Road—soundtrack

Johnny Cash sings inspirational songs

Amazing Grace—Aretha Franklin with James Cleveland

and the Southern California Community Choir perform gospel favorites

Mormon Tabernacle Choir

"Messiah"

"Lord's Prayer"

"Bless This House"

"Climb Every Mountain"

"A Jubilant Song"

"Jesu, Joy of Man's Desiring"

"Requiem"—Mozart

Mass in C minor—Mozart

Tennessee Ernie Ford sings Spirituals and Hymns

Mahalia Jackson sings Americas Favorite Hymns

Concert for the Earth—Paul Winter Consort
> (recorded live at the U.N. on World Environment Day, June 5, 1984....glorious music and the love for our earth and all living creatures)

We Are The World—USA for Africa
> (Lionel Ritchie, Michael Jackson, Quincy Jones, et al.)

1812 Overture—Tchaikovsky

Cantatano Numbers 11 and 80—J.S. Bach

Panis Angelicus—Franck

"Ave Maria"—Schubert

Toccata & Fugue in D—J.S. Bach

Symphony Number 5—Beethoven

"Te Deum"—Berlioz

Symphony Number 9—Bruckner

"America the Beautiful"

"Battle Hymn of the Republic"

"Star-Spangled Banner"

"The Marseillaise"

"Pomp and Circumstance"

"O Holy Night"

"Angels We Have Heard on High" (Gloria)

"Ride of the Valkyries"—Wagner

Morning Like This—Sandi Patti

"Twilight at Rhodes"—(*Fresh Aire VI*)—Mannheim Steamroller

"Miracles"—(*Powerlight* album)—Earth, Wind & Fire

"That's What Friends Are For"—Dionne Warwick and friends
> (c. Burt Bacharach and Carole Bayer Sager to help victims of AIDs)

"The Sound of One Song"—(*Confetti* album)—Sergio Mendes

"One Voice"—Barry Manilow's Greatest Hits Volume II

To The Unknown Man—(title song)—Vangelis

Self-awareness

Often we think we are alone in the world, that no one has the same problems we have, or is as frustrated by unfulfilled wishes and dreams as we are. Sometimes we lose faith in our abilities and doubt our self-worth. Music by itself or combined with positive, reaffirming lyrics inspires us to greater achievements and revitalizes our connection with the Universal Life Force. Through music we can rid ourselves of depression and fear, and overcome challenges to our willpower and our character.

Music can aid you greatly in a self-awareness "self-therapy" session when you feel you would like to have a stronger sense of identity. This exercise is not to be substituted for a professional therapy session if you have deep-rooted psychological problems, but it can help you learn to open up and discover the true you—what makes you happy, what makes you sad, what stirs your reverie, what hidden or repressed emotions are in need of being expressed.

For this exercise, choose a wide variety of songs that offer a broad spectrum of emotions and responses. Play each music clip (you can string them all together on one cassette if you like, or play them one by one) and write down the first thought that comes into your mind. Then go back and spend more time on each one, stopping your tape if you have to, to give you a chance to spill out all your feelings. Do this exercise at least twice a week and compare your notes from the last time you did it. See if there are some new emotions or feelings you are expressing that you did not ventilate before.

As time goes by, you will become more adept at this exercise and learn to bring forth your feelings more easily. Then you will know what music will elicit a certain response in you that you desire at the time. It will also help you to recognize what music *not* to play at those times when you are sad, depressed, agitated, or feeling any other negative emotions—unless you wish to use the music as a cathartic. When you do this, be sure to follow up with some music to lift your mood back up again.

Here are some suggestions to help your self-awareness develop: try applying some of the following adjectives to the music you hear, and at the same time apply these descriptive words to your own feelings and emotions:

bright, cheerful, gay, happy, merry, joyous
agitated, dramatic, exhilarated, passionate
serious, sober, solemn, spiritual
dreamy, longing, sentimental, tender, yearning
light, playful, whimsical, humorous

calm, serene, tranquil

depressed, frustrated, melancholy, sad, tragic

Here are the music suggestions:

Camelot—soundtrack (Alan Jay Lerner/Frederick Lowe)

> The tender, poignant, triangular love story of Lancelot, Guenevere, and King Arthur includes these songs: "Camelot," "I Loved You Once in Silence," "If Ever I Would Leave You."

Cats—soundtrack (Andrew Lloyd Webber)

> Based on "Old Possum's Book of Practical Cats" by T.S. Eliot, the words and music imply *furry* cats are not much different from *human* cats. Includes the haunting, "Memory," also recorded by Barry Manilow and Barbra Streisand.

Fantastiks—soundtrack (Harvey Schmidt/Tom Jones)

> The longest running musical in the world gave us favorites like "Try to Remember" and "Soon It's Gonna Rain."

Funny Girl—soundtrack—(Julie Styne)

> Barbra Streisand in the role of Fanny Brice sings "My Man," "People," "Don't Rain On My Parade," "The Music that Makes Me Dance."

The King and I—soundtrack—(Rodgers and Hammerstein)

> Yul Brynner's immortal triumph includes "I Have Dreamed," "We Kiss in a Shadow," "Hello Young Lovers."

Oliver—soundtrack

> Lionel Bart's delightful musical version of Oliver Twist includes "Where is Love," "As Long as He Needs Me," "Who Will Buy."

Porgy and Bess—soundtrack (George Gershwin)

> The heart-rending story of the crippled beggar, Porgy, and his love for the beautiful, loose-living Bess includes "My Man's Gone Now," "Bess You Is My Woman Now," "Summertime," "I Loves You, Porgy."

The Color Purple—soundtrack—music produced by Quincy Jones

> Black music circa 1909–1943 blends with Jones's lush score, all of which complement Alice Walker's Pulizter Prize-winning story of a poor black woman's triumph over life's agonies. Includes "Miss Celie's Blues" and "Body and Soul."

Yentl—soundtrack—(Michel Le Grand/Alan and Marilyn Bergman)

Barbra Streisand produced, directed, co-wrote, and starred in this engrossing story of a young Jewish woman's quest to realize her full potential as a human being. Very mind-expanding lyrics, marvelous music, includes: "Where Is It Written," "Papa, Can You Hear Me?" "No Wonder," "A Piece of the Sky."

The Broadway Album—Barbra Streisand sings some of the

greatest songs ever written by some of the greatest composers of the Broadway stage, each song emitting and evoking a wide breadth of emotions. Includes "Somewhere" (*West Side Story*—Leonard Bernstein) "Send in the Clowns" (*A Little Night Music*—Steven Sondheim) "Can't Help Lovin' That Man"—(Kern/Hammerstein).

West Side Story—soundtrack—(Leonard Bernstein/Steven Sondheim)

The twentieth-century version of *Romeo and Juliet.* Innovative, magnificent in musical scope, offers a vast array of emotions and thought-provoking lyrics. Includes "Something's Coming," "Maria," "Tonight," "America," "I Feel Pretty."

Jesus Christ Superstar—soundtrack—(Andrew Lloyd Webber/Tim Rice)

The brilliant rock opera depicting the persecution and crucifixion of Christ. Music ranges from riveting to tender, including "I Don't Know How To Love Him," "Everything's All Right," "Hosanna," "This Jesus Must Die."

Music of Neil Diamond, including:

"Yes, I Will"

"I've Been This Way Before"

"The Story of My Life"

"Holly Holy"

Jonathan Livingston Seagull soundtrack

"I Am, I Said."

"Stones"

"I Think It's Going To Rain Today" (Randy Newman)

Music of Billy Joel, including:
> "Piano Man"
> "Everybody Has A Dream"
> "I've Loved These Days"
> "Scenes From An Italian Restaurant"

Music of Paul Simon, including:
> "Bridge Over Troubled Waters"
> "Homeless" (on *Graceland* album)
> "Sounds of Silence"
> "Mother and Child Reunion"

Music of Elton John, including:
> "Breaking Hearts"
> "In Neon"
> "Burning Buildings"

John Lennon Collection (Geffen Records)
> "Give Peace A Chance"
> "Imagine"

Music of Bob Dylan, including:
> "Blowin' In The Wind"
> "Like A Rollin' Stone"

Symphony Number 8 in B minor (unfinished)—Schubert

Iberia—Debussy

"An American in Paris"—George Gershwin

"Rite of Spring"—Stravinsky

"Scorcerer's Apprentice"—Paul Duka (*Fantasia* soundtrack)

"Night On Bald Mountain"—Mussorgsky (*Fantasia* soundtrack)

"Happy Days Are Here Again/My Buddy"—sung by Barbra Streisand

"My Way"—Paul Anka

"The Times of Your Life"—Paul Anka

Saving the Wildlife—soundtrack, PBS special—Mannheim Steamroller
> includes the moving and dramatic tribute to "Dolphins and Whales"

Fresh Aire VI—Mannheim Steamroller

> An exceptionally image-provoking album, depicting the composers' impressions of Greek Mythology. Highlights for this exercise include "Twilight at Rhodes" and "Sunrise at Rhodes"

Songs in the Key of Life—Stevie Wonder

> The pop beat may obscure some of the lyrics, but a full songbook is enclosed in the album, with moving tributes to people who have suffered in this life, as well as contributed greatly to it. Includes,

"Isn't She Lovely"

"Sir Duke"

"Black Man"

"As"

"Have A Talk With God"

"Miracles"—(*Powerlight* album) Earth, Wind & Fire

> Always spiritual, even with a jazz/rock beat, Earth Wind and Fire have included this extremely soul-stirring ballad in their album, truly a memorable song.

"Somewhere Out There"—(An American Tail), sung by Linda Ronstadt and James Ingram, this lovely song never fails to touch me deeply. How about you?

Graceland—Paul Simon (and Lady Blacksmith Mambaza)

> 1986 Grammy-winning album of the year, it incorporates Simon's thought-provoking poetry and the harmonies and rhythms of Black South Africa. Listen carefully, especially to "Homeless," "Boy in the Bubble," "Diamonds on the Soles of Her Shoes"

"Water Music"—Handel

Piano Concerto Number 2—Rachmaninoff

Prelude to Rosamunde—Schubert

"The Greatest Love of All"—Whitney Houston or George Benson

Physical Energy

Most any music that is bright and lively will give you physical energy, from the classics to marches to foot-stompin' country. Whether you want to invigorate your body or your mind, choose music that pleases you, that relieves boredom and the blahs and changes your behavior from inert to vivacious. Remember, however, to avoid prolonged exposure to hard rock or pop music, and monitor how you feel: there is a difference between feeling *energetic* and feeling *jittery.*

Adrenaline is a drug and you can become addicted to it. When the outpouring of adrenaline is too high (such as happens when you listen for long periods of time to very fast, intense music), the body has a craving for more. People may think they "feel good," but in reality they are hooked on a stimulus. As long as you are aware that this is happening, and take measures to reverse it (by varying your music often) so your mind and body can rest, there is no real harm done.

If you are in need of some mild stimulation to lift you up from your "I'm too tired to move" mood, try some of the following:

Slavonic Dances—Dvorak

Strauss waltzes and marches

Arthur Fiedler and the Boston Pops

John Williams and the Boston Pops

Scott Joplin rags

"Rodeo"—Aaron Copland

Drums and Chants—Mongo Santa Maria and his Afro-Cuban Band

Sousa, Ives, Joplin marches

Military Bands, Pipe, and Drums of Scotland

Military marches

Spanish Flamenco music

Graceland—Paul Simon

Best of the Beach Boys

Chuck Berry classics

Stand Your Ground—Jaluka (exciting Afro-Latin-Rock)

The Motown Story—The First Decade

> (Anthology and chronology of hits by some of the most popular and talented black artists of this era including Marvin Gaye, Smoky Robinson, Temptations, Diana Ross, etc.)

Music by Stevie Wonder

Music by Ray Charles

New Weave—Rare Silk

Music of Elvis Presley

Golden Hits—Ramsey Lewis

Music of Spyro Gyra

Sinatra-Basie—Frank Sinatra & Count Basie

Breakin' Away; Jarreau—Al Jarreau

Breezin'—George Benson

West Side Story—André Previn/Shelly Mann/Red Mitchell

Credence Clearwater Revival (various albums)

Three Dog Night (various albums)

Chicago's Greatest Hits

Best of the Doobies—Doobie Brothers

Music of Alabama

Mozart Symphony Number 40 in G minor

"Gaite Parisienne"—Offenbach

"Don Quixote Pas De Deux"—Minkus

"Black Swan Pas De Deux"—Tchaikovsky

Vienna Overtures: "Die Fliedermaus," "Merry Wives of Windsor," "Donna Diana," "Prinz Methusalem," "The Opera Ball"

Overtures from Broadway shows

Big Band classics by Duke Ellington, Glenn Miller, Dorsey Brothers, Benny Goodman, etc.

Dixieland music by Pete Fountain, Dukes of Dixieland, etc.

Bluegrass music

Blues by B.B. King, Bobby Bland, etc.

Music of Charlie Daniels Band

Jungle Garden—Dave Valentin

Music by the Rippingtons

Music by David Sanborn

Exercise

In recommending music for exercise classes, I use the following criteria when making selections: exciting rhythms, appropriate exercise energy (for specific body parts), creative use of instruments, quality of recording, quality of vocal performance, and absence (or minimum) of harsh sounds and vibrations.

The music you use in exercise class (or at home for your workouts) can spell the difference between peak performance or frustration and indifference. Music not only stimulates the body to move, it stimulates the brain psychologically and emotionally, creating chemical changes that give you a musical "high" or "low."

The following are some of the albums I have recommended to members of the Aerobics and Fitness Association of America in my bimonthly *MUSIC POWER tip sheets* (AFAA Journal). Note that some of the selections are especially good for weight training.

The Main Event (soundtrack)
Barbra Streisand

"Main Event" (long and short versions)—jog/aerobic dance

"Body Shop"—standing/floor legs

"Big Girls Don't Cry"—warm-up

"Angry Eyes"—Sit-ups/buttocks

"Main Event" (ballad)—relax/stretch

Fame (movie soundtrack)
Irene Carra and cast

"Fame"—warm-up

"Out Here On My Own"—relax/stretch

"Hot Lunch Jam"—jog/aerobic dance

"Dogs in the Yard"—cool-down stretch

"Red Light"—sit-ups/buttocks

Barry Manilow I
Barry Manilow

"I Want To be Somebody's Baby"—warm-up

"Early Morning Strangers"—pre-jog stretch

"It's A Miracle"—jog/aerobic dance

"My Baby Loves Me"—cool-down stretch

The Turn Of a Friendly Card
Alan Parsons Project
(This album is good for working with free weights and weight machines. Often very dramatic orchestral arrangements)

"May Be A Price To Pay"—warm-up

"Games People Play"—floor legs
"Time"—relax/stretch
"I Don't Wanna Go Home"—sit-ups/buttocks
"Gold Bug"—prejog stretch

Life is a Song Worth Singing
Teddy Pendergrass

Title song—warm-up
"Only You"—sit-ups/buttocks/legs
"Cold, Cold World"—prejog stretch
"Get Funky, Get Loose"—floor legs
"When Somebody Loves You Back"—lively stretch

Best of Earth Wind and Fire, Vol. I
(The unique vocal blend and the inspiring lyrics of EWF, make this album—and the following one—a brilliant collection of rhythm and blues songs with African and American jazz rhythms and harmonies. Strong brass section; wide range of emotional dynamics.)
"Got To Get You Into My Life"—standing legs
"Fantasy"—standing hips/buttocks
"Can't Hide Love"—cool-down stretch
"Get Away"—prejog stretch
"That's the Way of the World"—cool-down
"September"—arms/floor legs
"Shining Star"—standing stretches

Gratitude
Earth Wind and Fire
"Africano/Power Medley"—aerobic dance
"Yearnin' Learnin'"—arms, legs
"Devotion"—standing stretches
"Sun Goddess"—warm-up or cool-down
"Reason"—cool-down, floor stretches
"Sunshine"—warm-up
"Sing a Song"—floor legs/buttocks or standing legs
"Gratitude"—sit-ups

Extensions
Manhattan Transfer
(Jazzy, swingy album with the expert vocal harmonies reminiscent of the thirties and forties)

"Birdland"—aerobic dance

"Wacky Dust"—warm-up/waist

"Nothing You Can Do About it"—prejog stretch

"Twilight Zone"—standing legs/hips

"Shaker Song"—standing hips/buttocks

Playing to win
Little River Band (LRB)
(The usually mellow LRB goes hard rock with strong, high-energy sounds. Progressive rhythms are slightly syncopated, but, if you have a good sense of timing, you'll be able to keep a consistent flow of movement. Very creative and musically exciting.)

"Paying to Win"—wasit/standing legs

"Relentless"—buttocks

"Blind Eyes"—standing stretches

"Piece of the Dream"—fast arms

"Don't Blame Me"—sit-ups

Primitive
Neil Diamond
(Diamond moves slightly to the left of his folk/rock mode into a sound that is earthy, sensual—as well as romantic and poetic.)

"Turn Around"—relax/stretch

"Primitive"—warm-up

"Fire on the Tracks"—arms

"Brooklyn on a Saturday Night"—standing legs

"Sleep With Me Tonight"—relax/stretch

"Crazy"—sit-ups/buttocks

"My Time With You"—relax/stretch

"Love's Own Song"—waist

"It's A Trip"—legs/hips

"One By One"—waist/standing legs

Headed for the Future
Neil Diamond
(Collaborators on this album include Stevie Wonder, Maurice White, and David Foster. A good cross section of music from contemporary to romantic and poetic.)

"Headed For The Future"—standing or floor legs

"The Man You Need"—floor stretches

"I'll See You On the Radio (Laura)"—standing stretches

"Lost In Hollywood"—aerobic dance

"The Story of My Life"—relax/stretch

"Angel"—floor legs

"Me Beside You"—cool-down/floor stretches

Relight my Fire
Dan Hartman
(A sensual, earthy disco/rock album with jazz, blues, and Latin influences. Long cuts, from four to ten minutes, for choreographed routines.)

"Hands Down"—fast arms

"Love Strong"—aerobic dance

"Just For Fun"—arms, legs, sit-ups

"I Love Making Music"—sit-ups/buttocks/legs

"Vertigo/Relight My Fire"—dance exercises, lively stretches, standing legs, etc.

"Free Ride"—my favorite for dancing, strutting, and sweating up a storm

Knee Deep in the Hoopla
Starship
(A creative, dynamic album with blood-pumping rhythms and motivating melodies)

"We Built This City"—standing legs, aerobic dance

"Sara"—stretch

"Tomorrow Doesn't Matter Tonight"—arms, weight training

"Before I Go"—floor legs

"Love Rusts"—leg stretches, sit-ups, weight training

Brothers in Arms
Dire Straits
(softly it rocks with a touch of jazz and folk. Some fun lyrics.
Good for all ages)

"So Far Away"—warm-up

"Money For Nothing"—standing or floor legs

"Walk of Life"—aerobic dance

"Why Worry"—floor stretches

"Ride Across the River"—standing stretches

"One World"—sit-ups/buttocks

"Brothers in Arms"—relax/stretch

Confetti
Sergio Mendes
(Outstanding album with excitement, drama, and sensitivity.
Writers include Cynthia Weil, Marilyn and Alan Bergman, and Barry
Mann. Vocals by Joe Pizzulo, but you'll also recognize James
Ingram and Jeffery Osbourne)

"Olympia"—aerobic dance

"Say It With Your Body"—aerobic dance

"Let's Give a Little More This Time"—cool-down, stretch

"Alibis"—floor legs, arms, weight training

"Dance Attack"—aerobic dance

"Kisses"—stretch

"Real Life"—floor or standing legs

"Morrer De Amor"—relax/stretch

"Sound of One Song"—find something to do with this one—warm
up, cool-down, dance, or *sing* to it. It is a moving, charming
musical experience

The Other Side of Life
Moody Blues
(The preeminent British art-rock group goes a bit more
commercial in this album. Good for all ages)

"Your Wildest Dreams"—standing legs

"Talkin' Talkin'"—aerobic dance

"Rock and Roll Over You"—aerobic dance

"I Just Don't Care"—standing stretches

"Running Out of Love"—arms, floor legs, weight training

"The Other Side of Life"—sit-ups/buttocks

"The Spirit"—aerobic dance

"Slings and Arrows"—standing legs, waist

"It May Be a Fire"—cool-down, stretch

JARREAU
Al Jarreau
(Pop-jazz classics by a vocal master. Good R&B beats for exercise and dance class)

"Morning"—warm up

"Trouble in Paradise"—warm-up

"Black and Blue"—waist/standing legs

"Love is Waiting"—waist/standing legs

"I Will Be Here For You"—standing stretches

"Boogie Down"—fast sit-ups

BENSON COLLECTION
George Benson
(Very exciting jazz/R&B rhythms good for dance and exercise classes. Some very moving vocal performances)

"Turn Your Love Around"—warm-up

"On Broadway"—standing hips, legs

"Never Give Up on A Good Thing"—waist/standing legs

"Give Me the Night"—sit-ups-buttocks

"Here Comes the Sun"—relax/stretch

"The Greatest Love of All"—floor stretches

"Breezin"—warm-up or cool-down dance

Best of the Doobies
Doobie Brothers
(A little rock and roll, R&B, spiritual, and country sounds blend to make this a great album for exercise as well as listening)

"Takin' it to the Streets"—warm-up

"Black Water"—standing stretches

"It Keeps You Runnin"—standing stretches

"China Grove"—arms

"Long Train Runnin'"—legs/hips

"Listen to the Music"—legs/hips

"Rockin' Down the Highway"—aerobic dance

"Take Me in Your Arms"—aerobic dance

Breaking Hearts
Elton John
(Incredibly versatile—from blues to ballads to rock. Good rhythms and sounds for all ages)

"Passengers"—warm-up

"Slow Down, Georgie"—arms

"Who Wears These Shoes?"—aerobic dance

"Lil' Refrigerator"—aerobic dance

"Breaking Hearts"—cool-down/stretch

"In Neon"—stretch

Toto IV
Toto
(Winner of six Grammies, it's a prime example of modern rock with appealing melodies and vibrant syncopated rhythms.)

"Rosanna"—warm-up/standing stretches

"Make Believe"—sit-ups/buttocks

"I Won't Hold You Back"—floor stretches

"Good for You"—slow arms, weight training

"It's A Feeling"—standing stretches

"Afraid of Love"—fast arms/standing legs

"Lovers in the Night"—floor legs/hips

"We Made It"—aerobic dance

"Waiting for Your Love"—sit-ups/buttocks

"Africa"—waist/standing legs and hips

The Best of the Guess Who Live!
Guess Who
(The historic group reunites to perform their classic hits from the sixties. Lively, upbeat; good for all ages, including prenatal classes. Lyrics are free-spirited and colorful)

"What's Going to Happen To The Kids?"—arms, sit-ups/buttocks

"Let's Watch the Sun Go Down"—warm up

"No Time"—standing or floor legs

"These Eyes"—warm up, standing stretches

"Creepin' Peepin' Baby Blues"—aerobic dance

"Rain Dance"—abdominals/waist

"Running Back to Saskatoon"—floor legs/hips

"Sour Suite"—cool-down stretches

"Albert Flasher"—arms

"Clap for the Wolfman"—sit-ups/buttocks

"C'mon and Dance"—slow arms, weight training

"American Woman"—standing hips/buttocks, slow arms, weight training

Fresh Aire IV
Mannheim Steamroller
(A compelling mixture of free-floating melodies—ideal for stretch and meditation—and powerful Baroque-inspired music with a contemporary beat. Lots of drama in the following songs, good for strong body moves and weight training)

"G Major Toccata" (pipe organ provides the liturgical quality; contemporary rhythm provides movement energy)

"Four Rows of Jacks" (harpsichord adds flair and charm; strong percussion, synthesizer and strings provide high energy)

To the Unknown Man
Vangelis
The master of the synthesizer has created an inspiring piece of music that begins gently and builds dramatically. Ideal for stretch class or for weight training. Good warm-up song. Put it on tape and play on your Walkman while you jog outside or use the indoor treadmill.

Sunrise
Paulinho da Costa
Wonderful Latin/jazz rhythms; light and breezy; interesting percussions. Great for dance/exercise class.

Back in the High Life
Steve Winwood
Exciting earthy rhythms with an Afro-Cuban flavor, mixed with rock beats and a blues feeling, so exciting you want to dance without restraint. Just what is needed for exercise motivation in a high-energy (intermediate, advance) class.

"Higher Love"—warm-up

"Take it As it Comes"—arms, legs

"Freedom Overspill"—floor work (fast sit ups, legs, buttocks)

"Back in the High Life"—weight training

"The Finer Things"—floor legs

"Wake Me Up On Judgment Day"—arms, floor work

"Split Decision"—weight training

"My Love's Leavin'"—cool-down stretch

Walk a Fine Line
Paul Anka
Paul Anka teams with David Foster and Michael McDonald to create one of his finest contemporary albums. Lively tempos with light rock beats and nice melodic lines make this a good choice for all ages; beginner- to intermediate-level classes.

"Second Chance"—warm-up

"Hold Me Till the Morning Comes"—final stretch

"Darlin' Darlin'"—sit-ups/buttocks; weight training

"No Way Out"—stretch

"Walk a Fine Line"—standing legs and hips

"Take Me in Your Arms"—arms, standing or floor legs, waist/abdomen

"This is the First Time"—stretch

"Gimme the Word"—aerobic dance

"Golden Boy"—aerobic dance

Laughter

The best medicine—besides music—is definitely laughter. *Combined* with music, it is unbeatable. Of the many functions of music, to evoke laughter and smiles is as fundamental and important as to provide relaxation or inspiration. When your spirit of whimsy is high, when you can laugh at yourself and the absurdities of life, all of your energy centers are balanced and you experience a very special kind of healing. The following popular songs have brought a smile or chuckle to all of us through the years.

1900–1910	*composers*
"In My Merry Oldsmobile"	Vincent Bryan/Gus Edwards
"Wait Till the Sun Shines Nellie"	Sterling/Tilzer
"Harrigan"	George M. Cohan
"Put on Your Old Grey Bonnet"	Murphy/Winrich

1911–1920

"Be My Little Baby Bumble Bee"	Marshall/Murphy
"When the Midnight Choo Choo Leaves For Alabam'"	Irving Berlin
"Aba Daba Honeymoon"	Donovan/Fields
"If You Don't Want My Peaches, You'd Better Stop Shakin' My Tree"	Irving Berlin
"If I Knock The 'L' Out of Kelly"	Grant/Lewis/Young
"Since Maggie Dooley Learned the Holley Hooley"	Kalmar/Leslie/Meyer
"Everybody Ought to Know How to Do the Tickle Toe"	Harbach/Hirsh
"Would You Rather Be a Colonel with an Eagle on Your Shoulder or a Private With a Chicken on Your Knee?"	Gottler/Mitchell

1920–1940

"Does the Spearmint Lose Its Flavor on the Bedpost Overnight?"	Bloom/Brewer/Rose
"Minnee The Moocher"	Calloway/Gaskill/Mills

"Inka Dinka Doo"   Durante/Ryan
"The Dipsy Doodle"   Larry Clinton
"Flat Foot Floogie"   Green/Gaillard/Stewart

1940–1960

"Mairzy Doats"   Drake/Hoffman/Livingston
"All I Want For Christmas is My
  Two Front Teeth"   Don Gardner
"I've Got A Lovely Bunch of
  Coconuts"   Fred Heatherton
"Bibbidi-Bobbidi-Boo"   David/Hoffman/Livingston
"Huckle Buck"   Alfred/Gibson
"Somebody Bad Stole De
Wedding Bell"   Hilliard/Mann
"Hot Diggity"   Hoffman/Manning
"Chipmunk Song"   Ross Bagdasarian
"Witch Doctor"   Ross Bagdasarian
"Kookie, Kookie, Lend Me Your
  Comb"   Irving Taylor

1960–Present

"Kids" (*Bye Bye Birdie*)   Adams/Strouse
"Ahab the Arab", "Guitarzan,"
  "The Streak"   Ray Stevens
"Coconut"   Harry Nilsson
"Short People"   Randy Newman
"Coalition to Ban Coalitions" Hank Williams
"50 Ways To Leave Your Lover" Paul Simon
"You Can Call Me Al"   Paul Simon
"The Future's So Bright, I Gotta
  Wear Shades"   Timbuck Three
"Born in East L.A."   Cheech and Chong
"Vanna, Pick Me A Letter"   Doctor Dave
Anything by Weird Al Yankovich
"Would Jesus Wear A Rolex on
  His Television Show"   Ray Stevens

Music And Color

Everything in the universe vibrates at a certain pitch, which in turn gives forth a light energy, or color equivalent. As music moves in its vibratory patterns of notes and combinations of notes, it emanates an array of colors that correspond to the mood and meaning of the music, as well as to their frequency levels of sound. The colors with which we surround ourselves can reflect or change our moods, for better or worse, for everyone responds differently emotionally and physically to the colors in their environment.

The science (or art) of color and music therapy is an ancient one. In ages past, there were temples where music, color, and precious gems were used for healing (those rubies and emeralds you admire are not red and green by accident—but by cosmic design!) Today, one of the most popular consulting businesses is that of color analysis, where a person trained in the psychological influences of color will advise you on your wardrobe, makeup, and office or home decor. Music and color therapy for health purposes is also performed by trained experts, and is being used to treat even the most deep-rooted emotional and physical problems.

Most of us cannot see the colors vibrating forth from music. Some very "attuned" people, however, can sense or feel them clairvoyantly, just as they can "read" the human aura that surrounds the body. A sensitive composer, artist, or music listener can actually "get inside" the music, experience its essence, its form, and its color vibrations, and thus discover the deepest mysteries and powers that the music possesses. During those moments in time and space, one can actually *become* the music and its power, and resonate in harmony with its color vibrations.

Since music's vibrational energy is not actually seen with the naked eye, but felt intuitively, there are some variances in people's perceptions of the actual color it sends forth. Also, most music is a combination of various notes (chords) and melodies, and is played by more than one instrument, giving off kaleidoscopic blends of pitches and light energy colors. Instead of being specifically red or blue, the music will be a gradation or hue variation of the basic color.

As noted in Chapter Six, each of the seven notes of the (do-re-mi, etc.) scale corresponds to one of the body's energy centers (chakras), and each vibrates at its own frequency, giving off a color of the light spectrum. These seven chakras, seven tones, and seven spectral colors are related to the seven heavenly bodies (planets) in the universe. And all of them co-exist harmoniously (when we are in good health) or discordantly (when we are ill or in distress). The chakras themselves, while predominantly one color vibration (such as the *red* chakra, or *green* chakra, etc.), may also have tinges of other colors in them.

The basic philosophy behind music and color healing is to bring the chakras into harmony with their universal counterparts, thus balancing our lives physically, emotionally, and spiritually. While serious emotional and physical disorders are best treated by a trained music/color therapist, you and I can derive great benefit by meditating or relaxing to various pieces of music that will help balance our energy centers, refresh, and reenergize us.

In 1797, composer Andre Gretry published a list of musical keys, their psychological characterizations, and color vibrations as perceived by composers Rimsky-Korsakov and Alexander Scriabin, respectively. These keys comprise all the 12 tones of the chromatic scale:

C major—fine and outspoken	white	red
C minor—pathetic		
D major—brilliant	yellow	yellow
D minor—melancholy		
E-flat major—noble and sad or gloomy		
E major—bright	sapphire-blue	bluish-white
E minor—slightly melancholy		
F major-moderately sad		
F-sharp major-	gray-green	bright blue
G major—warlike	brownish-gold	orange-rose
G minor—very sad		
A major—brilliant	rosy	green
A minor—graceful		
B-flat major—noble, but less great than C		

B major—brilliant
and less playful   dark blue   bluish white

All pieces of music are written in a specific key, but the key is not always designated in the song's title, except in some "classical" pieces (Vivaldi's Concerto in D major, for example). A good place to begin your home color therapy session may be in choosing some classical works written in keys that will stimulate the emotion, mood, or experience you desire. Or try some of the following selections, recommended by Dr. Mary Bassano, music therapist. (See Chapter Six for the location and description of the chakras, basic corresponding colors and musical notes.)

To stimulate the red chakra:
    Sousa Marches
    "Mars" music from *The Planets* by Holst
    "Ride of the Valkyrie"—Wagner
    "Fire Bird Suite"—Stravinsky
    "March Militaire"—Franz Schubert
    (also see music for PHYSICAL ENERGY, EXERCISE)

To open the orange chakra:
    "Capriccio Espagnole"
    "Gaite Parisienne"
    "The William Tell Overture"
    "Jupiter" music from *The Planets*
    "Habanera" from *Carmen* by Bizet
    (also see music for PHYSICAL ENERGY, CREATIVE STIMULATION)

For the yellow chakra:
    "Fountains of Rome" by Respighi
    Mozart's "Piano Concerto #26"
    Some of the Chopin Etudes
    "Lemurian Sunrise"
    "Mercury" music from *The Planets*
    Chopin's "Polonaise"
    (also see music for MENTAL CLARITY)

The green chakra:

    "Clair de Lune," "Images"—Debussy

    "Spring Song" by Mendelssohn

    "Midsummer Night's Dream"

    "Neptune" music from *The Planets*

    "Waterfall Music" by Paul Lloyd Warner

    Any of the Strauss waltzes

    "Ocean" by Larkin

    (also see music for MENTAL CLARITY, RELAXATION, LEARNING)

To open the blue chakra:

    "Air on a G String" by Bach

    "Prelude Op. 28, #9"—Chopin

    "Pranava" by Heidemarie Garbe

    Tchaikovsky's piano concertos

    "Ave Marie"—Schubert

    (also see music for RELAXATION, SELF AWARENESS, COURAGE/INSPIRATION. Singing also opens up the blue "throat chakra")

To balance the indigo chakra:

    "Panis Angelicus"

    "Venus" music from *The Planet*

    "German Mass" by Schubert

    Gregorian Chants

    "Inside the Taj Mahal"

    "Evening Star" by Wagner

    (also see music for CREATIVE STIMULATION, COURAGE/INSPIRATION)

For the divine violet chakra:

    The Parsifal music by Wagner

    "Requiem" by Verdi

    "Neptune" music from *The Planets*

    Gregorian chants

    "Inside the Great Pyramid"

    Hallelujah Chorus from *Messiah*—Handel

    (also see music for MEDITATION AND COURAGE/INSPIRATION)

As you listen to the music, visualize the color energy, then direct that color into the chakra you wish to open and balance. Some people use strips of colored fabric and lay it over their closed eyes so they can feel the color energy more intensely. *Visualization* is the key here, for the stronger you can imagine the light energy of the music and focus it on the desired energy center, the more deeply you will become enveloped in the power and strength of the music, providing much more therapeutic value.

A Final Note: Silence

If silence is golden, it is also necessary. Just as the plants in Dorothy Retallack's experiments withered and died when exposed to harsh sounds, they also expired when subjected to unceasing *healthful* tones. Like the plants, your brain and body need a rest now and then from the constant intrusion of voices, environmental noises, and, yes, even musical sounds.

But it isn't a lonely, withdrawn silence we need; it is an alert, finely tuned sense of self, acquired only through a connection with the universe and its Creative Life Forces.

Silence as we think of it doesn't really exist. Our environment is never completely without sound, even though we think all is quiet. And the world is never truly devoid of music (Remember, there is music even in the "silent" growing of a blade of grass). If you sat in a room insulated from all external sound, still there would be music—in the rhythm of your heartbeat and the melody of your soul.

The world of the deaf is completely without sound—as *we* know it.

199

But they "hear" things that we do not. They feel rhythms and vibrations, and can respond as well as hearing persons to these stimuli.

In the beautiful film *Children of a Lesser God,* William Hurt portrayed a teacher (James) of hearing-impaired teenagers. His unorthodox methods of teaching included the use of music to connect the kids to the hearing world. Through their ability to feel the vibrations and the rhythm of the song, they learned to dance and "sing." One of the most delightful scenes of the film had the teenagers performing a lip-sync to the rock song, "Boomerang." The kids boogied, strutted, and mouthed the words perfectly, thrilling their parents in the audience.

In more poignant moments in the film, James was sad that his deaf lover Sarah (Marlee Matlin) could not enjoy listening to music with him. But she could hear and feel things that he could not. Once sensing the vibration and flow of the music, she could dance more fluidly and sensuously than the hearing people on the dance floor. And when James asked her what ocean waves "sounded" like to her, Sarah made caressing movements on her body with her hands. James replied, astonished, "Yes, that's exactly how they sound."

While James was responding to the physical sense of sound, Sarah was expressing the inner sounds—the inner *music*—that she experienced in her silent world.

Many people are afraid of being in complete silence, just as they are afraid to be alone. For in both instances they must be alone with themselves and their own thoughts, their own fears, their own truths. But unless we can face ourselves—alone and in silence—we can never truly know the joys of life, of love, and of the Spirit. And we can never hear the music of our own creation.

We often hear of "runner's high," the euphoria that comes while running over a long distance. It is at this time the runner needs no external music playing to spur him on, for he now hears a harmony of his own created by the steady, driving rhythm of his stride and breathing. If he lets go completely, he can take flight, become weightless, soar to another dimension, hear the Music of the Spheres within and around himself. We are not all runners, but we can create our own "runner's high" of inner music by letting the song play on inside of us.

When we are silent and still, we can close our eyes and see visions of color and music with our Third Eye. These are the electromagnetic images of thought entering our mind from the universe. We are seeing the sounds of our own soul, of our own knowing and of our own creation. If we listen to this music from within, we can also see and feel our vibratory rate change, going higher and higher into the Light of a profound state of consciousness.

When you are playing your favorite meditation or relaxation music, allow your mind to focus in on the last few melodic strains. Listen for the final tone (it could be a musical note, a bell tone, the sound of wind chimes, but be sure it is the *final* tone), and let it resonate through your body, traveling upward through the top of your head. Even after the music is gone and there is "silence," you will still hear and feel the vibration of the note and will be lifted upward to become "at one" with the universe.

Like the runner, take flight, soar to another dimension, and listen to the celestial silence. It's playing your song.

About the Author

Barbara Anne Scarantino performed as a vocalist for twelve years with jazz bands and orchestras (including the Glenn Miller Orchestra under the direction of Buddy DeFranco). Born in Philadelphia, Pennsylvania in 1942, she later moved to Las Vegas, Nevada, to pursue her singing career. She subsequently attended the University of Nevada, Las Vegas, majoring in communications studies and has worked as a fine arts publicist and creative writer for the past thirteen years.

In addition, she began writing music, and is a composer/lyricist and member of ASCAP. In 1984, she was certified as an aerobics instructor through the Aerobics and Fitness Association of America (AFAA) and her MUSIC POWER tip sheets have appeared as a regular feature in the AFAA Journal.

Barbara has one son, Jonathan, who is a professional musician.

Selected
Bibliography

Apel, WIlli and Ralph T. Daniel. *Harvard Brief Dictionary of Music,* New York: Simon and Schuster, 1961.

Ardley, Neil. *Music, An Illustrated Encyclopedia,* New York, Facts on File Publications, 1986

Bassano, Dr. Mary, D.D. *In the Flow.* Kissimmee, Florida: self-published, 1983.

Chagall, David. "How Music Soothes, Stirs and Slims You." *Family Weekly,* January 30, 1983.

Christy, Van A. *Foundations in Singing.* Dubuque, Iowa: Wm. C. Brown Company, 1979.

Clynes, Dr. Manfred. *Sentics.* New York: Anchor Press/Doubleday, 1977.

Diamond, John, M.D. *Your Body Doesn't Lie.* New York: Warner Books, 1979.

Diamond, John, M.D. *Life Energy in Music,* Vol. I and II. Valley Cottage, New York: Archaeus Press, 1981, 1983.

Frith, Simon, *Sound Effects—Youth, Leisure and the Politics of Rock and Roll,* New York: Pantheon Books, 1981.

Halpern, Steven, Ph.D. *Tuning the Human Instrument.* Belmont, California: Spectrum Research Institute, 1978.

Halpern, Steven, Ph.D., and, Louis Savary. *Sound Health.* San Francisco, California: Harper and Row, 1984.

Hedges, Michael. "Radio's Lifestyles." American Demographics, Ithaca, N.Y. 1986.

Heline, Corinne. *Healing and Regeneration Through Music,* Marina Del Rey, California: DeVorss & Co., 1978.

Kamien, Roger. *Music—An Appreciation.* New York: McGraw-Hill, 1984.

Keys, Laurel Elizabeth. *Toning: The Creative Power of the Voice.* Marina Del Rey, California: DeVorss & Co., 1982.

Kupferberg, Herbert. *The Book of Classical Lists,* New York, Facts on File Publications, 1985

Lingerman, Hal A. *The Healing Energies of Music.* Illinois: Theosophical Publishing House, 1983.

Menuhin, Yehudi, and Davis, Curtis W. *The Music of Man,* New York, Simon and Schuster, 1979.

Meyer, Leonard B. *Emotion and Meaning in Music.* Chicago: University of Chicago Press, 1956.

Miller, Jim, ed. *History of Rock and Roll.* New York: Random House/Rolling Stone Press, 1976, 1980.

Miller, William Hugh. *Everybody's Guide to Music.* Pennsylvania: Chilton Company, 1961.

Milliman, Ronald E. "Using Background Music to Affect the Behavior of Supermarket Shoppers," *Journal of Marketing,* Summer 1982 (Vol 46).

Motoyama, Hiroshi. *Theories of the Chakras,* Theosophical Publishing House, Illinois, 1981.

Ostrander, Sheila and Lynn Schroeder with Nancy Ostrander. *Superlearning.* New York: Dell Publishing, 1982.

Pearce, Kathy A. "Effects of Different Types of Music on Physical Strength. *Perceptual Motor Skills,* Volume 53, 1981.

Pierce, John R. *The Science of Musical Sound.* New York: Scientific American Library, 1983.

Radocy, Rudolph E. and J. David Boyle. *Psychological Foundations of Musical Behavior.* Illinois: Charles C. Thomas, 1979.

Retallack, Dorothy. *The Sound of Music and Plants.* Marina Del Rey, California: DeVorss & Company, 1973.

Rosenfeld, Anne H. "Music, the Beautiful Disturber." *Psychology Today,* December, 1985.

Schoen, Max. *The Effects of Music.* New York: Books for Libraries Press, 1969.

Shaw, Arnold. *Dictionary of American Pop/Rock.* New York: Shirmer Books, 1982.

Simels, Steven. "Sound's Hidden Strengths." *Self* magazine, April 1983.

Strachen, Dorothy. *Music.* Fitness Ontario Leadership Program, Ministry of Tourism and Recreation. Ontario: 1984.

Tame, David. *The Secret Power of Music.* New York: Destiny Books, 1984.

Tanner, Paul O.W. and Maurice Gerow. *A Study of Jazz.* Dubuque, Iowa: Wm. C. Brown Company, 1984.

Taylor, Charles. *Sounds of Music.* New York: Charles Scribner's Sons, 1976.

White, Mark. *You Must Remember This.* New York: Charles Scribner's Sons, 1985.

Winston, Shirley Rabb. *Music as the Bridge.* Virginia: A.R.E. Press, 1972.

Wold, Milo, and Edmund Cykler. *An Outline History of Music.* Dubuque, Iowa: Wm. C. Brown Company, 1966.

Index